DONALD D. SPENCER is an internationally known computer-science consultant, educator, and writer. The author of over 100 computer science books, he holds a Ph.D. in computer science and has worked in the field for over twenty-five years. Dr. Spencer has taught computer science in college and industry and has lectured widely to international educational and professional audiences. He is a member of several professional and educational societies including the Association for Computing Machinery, the National Council of Teachers of Mathematics, the Association for Educational Data Systems, the Institute for Electrical and Electronics Engineers, the World Future Society, and the American Robotics Society. His books have been used by students, teachers, computer users, professionals, and lay readers all over the world. His other titles include *BASIC Programming, Understanding Computers, What Computers Can Do, Second Edition,* and *Problem Solving With BASIC.*

For Reference

Not to be taken from this room

*Spencer's Computer
Dictionary for Everyone*

Also by Donald D. Spencer
BASIC Programming
Problem Solving With BASIC
Understanding Computers
What Computers Can Do

Spencer's Computer Dictionary for Everyone

Third Edition

DONALD D. SPENCER

CHARLES SCRIBNER'S SONS · NEW YORK

Copyright © 1985, 1979, 1977 Camelot Publishing Company, Inc.

Library of Congress Cataloging in Publication Data

Spencer, Donald D.
  Spencer's computer dictionary for everyone.

  Rev. ed. of: Computer dictionary for everyone. © 1979.
  1. Computers—Dictionaries. I. Spencer, Donald D.
Computer dictionary for everyone. II. title.
QA76.15.S674 1985   001.64'03'21   84–22131
ISBN 0–684–18250–5
ISBN 0–684–18251–3 (pbk.)

1 3 5 7 9 11 13 15 17 19 H/C 20 18 16 14 12 10 8 6 4 2

1 3 5 7 9 11 13 15 17 19 H/P 20 18 16 14 12 10 8 6 4 2

Printed in the United States of America.

Front cover:
Photograph courtesy Radio Shack, a division of Tandy Corp.

To Michael

CONTENTS

PREFACE

Like it or not, computers are here to stay. Anyone involved in work, art, sports, or recreation in this decade—and that means all of us—will have to adjust to the rapidly growing world of digital displays, keyboards, robots, and computer-generated speech. As computer technology continues to infiltrate our society, there is an increasing need for an easy-to-understand guide to the language used by computer users.

Spencer's Computer Dictionary for Everyone contains more than 3000 of the most frequently used terms, words, acronyms, and abbreviations involved in using computers. It contains all of the terms that most often confuse a beginner. All definitions are given in clear, easy-to-understand language. In many cases, definitions are supported by photographs or drawings.

This book is intended for several kinds of readers. It is a basic reference book for the person who knows little or nothing about computers but wants to learn. It is hoped that business people, professionals, students, teachers, and others will find it a useful source book. Programmers, systems analysts, and other computer professionals will find it a handy reference book. Prospective computer users can use it when evaluating available machines and accessories.

The keynote of this book is clarity—without sacrifice of authority and precision. All definitions are simple and stand as independent units of explanation. Technical terms are kept out of the definitions as much as possible. In a few cases where a special terminology is required, the expressions used are carefully defined, and related terms or concepts are indicated by cross-references.

I have been in the front lines of the computer revolution since the late 1950s. Computer models, programming languages, computer manufacturers, and programming techniques have come and gone since those days of "vacuum tube" computers and machine language programming. Today's computer-based systems and equipment are literally generations ahead and orders of magnitude more effective than their early predecessors. Because of my close involvement with computer science education and the design and use of computer-based systems, I have long recognized the need for a current and comprehensive dictionary of computer terminology that would present all terms in a simple, understandable manner.

The selection of words for a dictionary inevitably involves a personal choice, and one has to balance a desire to be comprehensive against the need to be concise. The task of preparing this dictionary involved the collection, correlation, and analysis of more than 30,000 words, phrases, and acronyms used in connection with computers. If you come across a term you think should be in this book, drop me a line in care of Charles Scribner's Sons, and I'll try to include it in any future edition.

HOW TO USE THIS DICTIONARY

The terms in this dictionary appear in alphabetical order of the complete term (spaces and hyphens don't count); for example, **computerization** comes between **computer graphics** and **computer literacy**. This order contrasts with some dictionaries in which the alphabetical order is based on a heavier weighing of the first word in a term; for example, all terms commencing with "computer" precede all terms commencing with "computerization."

All terms listed in the dictionary are in **boldface**. Cross-references that are important to an understanding of any term are given in *italics*.

If you cannot find a word, it might be listed in a slightly different form. For example, you might try looking for "flowcharting" and find the description under "flowchart." I have included only one definition to keep from cluttering the book with the obvious.

The terms normally appear in boldface lower case characters. Proper names and nouns are headed by an upper case letter; for example, **Pascal, Blaise**. Acronyms are presented in boldface caps and the proper letters are amplified in the text; for example, **BASIC** stands for Beginners All-purpose Symbolic Instruction Code.

DICTIONARY OF TERMS

A

AAAI (American Association for Artificial Intelligence) A professional organization concerned with advancing the field of artificial intelligence.

abacus An ancient device for doing simple calculations that uses movable beads threaded on a grid of wires. Still widely used in many Oriental countries.

abbreviated addressing A modification of the direct address mode that uses only part of the full address and provides a faster means of processing data because of the shortened code.

ABC (Atanasoff-Berry Computer) An early electronic digital computer built in 1942 by Dr. John V. Atanasoff and his assistant, Clifford Berry.

abend (ABnormal ENDing) An early termination of a program due to an error condition. For example, division by zero or trying to add a number and a letter.

abort The procedure for terminating a program when a mistake, malfunction, or error occurs.

absolute address An address that is permanently assigned by the machine designer to a particular storage location. For example, the addresses 0000, 0001, 0002, and 0003 might be assigned to the first four locations in a computer's storage. Also called machine address.

absolute coding Coding that uses machine instructions and ab-

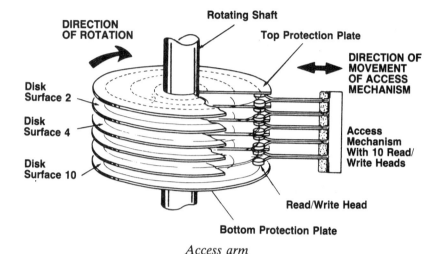

Access arm

solute addresses; therefore, it can be directly executed by a computer without prior translation to a different form. Contrast with *symbolic coding.*

absolute value   The magnitude of a number without regard to sign; that is, the absolute value of -9 is 9.

acceptance test   A test used to demonstrate the capabilities and workability of a new computer system. It is usually conducted by the manufacturer to show the customer that the system is in working order.

access   Generally, the obtaining of data. To locate the desired data.

access arm   A mechanical device in a disk file storage unit that positions the reading and writing mechanisms.

access code   A group of characters or numbers that identifies a user to the computer system.

access method   Any of the data management techniques available to the user for transferring data between storage and an input/ output device.

access time   The time the computer takes to locate and transfer data to or from storage.

accumulator   A register or storage location that forms the result of an arithmetic or logic operation.

accuracy   The degree of exactness of an approximation or measurement. Accuracy normally denotes absolute quality of computed results; precision usually refers to the amount of detail used in representing those results. Thus, four-place results are less precise than six-place results; nevertheless, a four-place table might be more accurate than an erroneously computed six-place table. See *precision.*

ACH (Association for Computers and the Humanities) An international organization devoted to the encouragement of computer-aided research in language and literary studies, history, anthropology, and related social sciences, as well as the use of computers in the creation and study of art, music, and dance.

ACI (Automatic Car Identification) A system used by railroad companies to automatically identify railroad cars.

ACK (ACKnowledge) An international transmission control code that is returned by a receiving terminal to a transmitting terminal to acknowledge that a frame of information has been correctly received. Contrast with *NAK*

ACM (Association for Computing Machinery) A professional computer science organization. Its function is to advance the design, development, and application of information processing and to promote the interchange of such techniques between computer specialists and users.

ACMST (Association for Computers in Mathematics and Science Teaching) This professional organization directs itself toward college and secondary school mathematics, and science teachers interested in educational uses of computers.

acoustic coupler A data communications device that converts electrical data signals to/from tones for transmission over a telephone line using a conventional telephone headset. Contrast with *direct-connect coupler.*

ACPA (Association of Computer Programmers and Analysts) A professional computer science organization.

activity ratio When a file is processed, the ratio of the number of records in a file that have activity to the total number of records in that file.

actuator In a disk drive, a mechanism that moves the read/write head to the desired position over the disk surface.

ACU (Automatic Calling Unit) A device that allows a business machine to make dial calls on a telephone network.

Ada A high-level programming language developed by the Department of Defense for use in military systems. The language was named after Ada Augusta Lovelace, the first woman programmer.

ADAPSO (Association of Data Processing Service Organizations) A trade association for vendors of computer systems, software, and services.

adapter A device that allows compatibility between different equipment.

adaptive systems Systems displaying the ability to learn, change their state, or otherwise react to a stimulus. Any system capable of adapting itself to changes in its environment.

A-D converter See *analog-to-digital converter*.

adder A device capable of forming the sum of two or more quantities. See *parallel adder* and *serial adder*.

add-in Refers to a component that can be placed on a printed circuit board already installed in a computer. For example, the addition of additional memory chips to empty slots in a microcomputer.

adding wheel A toothed gear that allows the process of "carrying" to be accomplished mechanically. Adding wheels were used in Pascal's calculator.

add-on The ability to increase a computer system's storage capacity, to modify its architecture, or to upgrade its performance by adding components or devices.

address An identification (e.g., a label, number, or name) that designates a particular location in storage or any other data destination or source.

address modification An operation that causes an address to be altered in a prescribed way by a stored program computer.

address register A register containing the address of the instruction currently being executed.

address space The complete range of addresses available to a computer user.

address translation The process of changing the address of an instruction or item of data to the address in internal memory at which it is to be loaded or relocated.

add time The time required for a computer to perform an addition, exclusive of the time required to obtain the quantities from storage and put the sum back into storage.

administrative data processing The field of data processing concerned with the management or direction of an organization. See *business data processing*.

ADP (Automatic Data Processing) Data processing performed largely by automatic means.

AEDS (Association for Educational Data Systems) A professional organization interested in sharing information related to the effect of data processing on the educational process.

AFCET (Association Française pour la Cybernetique Economique et Technique) A professional organization whose purpose is to bring

ALGORITHM   7

together French scientists, computer users, computer manufacturers, and engineers working and interested in computer technology and applied mathematics.

AFIPS   (American Federation of Information Processing Societies) A society whose primary purpose is to advance understanding and knowledge of the information processing sciences through active engagement in various scientific activities and through cooperation with state, national, and international (called IFIPS) organizations on information processing.

AI   An abbreviation for artificial intelligence, the branch of computer science that works on getting computers to think like human beings.

Aiken, Howard Hathaway   (1900–1973) Headed the team of people who designed and built the first electromechanical computer, the Automatic Sequence Controlled Calculator at Harvard University. See *ASCC*.

airline reservation system   An on-line, direct access application in which a computing system is used to keep track of seat inventories, flight schedules, and other information required to run an airline. The reservation system is designed to maintain up-to-date data files and to respond, within seconds or less, to inquiries from ticket agents at locations remote from the computing system.

AISP   (Association of Information Systems Professionals) Membership is intended for professionals involved in any aspect of information systems—including design, analysis, manufacture, sales, management, education, and consultation.

algebra   The study of mathematical structure. Elementary algebra is the study of numeral systems and their properties. Algebra solves problems in arithmetic by using letters or symbols to stand for quantities.

algebra of logic   A system of logical relations expressed as algebraic formulas; first introduced by George Boole. See *Boolean algebra*.

ALGOL   (ALGOrithmic Language) An international high-level programming language used to code problem-solving algorithms.

algorithm   A prescribed set of well-defined, unambiguous rules or processes for the solution of a problem in a finite number of steps; for example, a full statement of an arithmetic procedure for evaluating cosine *x* to a stated precision. Contrast with *heuristic*.

Example of an algorithm:

1. Dial 1.
2. Dial the area code, if it is different from your local area code.
3. Dial the 7-digit telephone number for the place you want.

algorithmic language A language designed for expressing algorithms.

alias A user-supplied name interpreted by the system to represent a program or command.

aliasing Undesirable visual effects in computer-generated images caused by improper sampling techniques. The most common effect is a jagged edge along object boundaries.

allocation The process of reserving computer storage areas for instructions or data.

alphabetic Pertaining to a character set that includes the letters of the alphabet.

alphabetic string A string in which the characters are letters, or pertain to an agreed alphabet set.

alphameric A contraction of alphanumeric.

alphanumeric A general term for alphabetic letters (*A* through *Z*), numerical digits (0 through 9), and special characters (-,/,*,$,(,), +, etc.) that are machine-processable.

alpha testing Trying a new product out on the employees of one's own company. Contrast with *beta testing*.

ALU (Arithmetic-Logic Unit) The portion of the central processing unit (CPU) where arithmetic and logical operations are performed. A basic element of the *CPU*.

ambient temperature The temperature surrounding a piece of equipment.

American National Standards Institute (ANSI) An organization that acts as a national clearing-house and coordinator for voluntary standards in the United States.

American Standard Code for Information Interchange See *ASCII*.

ampere Base unit of electric current in the SI metric system. A current of 1 ampere means that 6.25×10^{18} electrons are flowing by a point each second, 1 ampere equals 1 coulomb per second.

amplifier An electronic circuit that increases the voltage, current, or power of an input signal, or that isolates one part of a system from another.

analog Pertaining to representation by means of continuously variable physical quantities. Contrast with *digital*.

analog computer A device that operates on data in the form of continuously variable physical quantities. See *computer*. Contrast with *digital computer*.

analog data A physical representation of information such that the representation bears an exact relationship to the original information. For example, the electrical signals on a telephone channel are analog-data representation of the original voice data.

analog model A model that relates physical similarity to the actual situation.

analog-to-digital converter (A-D converter) A mechanical or electrical device used to convert continuous analog signals to discrete digital numbers Opposite of *digital-to-analog converter*. See *digitize*.

analyst/programmer A person whose major tasks involve the combining of systems analysis and design functions with programming activities. Most frequently referred to as a programmer analyst.

analytical engine A device invented in the mid-1800s by Charles Babbage, a British mathematician, to solve mathematical problems. This machine was a forerunner of the modern digital computer. See *Babbage, Charles*.

AND A logical connection, as in the statement A AND B, which means that the statement is true if, and only if, A is true and B is true simultaneously.

AND-gate (1) A binary circuit with two or more inputs and a single output, in which the output is logic 1 only when all inputs are logic 1, and the output is logic 0 if any one of the inputs is logic 0. (2) In a computer, a *gate* circuit with more than one input terminal. No output signal will be produced unless a pulse is applied to all inputs simultaneously.

android A humanlike male robot.

angstrom A unit of measurement, 1/250 millionth of an inch. Angstroms are used to measure the elements in electronic components on a chip.

animation Making an object appear to move by rapidly displaying a series of pictures of it, each one in a slightly different position. The technique used for producing computer-generated movies.

annotation symbol A symbol used to add messages or notes to a flowchart. It is attached to flowcharting symbols by dotted lines.

ANSI (American National Standards Institute) An organization that acts as a national clearing-house and coordinator for voluntary standards in the United States.

answer mode The ability of a modem to accept an incoming call from another modem.

anthropomorphic image A figure of speech used to describe a computer, and devices controlled by computers, as though the computer were a person.

Apple IIc computer. Courtesy Apple Computer, Inc.

anti-aliasing A filtering technique to give the appearance of smooth lines and edges in a raster display image.

antistatic mat A floor mat placed in front of a device, such as a disk unit that is sensitive to static, to prevent shocks that could cause loss of data during human handling of the unit.

aperture card A punched card with an opening specifically prepared for the mounting of a frame or frames of microfilm.

APL (A Programming Language) A mathematically structured programming language developed by the IBM Corporation. In its simplest mode of operation, APL performs the functions of an intelligent calculator. The power of the language is demonstrated by its extended single operators that allow a user to directly perform such calculations as taking the inverse of a matrix or solving a set of linear equations.

Apple II, IIc, and IIe Popular microcomputer systems manufactured by Apple Computer, Inc.

Apple Computer, Inc. A manufacturer of microcomputer systems.

application Task to be performed by a computer program or system. Broad examples of computer applications are engineering design, numerical control, airline seat reservations, business forecasting, and hospital administration.

application-oriented language A problem-oriented programming language whose statements contain or resemble the terminology of the computer user.

applications programmer A computer programmer who develops applications programs.

applications programming The preparation of programs for application to specific problems in order to find solutions. Contrast with *systems programming*.

applications programs The programs normally written by an organization that enable the computer to produce useful work; for example, inventory control, attendance accounting, linear programming, and medical accounting. Contrast with *systems programs*.

applications software See *Applications programs*.

APT (Automatic Programmed Tool). A programming system that is used in numerical control applications for the programmed control of machine functions. The APT language allows a user to define points, lines, circles, planes, conical surfaces, and geometric surfaces. See *numerical control* and *parts programmer*.

architecture The physical structure of a computer's internal operations, including its registers, memory, instruction set, input/output structure, and so on.

archive To copy programs and data onto an auxiliary storage medium (disk, tape, and so forth) for long-term retention.

area search The examination of a large group of documents to select those that pertain to one group, such as one category, class, and so on.

argument A variable to which either a logical or a numerical value may be assigned.

arithmetic Refers to the operations of addition, subtraction, multiplication, and division, or to the section of the computer hardware that performs these operations. See *arithmetic-logic unit*.

arithmetic-logic unit A basic element of the central processing unit (CPU). The portion of the CPU where arithmetic and logical operations are performed.

arithmetic shift To multiply or divide a quantity by a power of the number base; for example, if binary 1101, representing decimal 13, is arithmetically shifted twice to the left, the result is 110100, representing 52, which is also obtained by multiplying 13 by 2 twice; however, if the decimal 13 were to be shifted to the left twice, the result would be the same as multiplying by 10 twice, or 1300.

arithmetic unit Same as *arithmetic-logic unit*.

ARPANET (Advanced Research Projects Agency NETwork) A government computer network that links Department of Defense sites, research centers, and computer think tanks. Its goals are to permit computer resource sharing, develop highly reliable and economic digital communications, and enable access to unique and powerful facilities that become economically feasible when widely shared.

ARQ   (Automatic Repeat ReQuest) A data transmission checking function.

arrangement   Order of index terms or items of data in a system.

array   (1) A series of related items. (2) An ordered arrangement of pattern of items or numbers, such as a determinant, matrix, vector, or table of numbers. See *matrix* and *vector*.

array processor   A processor that performs matrix arithmetic much faster than standard computers. It is capable of performing operations on all the elements in large matrices at one time.

arrival rate   The number of characters or messages arriving over a data communications medium per unit of time.

artificial intelligence   The capability of a device to perform functions that are normally associated with human intelligence, such as reasoning, learning, and self-improvement. See *heuristic* and *machine learning*.

artificial language   A language based on a set of prescribed rules that are established prior to its usage. Contrast with *natural language*.

ARTSPEAK   A programming language designed to help inexperienced users produce computer drawings on digital plotters.

ASA   (American Statistical Association) A professional organization for statisticians, quantitative scientists, and users of statistics. ASA also is an acronym for American Standards Association, which was replaced by ANSI.

ASCC   (Automatic Sequence Controlled Calculator) First electromechanical computer developed under the direction of Howard Aiken at Harvard University.

ASCII   (American Standard Code for Information Interchange) Acronym pronounced "asskey." A 7-bit standard code adopted to facilitate the interchange of data among various types of data processing and data communications equipment. *See opposite.*

ASIS   (American Society for Information Science) This professional organization provides a forum for librarians, information specialists, scientists, and others who seek to improve the communication of information.

ASM   (Association of Systems Management) This organization represents members of the industry who are concerned with the promotion of effective management of people and equipment in data processing fields.

Character	ASCII
0	011 0000
1	011 0001
2	011 0010
3	011 0011
4	011 0100
5	011 0101
6	011 0110
7	011 0111
8	011 1000
9	011 1001
A	100 0001
B	100 0010
C	100 0011
D	100 0100
E	100 0101
F	100 0110
G	100 0111
H	100 1000
I	100 1001
J	100 1010
K	100 1011
L	100 1100
M	100 1101
N	100 1110
O	100 1111
P	101 0000
Q	101 0001
R	101 0010
S	101 0011
T	101 0100
U	101 0101
V	101 0110
W	101 0111
X	101 1000
Y	101 1001
Z	101 1010

aspect card A card containing the accession numbers of documents in an information retrieval system.

aspect ratio In computer graphics, the relationships of the height and width of the video display screen frame or image area.

ASR (Automatic Send/Receive) A teletypewriter with keyboard, printer, paper tape reader, and paper tape punch that allows tape to be produced and edited off-line for automatic transmission.

assemble To gather, interpret, and coordinate data required for a computer program, translate the data into computer language, and project it into the final program for the computer to follow.

assembler A computer program that takes nonmachine language instructions prepared by a computer user and converts them into a form that may be used by the computer.

assembler directive A statement placed in an assembly language program to give directions to the assembler.

assembling The automatic process by which a computer converts a symbolic source language program into a machine language, usually on an instruction-by-instruction basis. See *cross-compiling/ assembling.*

assembly language A programming language that allows a computer user to write a program using mnemonics instead of numeric instructions. It is a low-level symbolic programming language that closely resembles machine code language. Same as low-level language. Contrast with *problem-oriented language* and *procedure-oriented language.*

assembly listing A printed output produced by an assembler. It lists the original assembly language program, the machine language version of the program, storage assignments, error messages, and other information useful to the programmer.

Association for Computing Machinery The major professional organization for computer scientists. See *ACM.*

associative storage A storage device whose storage locations are identified by their contents (rather than by names or positions, as in most computer storage devices). Same as *content-addressable memory* and *search memory.*

asterisk The symbol *. Used to represent a multiplication operator in many programming languages.

asynchronous communications adapter A device attached to a computer that enables it to effect asynchronous data communications over standard telephone facilities.

asynchronous computer A computer in which each operation starts as a result of a signal generated by the completion of the previous operation or by the availability of the equipment required for the next operation. Contrast with *synchronous computer.*

asynchronous input Input data having no time-dependable pattern or cycle when related to the computer system.

asynchronous transmission Transmission of data that requires the use of start and stop elements for each character because the interval of time between characters can vary.

Atanasoff, John V. (born 1903) Designed an electronic digital computer in 1942. An engineer, he was interested in finding faster ways of performing computations for physics problems. See *ABC.*

Atari A manufacturer of personal computers and related peripheral devices.

ATM (Automatic Teller Machine) A special-purpose banking terminal that allows users to make deposits and withdrawals.

atom The elementary building block of data structures. An atom corresponds to a record in a file and many contain one or more fields of data.

attach To connect a peripheral to a computer in order to increase its capacity.

attenuation The decrease in the strength of a signal as it passes through a control system. Opposite of *gain.*

atto One quintillionth, or a billionth of a billionth, 10^{-18}.

attribute A word that describes the manner in which a variable is handled by the computer.

audio device Any computer device that accepts sound and/or produces sound. See *voice recognition* and *voice synthesis.*

audio output Computer output generated through voice synthesizers that create audible signals resembling a human voice.

audio response device An output device that produces a spoken response. See *voice output.*

audit trail A means for identifying the actions taken in processing input data or in preparing an output. By use of the audit trail, data on a source document can be traced to an output, and an output can be traced to the source items from which it was derived.

authoring system A computer system capable of executing an author language.

authorization A system control feature that requires specific approval before processing can take place.

authorized program A computer program capable of altering the fundamental operation or status of a computer system.

Audio device. Courtesy Radio Shack, a division of Tandy Corp.

author language A programming language that is used for designing instructional programs for computer-assisted instruction (CAI) systems. See *PILOT* and *PLANIT*.

authors People who design instructional material for *computer-assisted instruction* (CAI) systems.

auto-answer A modem that can automatically answer incoming telephone calls from computers and pipe the data into another computer.

autochart A type of documentor used for the automatic production and maintenance of charts, principally flowcharts.

AUTODIN (AUTOmatic DIgital Network) The data handling portion of the military communciations system.

auto indexing A system of indexing that superimposes additional information at any of several given addresses.

auto-load A key on some computer keyboards that activates the computer. It essentially boots the operating system into internal storage and starts execution of the system. See *operating system*.

automata The theory related to the study of the principles of operation and the application and behavioral characteristics of automatic devices.

automated data processing A process, largely self-regulating, in which information is handled with a minimum of human effort and intervention.

automated flowchart   A flowchart drawn by a computer controlled printer or plotter.

automated office   A general term that refers to the merger of computers, office electronic devices, and telecommunications technology in an office environment.

automatic   Pertaining to a process or device that, under specified conditions, functions without intervention by a human operator.

automatic carriage   See *carriage*.

automatic check   An equipment check built in specifically for checking purposes. Also called *built-in check*.

automatic coding   See *automatic programming*.

automatic computer   A computer that can process a specified volume of work, its assigned function, without requiring human intervention except for program changes. See *computer*.

automatic controller   A device or instrument that is capable of measuring and regulating by receiving a signal from a sensing device, comparing this data with a desired value, and issuing signals for corrective action.

automatic data processing   (ADP) See *data processing*

automatic error correction   A technique for detecting and correcting errors that occur in data transmission or within the system itself.

automatic loader   A hardware loader program, usually implemented in a special ROM, that allows loading of an auxiliary storage unit (disk or magnetic tape). See *bootstrapping*.

automatic message switching   See *message switching*.

automatic programming   (1) The process of using a computer to perform some stages of the work involved in preparing a program. (2) The production of a machine language computer program under the guidance of a symbolic representation of the program.

automatic quality control   Technique for evaluating the quality of a product being processed by checking it against a predetermined standard, and then automatically taking the proper corrective action if the quality falls below the standard.

automatic shutdown   Refers to the ability of some systems software to stop a network or a computer system as a whole in an orderly fashion.

automatic teller machine   A machine that provides bank customers with 24-hour teller service. The device is connected to the bank's computer system. To use the automatic teller, you insert a plastic identification card, log in with a special password code, and communicate with the system using a numeric keypad and a visual display. This machine allows you to cash checks, make deposits, and other banking transactions.

automaton A machine designed to simulate the operations of living things.

automonitor (1) A computer's record of its functions. (2) A computer program that records the operating functions of a computer.

autopilot A device used to fly an airplane or space vehicle automatically.

autopolling A contraction for automatic polling. Polling is a process whereby terminals in a computer network are scanned periodically to determine whether they are ready to send information. Auto-polling is a combination of hardware and software that polls the terminals in a computer network.

auto-repeat A feature of some keyboards that allows a key to automatically repeat when held down.

auto-restart The capability of a computer to perform automatically the initialization functions necessary to resume operation following an equipment or power failure.

autoscore In word processing, an instruction that causes text to be underlined.

auxiliary equipment Equipment not under direct control of the central processing unit. See *off-line.*

auxiliary function In automatic machine tool control, a machine function other than the control of the motion of a work-piece or cutter. Control of machine lubricating and cooling equipment are typical auxiliary functions.

auxiliary memory See *auxiliary storage.*

auxiliary operation An operation performed by equipment not under control of the central processing unit. See *off-line.*

auxiliary storage A storage that supplements the primary internal storage of a computer. Examples are magnetic disks, floppy disks, magnetic tapes, and magnetic drums. Same as *secondary storage.*

availability The ratio of the time that a hardware device is known or believed to be operating correctly to the total hours of scheduled operation. Often called *operating ratio.*

available time The time that a computer is available for use.

average search length An anticipated time or number of functions to be performed to locate an address.

AWC (Association for Women in Computing) The AWC has these purposes: to promote communication among women in computing;

to further the professional development and advancement of women in computing; and to promote the education of women and girls in computing.

axes   In a two-dimensional coordinate system, lines used as references for vertical (y) and horizontal (x) measurement.

B

Babbage, Charles   (1792–1871) A British mathematician and inventor. He designed a *Difference Engine* for calculating logarithms to 20 decimal places and an "analytical engine" that was a forerunner of the digital computer. Babbage was ahead of his time, and the engineering techniques of his day were not advanced enough to successfully build his machines. See *analytical engine*.

babble   The cross talk from a large number of channels in a system. See *cross talk*.

background   In multiprogramming, the environment in which low-priority programs are executed.

background job   See *background program*.

background noise   In optical scanning, electrical interference caused by such things as ink tracking or carbon offsetting.

background processing   The execution of low-priority computer programs during periods when the system resources are not required to process high-priority programs. See *background program*.

background program   A program that can be executed whenever the facilities of a multiprogramming computer system are not required by other programs of higher priority. Contrast with *foreground program*.

backing store   A backup memory to the computer main memory. More commonly called *auxiliary storage*.

backlash   In a mechanical operation, the "play" between interacting parts, such as two gears, as a result of tolerance.

backplane   The circuitry and mechanical elements used to connect the boards of a system. Also called *motherboard*.

backspace   A keyboard operation that moves the cursor one place to the left. Backspacing allows you to modify what you already typed.

backspace tape   The process of returning a magnetic tape to the beginning of the preceding record.

backtracking   The operation of scanning a list in reverse.

backup   Pertaining to procedures or equipment that are available for use in the event of failure or overloading of the normally used equipment or procedures. See *fail-safe system, fail-soft system, fall-back*, and *father file*.

backup programmer   The programmer who is an assistant to the chief programmer. See *chief programmer*.

Backus Normal Form (BNF)   A language used for describing languages.

backward read   A feature available on some magnetic tape systems whereby the magnetic tape units can transfer data to computer storage while moving in reverse.

badge reader   A terminal equipped to read credit cards or specially coded badges.

balance   The amount remaining at the end of one period or beginning of another period.

band   (1) In communications, a range of frequencies, as between two specified limits. (2) Range, or scope, of operation. (3) A group of circular recording tracks on a storage device such as a disk or drum.

bandwidth   In data communications, the difference (expressed in hertz) between the highest and lowest frequencies of a band.

bank   A unit of internal storage.

banked memory   A method of enlarging the usual 64K RAM memory. Space addressable by 8-bit microprocessors to a much larger range, usually to 1 megabyte. To avoid addressing confusion, boards above 64K are switched on only when needed by software control.

bar-code   A type of code used on labels to be read by bar-code scanner. Bar codes are used to identify retail sales items, library books, and railroad cars. See *UPC*.

bar-code scanner   An optical device that can read data from objects bearing characters recorded in the form of parallel bars. The characters are translated into digital signals for storage or processing.

bare board   A printed circuit board with no electronic components on it.

bar printer A printing device that uses several type bars positioned side by side across the line.

base (1) The radix of a number system. (2) The region between the emitter and collector of a transistor that receives minority carriers injected from the emitter. (3) On a printed circuit board, the portion that supports the printed pattern.

base 2 See *binary*

base 8 See *octal.*

base 10 See *decimal.*

base 16 See *hexadecimal.*

base address A specified address that is combined with a *relative address* to form the *absolute address* of a particular storage location.

baseband transmission A means of using low frequency transmission of signals across coaxial cables for short distance, local area network transmission.

baseline document A document that is a reference for changes to a data processing system.

BASIC (Beginner's All-purpose Symbolic Instruction Code) An easy-to-learn, easy-to-use, algebraic programming language. BASIC has a small repertory of commands and simple statement formats. For this reason, BASIC is widely used in programming instruction, in personal computing, and in business and industry. The BASIC language has been implemented on most microcomputers, minicomputers, and larger machines. See *BASIC-PLUS, integer BASIC, floating point BASIC and True BASIC.*

EXAMPLE OF A BASIC PROGRAM

```
100   REM METRIC CONVERSION
110   INPUT "METERS =",M
120   INPUT "CENTIMETERS =",C
130   LET X = M + C/100
140   LET I = 39.37*X
150   LET F + INT(I/12)
160   LET I = I - 12*F
170   PRINT F,I
180   END
```

Basic FORTRAN An approved American Standard version of FORTRAN programming language. See *FORTRAN*.

basic linkage A linkage that is used repeatedly in one routine, program, or system and that follows the same set of rules each time. See *calling sequence* and *linkage*.

BASIC-PLUS An extension of the BASIC programming language. BASIC-PLUS includes more powerful capabilities, especially for data manipulation.

batch A group of records or programs that is considered as a single unit for processing on a computer.

batch processing A technique by which programs that are to be executed are coded and collected together for processing in groups or batches. The user gives the job to a computer center, where it is put into a batch of programs and processed, and then the data are returned. The user has no direct access to the machine. See *remote batch processing*.

batch total A sum of a set of items in a batch of records that is used to check the accuracy of operations involving the batch.

Batten system A method of indexing invented by W. E. Batten that uses the coordination of single attributes to identify specific documents. Sometimes called the "peek-a-boo" system because of its method of comparing holes in cards by superimposing cards and checking the coincidence of holes.

baud A unit for measuring data transmission speed. One baud is 1 bit per second.

Baudot code A code for the transmission of data in which five bits represent one character. It is named for Emile Baudot, a pioneer in printing telegraphy. The name is usually applied to the code used in many teleprinter systems.

bay A cabinet or rack in which electronic equipment is installed.

BCD See *binary coded decimal*.

BCS (British Computer Society) A professional computer society in the United Kingdom.

BDOS (Basic Disk Operating System) In some operating systems, the part of the system that customizes it to a specific disk drive.

bebugging The intentional seeding of a program with known mistakes to measure the rates of debugging by student programmers.

bells and whistles An informal description of the special or extra features of a computer system; for example, graphics, color displays, sound, many peripherals, and so on.

BEMA (Business Equipment Manufacturers Association) This organization's main functions are to guide users of information processing equipment in solving problems and applying information for general benefit, and to sponsor the setting of standards for computers and information processing.

benchmark A point of reference from which measurements can be made; for example, the use of a program to evaluate the performance of a computer.

benchmark problem A problem to evaluate and compare the performance of digital computers.

benchmark tests Tests used in the measurement of computer equipment performance under typical conditions of use (i.e., a computer program run on several different computers for the purpose of comparing execution speed, throughput, and so forth).

beta testing Trying a new product out on people other than employees of one's own company. Contrast with *alpha testing*.

bias The amount by which the average of a set of values departs from a reference value.

bidirectional The ability of a print head to print right to left, as well as left to right, enabling a printer to operate quickly.

binary Pertaining to the number system with a radix of 2.

binary coded decimal (BCD) A computer coding system in which each decimal digit is represented by a group of four binary ones and zeros.

binary coded decimal number A number, usually consisting of successive groups of figures, in which each group of four figures is a binary number that represents, but does not necessarily equal arithmetically, a particular figure in an associated decimal number; for example, the decimal number 264 is represented as the binary coded number 0010 0110 0100.

binary device In computer science, equipment that records data in binary form or that reads the data so coded.

binary digit (*bit*) Either of the characters 0 or 1.

binary file A file containing programs in machine code.

binary notation A numeral system written in base 2 notation.

binary number A numeral, usually of more than one digit, representing a sum in which the quantity represented by each digit is based on a radix of 2. The digits used are 0 and 1.

binary point The radix point in the binary numeral. The point that separates the fractional part of a mixed binary numeral from the integer part. In the binary numeral 110.011, the binary point is between the two zeros.

binary search A search in which the series of items is divided into two parts, one of which is rejected, and the process repeated on the unrejected part until the item with the desired property is found. Also known as *dichotomizing search.*

binary system   A numeral system with a base or radix of 2; for example, the numeral 111 represents the quantity 1, plus 1×2^1, plus 1×2^2—7.

binary-to-decimal conversion   The process of converting a numeral written to the base 2 to the equivalent numeral written to the base 10.

binary-to-gray code conversion   A gray code equivalent of a binary numeral can be obtained by applying the following rule: the most significant gray code digit equals the corresponding binary digit, and the following gray code digit is 1 if the binary digit changes and 0 if it does not. For example, the binary value 0110100 equals the gray code value 0101110.

binary-to-hexadecimal conversion   The process of converting a numeral written to the base 2 to the equivalent numeral written to the base 16.

binary-to-octal conversion   The process of converting a numeral written to the base 2 to the equivalent numeral written to the base 8.

binding time   The stage at which a compiler replaces a symbolic name or address with its machine language form.

bionics   The study of living systems for the purpose of relating their characteristics and functions to the development of mechanical and electronic hardware (hardware systems).

BIOS   (Basic Input/Output System) In some operating systems, the part of the program that customizes it to a specific computer.

bipolar   The most popular fundamental kind of integrated circuit, formed from layers of silicon with different electrical characteristics. "Bipolar" literally means "having two poles" and is used to distinguish the earlier transistor from the MOS Field Effect Transistor (MOSFET), which is "unipolar" ("Having one pole"). As in MOSFET, the current flow of majority carriers goes in one direction only—for example, from source to drain. In a bipolar transistor, the current in the emitter region splits and flows toward two terminals (poles), the base and the collector.

bipolar read-only memory   See *BROM.*

biquinary code   A 7-bit weighted code used primarily to represent decimal numbers. It is a redundant code that may be used to provide error-checking features. A pair of bits represents the decimal number 5 or 0, and the remaining 5 bits are used to represent the decimal numbers 0 through 4.

bistable device A device with only two stable states, such as "on" and "off."

bi-state A situation in which a computer component takes on one of only two possible conditions.

bit A binary digit; a digit (1 or 0) in the representation of a number in binary notation. Several bits make up a byte, or a computer word.

bit density A measure of the number of bits recorded per unit of length or area.

bit manipulation The act of turning bits on and off. Sometimes called bit-flipping.

bit map An area in the computer's storage reserved for graphics. The bit map holds the picture that is continuously transmitted to the display screen.

bit rate The rate at which binary digits appear on communication lines or channels.

bit-slice processor This approach to microprocessors allows microcomputer organizations of variable word sizes, with processor units separated into 2- , 4- , or 8-bit slices on a single chip. These devices can be paralleled to yield an 8- , 12- , 16- , 24- , or 32-bit microcomputer when assembled with the other necessary overhead components of the system.

bit stream Referring to a binary signal without regard to groupings by character.

bit test A program check to determine whether a specific bit is on (1) or off (0).

bit transfer rate The number of bits transferred per unit time, usually expressed in bits per second.

bit twiddler A hacker. A person who enjoys working with computers.

BL (BLank) An empty space in text.

black box An electronic or mechanical device that alters input signals in a predictable manner but whose inner workings are often a mystery to the user.

blank A part of a medium in which no characters are recorded.

blank character A character used to produce a character space on an output medium.

block A group of digits, characters, or words that are held in one section of an input/output medium and handled as a unit (e.g., the data recorded between two interblock gaps on a magnetic tape).

block diagram A graphic representation showing the logical sequence by which data is processed. See *flowchart*.

blocking   Combining two or more records into one block, usually to increase the efficiency of computer input and output operations.

blocking factor   The number of logical records per physical record on a magnetic tape or disk.

block length   A measure of the size of a block, usually specified in units such as records, words, characters, or bytes.

block move   A feature in word processing systems that allows the user to identify a block of text and move it anywhere in a file. It is the electronic equivalent of "cut and paste."

block sorting   A sorting technique used to break down a file into related groups.

block structure   A programming concept that allows related declarations and statements to be grouped together.

block transfer   Relocating an entire block of data from one area of storage to another.

blow-up   A blow-up occurs when a program unexpectedly halts due to a bug or because it encounters data conditions it cannot handle.

blue ribbon program   A computer program that executes properly on the first try. Blue ribbon programs do not require any debugging.

BNF   (Backus Normal Form) A notation for describing the syntax of programming languages.

board   A card that contains circuitry for one or more specific functions.

board exchange warranty   A warranty that provides a customer with a new replacement board when the original needs fixing,

boldfacing   A feature of some printers and word processing systems that lets them imitate the look of a boldface font. On many printers, boldfacing is produced by shadow printing.

bomb   A term used to denote a spectacular failure in a program. A computer user "bombs" a system when he/she deliberately writes a program that will disrupt the system.

bookkeeping   See *housekeeping*.

Boolean algebra   A branch of symbolic logic that is similar in form to algebra, but instead of dealing with numerical relationships, it deals with logical relationships.

Boolean operator   A logic operator, each of whose operands and whose result has one of two values.

Boole, George   (1815–1864) The father of Boolean algebra. A British logician and mathematician. In 1847, he wrote a pamphlet, "Mathematical Analysis of Logic." In 1851, he wrote a more mature statement of his logical system in a larger work, "An Investigation of the Laws of Thought," in which are founded the mathematical theories of logic. Boolean algebra lay dormant until it could be usefully applied to the fields of relay switching and electronic computers. It has now become an important subject in logic design of electronic computers. See *Boolean algebra.*

boot   To start up a program.

bootstrapping   The process of using a small initialization program bootstrap to load another program and to start up an inactive computer.

bore   The diameter of a hole; for example, the diameter of the hole on a floppy disk or magnetic tape reel.

borrow   An arithmetically negative carry. It occurs in direct subtraction by raising the low order digit of the minuend by one unit of the next higher order digit.

BOT   (Beginning-Of-Tape) A mark that shows where to start recording on a magnetic tape.

bottleneck   See *limiting operation.*

bottom up technique   An implementation technique wherein the bottom level modules are written and tested, after which the next lowest level of modules are written and tested. This process continues until all of the modules have been completed.

bpi   Bits per inch or bytes per inch.

bps   Bits per second or bytes per second.

branch   The selection of one or more possible paths in the flow of control, based on come criterion. See *conditional transfer, jump,* and *unconditional transfer.*

branch instruction   An instruction to a computer that enables it to

A board

choose between alternative program paths, depending upon the conditions determined by the computer during the execution of the program.

branchpoint   A place in a program where a branch is selected.

breadboard   Usually refers to an experimental or rough model of a process, device, or construction.

break   An interruption of a transmission.

break key   On some computers, a keyboard key that will interrupt what the computer is doing.

breakpoint   A specified point in a program at which the program may be interrupted by manual intervention or by a control routine. Breakpoints are generally used as an aid in testing and debugging programs.

bridge   A device that connects several data communication lines to form a multipoint circuit.

bridgeware   Computer programs used to translate instructions written for one type of computer into a format that another type of computer understands.

briefcase computer   A briefcase-size computer that uses a flat panel liquid crystal display. It is larger than a hand-held computer but smaller than a desk size computer.

broadband   As applied to data communications, used to denote transmission facilities capable of handling frequencies greater than those required for high-grade voice communications. Broadband communication channels can transmit data at rates up to 120,000 bits per second; for example, microwaves, fiber optics, and laser beams.

broadcast   In data communications, the dissemination of information to a number of stations simultaneously.

BROM   (Bipolar Read-Only Memory) A read-only memory with no write function that uses bipolar semiconductor devices.

brush   In computer graphics, a blob of color that can be moved anywhere on the display screen by means of a joystick paddle or similar input device. As the brush moves, it leaves behind a trail of color.

brute-force technique   Any mathematical technique that depends on the raw power of a computer to arrive at a nonelegant solution to a mathematical problem. Most computer users try to avoid brute-force techniques unless they have no practical alternative.

BSC   (Binary Synchronous Communication) Procedure used for data transmission.

BTAM   (Basic Telecommunications Access Method) An access method that permits read/write communications with remote devices.

bubble memory   A method by which information is stored as magnetized dots (bubbles), which rest on a thin film of semiconductor material. Offers a compact storage capability.

bubble sort   A sort achieved by exchanging pairs of keys that begins with the first pair and exchanges successive pairs until the list is ordered. Also called ripple sort.

bucket   A term used to indicate a specific portion of storage.

buffer   A temporary storage area that is used to equalize or balance the different operating speeds. For example, a buffer can be used between a slow input device, such as a typewriter, and the main computer, which operates at a very high speed.

buffered computer   A computer that provides for simultaneous input/output and process operations.

bug   A term used to denote a mistake in a computer program or system or a malfunction in a computer hardware component. Hence to debug means to remove mistakes and correct malfunctions. See *malfunction* and *mistake*.

built-in check   See *automatic check*.

bulk eraser   See *degausser*.

bulk memory   See *auxiliary storage*.

bulletin board   See *electronic bulletin board*.

bundle   (1) Software that is supplied with hardware. (2) Products and services provided together as a package.

bundled   The position of a computer manufacturer that includes the entire line of computer products and services in a single price. Contrast with *unbundled*.

burn-in   The process of testing electronic circuits and components by running the circuits at elevated temperatures in an oven. For example, a typical test might be to run components continuously for a week at 50°C (122°F). This testing process causes weak links in the circuit to burn out; the failed circuitry is replaced with components that will withstand the test.

burning   The process of programming a read-only memory. See *PROM programmer*.

Burroughs Corporation   A large manufacturer of computer equipment.

burst   (1) In computer operations, to separate continuous-form paper into discrete sheets. (2) In data transmission, a sequence of signals counted as one unit.

burster   A mechanical device that takes apart a multipage computer printout. It separates copies and removes the carbon paper.

Business graphics. Courtesy Sperry Corp.

burst mode A method of reading or writing data that does not permit an interrupt to occur.

bus A channel or path for transferring data and electrical signals.

bus system A network of paths inside the computer that facilitates data flow. Important buses in a computer are identified as data bus, control bus, and address bus.

business applications Computer systems involving normal day-to-day accounting procedures such as payroll, accounts receivables, accounts payable, and inventory.

business data processing Data processing for business purposes (e.g., payroll, scheduling, accounting). See *administrative data processing*.

business graphics Pie charts, bar charts, graphs, and other visual representations of the operational or strategic aspects of a business, such as sales vs. costs, sales by department, comparative product performance, stock prices, etc.

business-oriented programming language A language designed for handling large data files in business applications; for example, COBOL.

business programming A branch of computer programming in which business problems are coded for computer solution. Business programming usually involves relatively few calculations with a large number of data inputs and outputs. See *business applications*.

bypass A parallel path around one or more elements of a circuit.

bypass capacitor A capacitor used to reduce electrical noise from the power supply.

byte (1) A grouping of adjacent binary digits operated on by the computer as a unit. The most common size byte contains 8 binary digits. (2) A group of binary digits used to encode a single character.

bytes per inch (BPI) The number of bytes that can be contained on 1 inch of magnetic tape.

C

C A programming language designed for use on microcomputers. The language combines high-level statements with low-level machine control to deliver software that is both easy to use and highly efficient.

cable An electrical wire or bundle of wires used to connect two parts of the system together. It carries electrical power or electrical signals.

cable connector Plugs (male/female) that are used for connecting cables between a computer and peripherals.

cache memory A small, high-speed buffer memory used in modern computer systems to hold temporarily those portions of the contents of the main memory that are (believed to be) currently in use.

CAD See *computer-aided design*.

CAD/CAM (Computer-Aided Design/Computer-Aided Manufacturing) A term applied to efforts to automate design operations and manufacturing operations.

cage A chassis in which printed circuit cards are mounted.

CAI See *computer-assisted instruction*.

CAI authors See *authors*.

CAL See *computer-augmented learning*.

calculating punch A machine designed to perform arithmetic operations with punch cards.

calculator Any mechanical or electronic machine used for performing calculations. Calculators, as distinguished from computers, usually require frequent human intervention. See *calculating punch* and *hand calculator*.

calculator mode Some interactive computer systems have an operating mode that allows the terminal (or keyboard/display in case of microcomputer systems) to be used as a desk calculator. The user types an expression, and the computer evaluates it and returns the answer immediately.

calibration The process of determining by measurement or by comparison with a standard the correct value of each scale reading on a meter or the correct value of each setting of a control knob.

call To transfer control to a specific closed subroutine. Synonymous with cue.

calligraphic display A system that generates images as collections of smooth straight lines.

calling sequence A specified set of instructions and data necessary to call a given subroutine.

call instruction An instruction that, after diverting execution to a new sequence of instructions (subroutine), permits a return to the program's original sequence.

CAM See *computer-aided manufacturing*.

Canadian Information Processing Society (CIPS) An organization formed to bring together Canadians with a common interest in the field of information processing.

cancel A keyboard operation that deletes the line you are currently typing.

canned routines Programs prepared by a computer manufacturer or software developer and provided to a user in a ready to use form.

canned software Programs prepared by computer manufacturers or another supplier and provided to a user in ready-to-use form. Contrast with *custom software*.

capacitance A measure of the ability to store electric charge, the basic unit of measurement being a farad.

capacitor An electronic component that stores a charge of static electricity and when properly stimulated releases this charge. This is the way bits are written to and read from computer storage.

capacity   The number of items of data that a storage device is capable of containing. Frequently defined in terms of computer words, bytes, or characters.

capstan   The rotating shaft within a magnetic tape drive that pulls the tape across the recording heads at a constant speed.

capture   (of data) The recording of data on a form or its entry into a computer.

card   A storage medium in which data is represented by means of holes punched in vertical columns in a 18.7 cm × 8.3 cm (7⅜ inches × 3¼ inches) paper card. See *Hollerith card, punched card, ninety-six column card.*

card cage   A rack inside the computer housing that holds the printed circuit boards.

card code   The combinations of punched holes that represent characters in a punch card. See *Hollerith code.*

card column   One of the vertical lines of punching positions on a punch card.

card deck   A collection of punch cards.

card face   The printed side of a punch card.

card feed   A mechanism that moves cards into a machine one at a time.

card field   A fixed number of consecutive card columns assigned to a unit of information.

card frame   An enclosure that holds a computer system's circuit boards in place.

card hopper   A device that holds cards and makes them available for the feeding mechanism of card handling equipment.

card image   A representation in storage of the holes punched in a card.

card punch   An output device that accepts information from the computer's memory and punches it into cards. A keyboard device by which an operator can punch cards. Also known as a *keypunch.*

card punching   See *keypunching.*

card reader   An input device that reads information punched into cards. The information read is transferred into the computer's memory.

card reproducer   A device that reproduces a punch card by punching a similar card. See *reproducing punch.*

card row   One of the horizontal lines of punching positions on a punch card.

card sorting   Separating a deck of punch cards into stacks in accordance with the holes punched into the individual cards.

card stacker   The receptacle into which cards are accumulated after passing through a punch card data processing machine.

card-to-disk converter   A device that converts data directly from punch cards to magnetic disk.

card-to-tape converter   A device that converts data directly from punch cards to magnetic tape.

card verification   A means of checking the accuracy of keypunching. A second operator verifies the original punching by depressing the keys of a verifier while reading the same source data. The machine compares the key depressed with the hole already punched in the card and, if they are not identical, indicates an error.

caret   (1) A symbol used to indicate the location of the radix point of a number. (2) ∧ or > mark, used on a screen as a cursor to show where text should be inserted. (3) A symbol used to represent exponentiation in many programming languages.

carousel   A rotary device that presents a data medium such as film or microfilm at an identified position for reading or recording.

carriage control tape   A tape that is punched with the information needed to control line feeding on a *line printer*.

carrier   A continuous frequency capable of being modulated with a signal.

carry   A process of bringing forward. The carry digit, or the digit that is to be added to the next higher column, or a special condition that occurs when the sum of two digits in a single column is equal to or greater than the numbering base.

carry register   A register of 1 bit that acts as an extension of the accumulator during rotation or carry operations.

Cartesian coordinate system   In a flat plane, a point can be located by its distances from two intersecting straight lines, the distance from one line being measured along a parallel to the other line. The numbers associated with the point are called the coordinates of the point.

cartridge   A plug-in module that contains software permanently stored in ROM memory. A cartridge is convenient, easy to use, soundless, and cannot be erased.

cascade control   An automatic control system in which the control units are linked chain-fashion, each feeding into (as well as regulating) the next stage.

cascade sort   An external tape sort that sorts by merging strings from all but one tape onto the remaining tape. Subsequent passes merge fewer tapes until one tape contains all items.

cashless society   A conceptual computerized system in which credit transactions would be settled instantaneously by transferring credits from the customer's bank account to the store's account via a point-of-sale terminal.

cassette A small, self-contained volume of magnetic tape used for data storage.

cassette interface The circuitry used to control data communications between a computer and a magnetic tape cassette recorder.

cassette recorder A device designed to use cassettes to record and store digital data and, at a later time, reload this data into the computer's internal storage. Used widely with microcomputers.

CAT Computer-Assisted Training.

catena A connected series. See *concatenate*.

cathode-ray tube (CRT) An electronic tube with a screen upon which information may be displayed. See *display, screen*, and *video terminal*.

CBASIC A compiler version of the BASIC language. Much faster in execution than the more popular interpreter BASIC. This high-level language is not interactive.

CBBS (Computerized Bulletin Board Service) See *electronic bulletin board*.

CBEMA Computer and Business Equipment Manufacturers Association.

CBI See *Charles Babbage Institute*.

CBL See *computer-based learning*.

CCD (Charge Coupled Device) A memory device within which stored information circulates rather than remains in fixed locations.

CCITT (Consultative Committee International Telegraph and Telephone) An organization established by the United Nations to develop worldwide standards for data communications.

CCP (Certificate in Computer Programming) The CCP examinations are given annually at test centers in colleges and universities in the United States, Canada, and several international locations. There are three separate examinations. Each of the three examinations tests a common core of programming knowledge and an area of specialization. The three areas of specialization are business programming, scientific programming, and systems programming. The common core of knowledge emphasizes such areas as data and file organization, techniques of programming, programming languages, interaction with hardware and software, and interaction with people.

CDC (Call Directing Code) Two- or 3-character code used to route automatically a message or command.

CDP   (Certificate in Data Processing) The CDP examination is given annually at test centers in colleges and universities in the United States, Canada, and several international locations. This broad-based examination consists of five sections and requires half a day to complete. In addition to having experience requirements and espousing the Code of Ethics, the CDP candidates must success-fully complete all five sections of the examination to receive the certificate.

CE   See *customer engineeer.*

cell   The storage for 1 unit of information, usually 1 character, 1 byte, or 1 word. A binary cell is a cell of 1 binary digit capacity. Also called *storage location.*

center   A keyboard function that places the information being typed in the center of the line.

centisecond   One hundredth of a second.

central information file   The main data storage system.

centralized data processing   A concept by which a company has all its computing equipment located at the same site and field-office operations have no effective data processing capability. Contrast with *distributed data processing.*

centralized design   An information structure in which a separate data processing department is utilized to provide data processing facilities for the organization.

centralized network configuration   The structure of a computer network whose dominating feature is a central computer that is involved in everything that happens in the system. Also called a *star network.*

central processing unit (CPU)   The component of a computer sys-tem with the circuitry to control the interpretation and execution of instructions. The CPU includes the arithmetic-logic and control sections. Synonymous with *central processor* and *mainframe.*

central processor   See *central processing unit.*

Centronics interface   A standard kind of parallel interface, origi-nally used to connect printers with microcomputers.

Certificate in Computer Programming   See *CCP.*

certification   Acceptance of software by an authorized agent, usually after the software has been validated by the agent, or after its validity has been demonstrated to the agent.

chad   A piece of material removed when forming a hold or notch in punched paper tape.

chadded tape   Perforated tape with the chad completely removed.

chadless tape   Perforated tape with the chad partially removed.

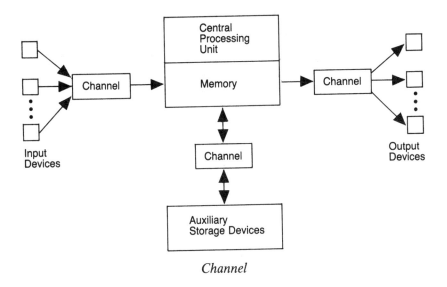

Channel

chain   (1) Linking of records by means of pointers in such a way that all like records are connected, the last record pointing to the first. (2) A set of operations that are to be performed sequentially.

chained files   Data files where data blocks are chained together using pointers.

chained list   A list in which each item points to the next item and the order of retrieval need not have any relation to the storage order.

chain field   A field in a record that defines the location and storage device of other data items logically related to the original record but not physically attached.

chaining   A process of linking a series of records, programs, or operations together.

chaining search   A technique that is used for retrieving data from a file by using addresses in the records that link each record to the next in the chain.

chain printer   A line printer in which the type slugs are carried by the links of a revolving chain. See *line printer*.

channel   (1) A path for electrical transmission between two or more points. Also called a path, link, line, facility, or circuit. (2) A transmission path that connects auxiliary devices to a computer.

channel adapter   A device that enables data communications between channels on different hardware devices.

channel capacity   In data communications, a term used to express the maximum number of bits per second that can be accommodated by a channel. This maximum number is determined by the bandwidth modulation scheme and certain types of noise. The channel capacity is most often measured in bauds, or bits per second.

character   Any symbol, digit, letter, or punctuation mark stored or processed by computing equipment.

character checking   The checking of each character by examining all characters as a group or field.

character code   A code designating a unique numerical representation for a set of characters.

character density   A measure of the number of characters recorded per unit of length or area.

characteristic   The part of a floating point number that represents the size of the exponent.

character pitch   In a line of text, the number of characters per inch. See *elite type* and *pica*.

character printer   A printer in which only a single character is composed and determined within the device prior to printing.

character reader   See *optical character reader*.

character recognition   The technology of using machines to automatically identify human-readable symbols, most often alphanumeric characters, and then to express their identities in machine-readable codes. This operation of transforming numbers and letters into a form directly suitable for electronic data processing is an important method of introducing information into computing systems. See *magnetic ink character recognition* and *optical character recognition*.

character set   Comprises the numbers, letters, and symbols associated with a given device or coding system.

character string   A string of alphanumeric characters.

character template   A device used to shape an electron beam into an alphanumeric character for a CRT display.

charactron   A special type of cathode-ray tube that displays alphanumeric and special characters on its screen.

charge   A quantity of unbalanced electricity in a body.

charged coupled device (CCD)   A memory device within which stored information circulates.

Charles Babbage Institute   An organization for the study of the "information revolution" from a historical perspective. It is intended as a clearing-house for information about research resources related to this history and a repository for archival materials.

chart   See *flowchart*.

chassis   The metal upon which the wiring, sockets, and other electronic parts of an electronic assembly are mounted.

check bit   A binary check digit; for example, a parity bit. See *parity checking*.

check digits   One or more digits carried within a unit item of information that provide information about the other digits in the unit in such a manner that, if an error occurs, the check fails, and an indication of error is given. See *check bit* and *parity checking*.

checkout   See *debug*.

checkpoint   A specified point at which a program can be interrupted either manually or by a control routine. Used primarily as an aid in debugging programs.

check problem   A testing problem designed to determine whether a computer or a computer program is operating correctly. See *bug, debug*, and *test data*.

check sum   A summation of digits or bits used primarily for checking purposes and summed according to an arbitrary set of rules.

chief programmer   An individual designated as the leader of a programming team who has the overall responsibility of seeing that an entire project is successfully completed.

chief programmer team   A team of programmers working together to produce error-free software systems.

child   A data record that can only be created based upon the contents of one or more other records (parents) already in existence. See *parent* and *parent/child relationship*.

chip   A common term for an integrated circuit etched on a tiny piece of silicon or germanium.

chip family   A group of related chips, each of which (except the first) evolved from an earlier chip in the family.

chop   To discard unneeded data.

chunking along   A slang term referring to the operation of a long-running, dependable program.

churning   See *thrashing*.

CICS   (Customer Information Control System) A widely used teleprocessing monitor.

CIM   (Computer Input Microfilm) A technology that involves using an input device to read the contents of microfilm directly into the computer.

cipher A secret method of representing information to ensure computer security.

CIPS (Canadian Information Processing Society) An organization formed to bring together Canadians with a common interest in the field of information processing.

circuit A general term referring to a system or part of a system of conducting parts and their interconnections through which an electric current is intended to flow. A circuit is made up of active and passive elements or parts and their interconnecting conducting paths.

circuit board A special board on which specific circuits have been etched or "printed."

circuit capacity The number of channels in a circuit that can be dealt with simultaneously.

circuitry A complex of circuits describing interconnection within or between systems.

circular list A linked list in which the last element points to the first one. Also called a *ring*.

circular shift A shifting operation whereby bits or characters shifted off one end of a register enter the register on the opposite end. Also called *end-around shift*.

CIU See *computer interface unit*.

C³L Complementary Constant Current Logic.

cladding In fiber optics, cladding is the second layer of the fiber optics unit that bounces the light waves back into the core of the unit.

classify To categorize or place data with similar characteristics into the same category.

clear A keyboard function that removes the contents from the display screen.

clearing Replacing the information in a register, storage location, or storage unit with zeros or blanks.

CLIP (Coded Language Information Processing) A scheme used by radiologists for entering their X-ray reports into a computer.

clipping The process of removing portions of an image that are outside the boundaries of the display screen.

clobber To write new data over the top of good data in a file or otherwise damaging a file so that it becomes useless. To wipe out a file.

clock (1) A timing device that gnerates the basic periodic signal used to control the timing of all operations in a synchronous computer. (2) A device that records the progress of real time, or some

Circuit board. Courtesy Sperry Corp.

approximation of it, and whose contents are available to a computer program.

clock rate   Time rate at which pulses are emitted from a clock.

closed loop   A loop that is completely circular. See *loop*.

closed routine   See *closed subroutine*.

closed shop   The operation of the data processing center by professional operators. Programs and data are carried by messengers or transmitted over telephone lines, avoiding the necessity of users entering the computer room. This enables a much more efficient use of the computer and is the opposite of the "open shop," in which each user puts her or his own program in the machine and fiddles with the switches on the console. Contrast with *open shop.*

closed subroutine A subroutine that can be stored at one place and linked to one or more calling routines. Contrast with *open subroutine.*

clustered devices Refers to a group of terminals that are all connected to a common controller.

clustering Refers to the process of grouping things with similar characteristics.

CMI See *computer-managed instruction.*

CML See *current mode logic* and *ECL.*

CMOS (Complementary MOS) A method of making MOS (metallic oxide semiconductor) chips that uses almost no power and works faster than MOS. CMOS is not very good for LSI (large scale integration), but it is used in electronic watches and clocks where power has to come from a battery.

CMU (Carnegie-Mellon University) An important computer and robotics research center.

coaxial cable A special type of communications cable that permits the transmission of data at high speed.

COBOL (COmmon Business Oriented Language) A higher-level language developed for business data processing applications. Every COBOL source program has four divisions, whose names and functions are as follows: (1) Identification Division, which identifies the source program and the output of a compilation; (2) Environment Division, which specifies those aspects of a data processing problem that are dependent upon the physical characteristics of a particular computer; (3) Data Division, which describes the data that the object program is to accept as input, manipulate, create, or produce as output; and (4) Procedure Division, which specifies the procedures to be performed by the object program by means of English-like statements.

CODASYL (COnference of DAta SYstem Language) The conference that developed the COBOL programming language.

code (1) A set of rules outlining the way in which data may be represented. (2) Rules used to convert data from one representation to another. (3) To write a program or routine (i.e., a programmer generates code). Same as *encode.*

code conversion A process for changing the bit groupings for characters in one code into the corresponding character bit groupings for a second code.

coded decimal number A number consisting of successive characters or a group of characters that usually represents a specific figure in an associated decimal number.

code level   The number of bits used to represent a given character.

coder   A person whose primary duty is to write (but not design) computer programs.

code set   The complete set of representations defined by a code; for example, all of the two-letter post office identifications for the fifty states.

coding   (1) The writing of a list of instructions that will cause a computer to perform specified operations. (2) An ordered list or lists of the successive instructions that will cause a computer to perform a particular process.

coding form   A form on which the instructions for programming a computer are written. Also called a coding sheet.

coding sheet   See *coding form.*

coercion   In programming language expressions, an automatic conversion from one data type to another.

COGO   (COordinate GeOmetry) A problem-oriented programming language used to solve geometric problems. Used primarily by civil engineers.

coherence   Assumption used in raster scan display technology that attributes the same value of an individual pixel to its adjacent pixel.

cold boot   The act of turning a computer on and loading an operating system into it.

cold fault   A computer fault that is apparent as soon as the machine is switched on.

Example of a COBOL Program

```
100   PROCEDURE DIVISION
110   PGM-VWGIN.MOVE ZEROS TO
         TOTAL-COUNT, INC.
120   LOOP. IF INC IS GREATER THAN 100
130      GO TO PGM-END.
140      ADD 1 TO INC.
150      ADD INC TO TOTAL-COUNT.
160      GO TO LOOP.
170   PGM-END. STOP RUN.
```

cold start The restart activity used when a serious failure has occurred in a real-time system, making the contents of the direct access storage inaccessible so that no trace of the recent processing can be used. The system must be reloaded and activity restarted as though at the beginning of a day.

collate To merge two (or more) sequenced data sets to produce a resulting data set that reflects the sequencing of the original sets. Same as *merge*.

collating sequence An ordering assigned to the characters of a character set to be used for sequencing purposes.

collating sorting A sort that uses a technique of continuous merging of data until one sequence is developed.

collator A machine used to collate or merge sets of cards or other documents into a sequence.

collector The section of a semiconductor device toward which electricity flows.

collision What happens when keys collide at the same address.

color camera An output device that is used to produce Polaroid instant photographs, color transparencies, or color slides.

color graphics Refers to a system that is used to create graphs, draw pictures, and so forth, using colors.

color graphics printer An output device that creates original color prints on plain paper directly from computer graphic systems. The printer combines laser scanning and xerography to produce computer-created images.

color map In computer graphics, a scheme whereby a limited number of bits can be made to do the work of more.

column (1) The vertical members of one line of an array. (2) One of the vertical lines of punching positions on a punched card. (3) A position of information in a computer word. Contast with *row*.

column split A device for distinguishing the pulses corresponding to an 11 or 12 punch from those corresponding to numeric punches in a card column and for making them separately available while reading or punching a card.

COLUSSUS A special-purpose electronic computer first used to decipher German codes during World War II. It was build in Great Britain.

COM (Computer Output Microfilm) A technology that permits the output information produced by computers to be stored on microfilm. See *computer output microfilm (COM) recorder*.

combination logic A circuit arrangement in which the output state is determined by the present state of the input. See *sequential logic*.

combinatorics   The study of methods of counting how many objects there are of some type, or how many ways there are to do something.

COMDEX   (COMmunications and Data processing EXposition) A large computer trade show held in the United States and in other locations.

COMIT   A string processing language. See *string processing languages*.

command   (1) A control signal. (2) Loosely, a mathematical or logic operator. (3) Loosely, a computer instruction. See *operation code*.

command-chained memory   A technique used in dynamic storage allocation.

command-driven software   Programs that make little or no effort to guide the terminal user with menus. Instead, command-driven software expects the operator to know what commands are available and when each is appropriate.

command key   A key on the keyboard that is used to perform specific functions.

command language   A computer-specific language used to instruct the operating system with respect to the way processing is to be performed. It consists of all the job control statements that can be used to control processing performed by a particular operating system and computer. In some computer systems, called a *job control language*.

command processing   The reading, analyzing, and performing of computer instructions.

comments   Verbal messages inserted into a computer program that do not trigger any computer processing steps but are helpful notes for future users who may later attempt to understand or alter the program.

Commodore Electronics Limited   A manufacturer of microcomputer equipment and software.

common carrier   A government-regulated private company that provides telephone, telegraph, and other telecommunications facilities for public use.

common language   A computer programming language that is sensible to two or more computers with different machine languages; for example, BASIC, Pascal, or FORTRAN.

common storage   A section of memory for each user that holds data or parameters that are accessible to all programs.

communicating   The process of transmitting information to point of use.

communicating word processors   A network of word processors used to transmit electronic mail.

communications channel   The physical means of connecting one location or device to another for the purpose of transmitting and receiving data.

communications control unit   Usually a small computer whose only job is to handle the flow of data communications traffic to and from a mainframe computer.

communications link   See *communications channel.*

communications processor   A computer that provides a path for data transfer between the computer system and the data communications network.

communications satellite   Earth satellites placed in different spots in the geostationary orbit 36,000 kilometers (22,250 miles) above the equator that serve as relay stations for communications signals transmitted from earth stations. These satellites orbit Earth once every twenty-four hours, giving the impression that they are "parked" in one spot over the equator. Once in this orbit, a satellite is capable of reaching 43 percent of Earth's surface with a single radio signal. Most communications satellites are launched by NASA, weigh several thousand pounds, and are powered by solar panels. A few communications satellites are Comstar, Westar, Intelsat V, Satcom, and Marisat.

Communications Satellite Corporation   A privately owned United States communications carrier company operating under a mandate from Congress. It is the American representative in the INTELSAT organization and provides technical and operational services for the global communications system. Traffic on the system is coordinated through an operations center located in Washington, D.C.

compaction   Packing of data structure to make room in storage.

comparative sort   A sort by comparison of two or more keys.

comparator   A device for checking the accuracy of transcribed data by comparing it with a second transcription, noting any variation between the two.

compare   To examine the representation of a quantity to determine its relationship to zero or to examine two quantities, usually for the purposes of determining identity or relative magnitude.

comparison   The act of comparing. The common forms are comparison of two numbers for identity, comparison of two numbers for relative magnitude, comparison of two characters for similarity, and comparison of the signs of two numbers.

compart   A term that means computer art.

compatibility   Pertains to the degree of interworking possible between two devices or systems. If an element in a system is fully compatible with the functional and physical characteristics of a system, it can be incorporated into the system without modification.

compatible   A quality possessed by a computer system that enables it to handle both data and programs devised for some other type of computer system.

compatible software   Programs that can be run on different computers without modification.

compilation time   The time during which a source language is translated (compiled) into an object program (machine language). Contrast with *run time*.

compile   To prepare a machine language program (or a program expressed in symbolic coding) from a program written in another higher-level programming language such as FORTRAN, COBOL, or Pascal.

compile-and-go   An operating technique by which the loading and execution phases of a program compilation are performed in one continuous run. This technique is especially useful when a program must be compiled for a one-time application.

compiler   A computer program that produces a machine language program from a source program that is usually written in a high-level language by a computer user. The compiler is capable of replacing single source program statements with a series of machine language instructions or with a subroutine. See *precompiler*.

compiler-compiler   See *metacompiler*.

compiler language   A source language that uses a compiler to translate the language statements into an object language. See *problem-oriented language* and *procedure-oriented language*.

compiler program   See *compiler*.

compile time   The time required to compile a program.

compiling   See *compile* and *cross-compiling/assembling*.

complement   A number used to represent the negative of a given number. A complement is obtained by subtracting each digit of the number from the number representing its base and, in the case of 2's and 10's complement, adding unity to the last significant digit.

complementary MOS (CMOS)   A method of making metallic oxide semiconductor (MOS) chips that uses almost no power and works faster than MOS.

completeness check   Establishes that none of the fields is missing and that the entire record has been checked.

component   A basic part; an *element*; a part of a computer system.

composite card   A multipurpose data card, or a card that contains data needed in the processing of various applications.

composite video   A signal composed of video information plus synchronizing pulses.

compound statement   A single instruction that contains two or more instructions that could be used separately.

CompuServe   A large commercial data base. It features timely news features, stock market reports, electronic mail, educational programs, programming aids, and more. Personal computer owners can reference the CompuServe network via the common telephone system.

computability   Property by which computational problems are classified.

compute-bound   A program or computer system that is restricted or limited by the speed of the central processing unit.

computer   A device capable of solving problems of manipulating data by accepting data, performing prescribed operations (mathematical or logical) on the data, and supplying the results of these operations. See *analog computer, briefcase computer, computer kit, desktop computer, digital computer, home computer, microcomputer, microprocessor, minicomputer, personal computer, portable computer, small business computer,* and *supercomputer.*

computer-aided design (CAD)   A process involving direct, real-time communication between a designer and a computer, generally by the use of a cathode-ray tube (CRT) display and a light pen.

computer-aided instruction (CAI)   See *computer-augmented learning.*

computer-aided manufacturing (CAM)   The use of computer technology in the management, control, and operation of manufacturing.

computer architecture   The area of computer study that deals with the physical structure (hardware) of computer systems and the relationships among these various hardware components.

computer art   Art form produced by computing equipment (usually plotters, printers, or visual display devices).

computer-assisted instruction (CAI)   The use of the computer to augment individual instruction by providing the student with programmed sequences of instruction under computer control. The

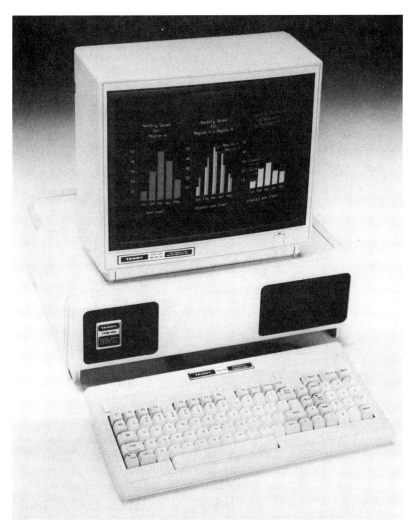

Computer. Courtesy Radio Shack, a division of Tandy Corp.

manner of sequencing and progressing through the materials permits students to progress at their own rate. CAI is responsive to the individual needs of the individual student. See *author language, authors, courseware, PILOT, PLANIT, PLATO,* and *TICCIT.*

computer-augmented learning (CAL)   A method of using a computer system to augment, or supplement, a more conventional instructional system. A typical example would be using simulation programs to aid in problem solving in a course of instruction.

computer-based learning (CBL)   A term used to embrace all the present forms of educational computing.

Computer-assisted instruction. Courtesy IBM Corp.

computer binder A binder designed to hold and protect printouts produced by printers.

computer center A facility that provides computer services to a variety of users through the operation of computer and auxiliary hardware, and through ancillary services provided by its staff.

computer center director An individual who directs the activities, operations, and personnel in a computer center.

computer circuits Circuits used in digital computers, such as gating circuits, storage circuits, triggering circuits, inverting circuits, power amplifying circuits, and others.

computer classifications Computers fall into two major classifications: digital and analog. A third classification, called hybrid, combines both digital and analog computers. Digital computers vary in size from huge supercomputers to minute microprocessors.

computer code A machine code for a specific computer.

computer control console See *console.*

computer control panel See *control panel.*

computer crime An intentional act to misuse a computer system. Computer crimes can range from simple fraud schemes to crimes of violence.

computer enclosure The cabinet or housing for a computer's circuit boards and power supply.

computerese The jargon of people working with computers.

computer family See *family of computers*.

computer flicks Movies made by a computer.

computer game Interactive software or firmware in which the input data consists of the human player's physical actions and the output is an interactive graphics display.

computer graphics A general term meaning the appearance of pictures or diagrams, as opposed to letters and numbers, on the display screen or hard-copy output device.

computer-independent language A high-level language designed for use in any computer equipped with an appropriate compiler (i.e., BASIC, FORTRAN, PL/I, Pascal, and so forth). See *problem-oriented language and procedure-oriented language.*

computer industry An industry composed of businesses and organizations that supply computer hardware, software, and computer-related services.

computer information system (CIS) A coordinated collection of hardware, software, data, people, and support resources to perform an integrated series of functions that can include processing, storage, input, and output.

computer input microfilm (CIM) A technology that involves using an input device to read the contents of microfilm directly into the computer.

computer instruction See *instruction*.

computer integrated manufacturing (CIM) The combining of data base technology with CAD/CAM applications.

Computer Classifications

Microprocessors
Hand-Held Computers
Portable Computers
Microcomputer Systems
Minicomputer Systems
Medium-Scale Mainframe Systems
Large-Scale Mainframe Systems
Supercomputer Systems

computer interface unit (CIU)   A device used to connect peripheral devices to a computer.

computerization   The application of a computer to an activity formerly done by other means.

computerized data base   A set of computerized files on which an organization's activities are based and upon which high reliance is placed for availability and accuracy.

computerized game playing   Computers (microcomputers, minicomputers, and larger machines) that have been programmed to play a wide variety of games such as tic-tac-toe, PACMAN, breakout, star raiders, space war, blackjack, hangman, backgammon, chess, and checkers, among others.

computerized mail   A technique of delivering mail in electronic form directly to homes and businesses through computer equipment.

computerized numerical control   See *numerical control*.

computer kit   A microcomputer in kit form. The user who purchases a computer kit is expected to "build" the microcomputer as he/she would "build" a model airplane or a stereo sound system. Computer kits are popular with computer hobbyists and are used in schools to help teach computer design. See *home computer, microcomputer*, and *personal computer*.

computer language   See *programming language*.

computer leasing company   A company that specializes in leasing computer equipment, which it purchases from a computer manufacturer.

computer letter   A personalized form letter produced by a word processing system or a special form letter program.

computer literacy   The nontechnical study of the computer and its effect upon society. This is an important area in computer education because it provides the student with some of the knowledge, tools, and understanding necessary to live in a computer-oriented society.

computer-managed instruction (CMI)   An application of computers to instruction in which the computer is used as a record keeper, manager, and/or prescriber of instruction.

Computer Museum   An archive for computer history, located in Boston, Massachusetts, whose collection contains many early computer systems and taped presentations of computer pioneers.

computer music   Music employing computer equipment at any stage of its composition or realization as sound. See *electronic music* and *musical language*.

computer network   A complex consisting of two or more interconnected computer systems, terminals, and communication facilities.

computer-on-a-chip   A complete microcomputer on an integrated circuit chip.

computer operations   That part of a computer installation responsible for the day-to-day collection, production, distribution, and maintenance of data.

computer operator   A person skilled in the operation of the computer and associated peripheral devices. A computer operator also performs other operational functions that are required in a computer center, such as loading a disk drive, placing cards in the card reader, removing printouts from the line printer rack, and so forth.

computer output microfilm (COM)   A technology that involves recording computer output on microfilm.

computer output microfilm (COM) recorder   A device that records computer output on photosensitive film in microscopic form.

computer process control system   A system that uses a computer connected to sensors that monitor a process in order to control that process for handling matter or energy. The system then uses its modification in order to produce a product at a profit.

computer processing cycle   The steps involved in using a computer to solve a problem: write the program in a programming language such as BASIC or FORTRAN; input the program into the computer; compile and execute the program.

computer program   The series of statements and instructions that cause a computer to perform a particular operation or task. See *program.*

computer programmer   A person skilled in the preparation of programs for a computer. A programmer designs, codes, debugs, and documents computer programs. Also called *programmer.* See *coder.*

computer revolution   See *information revolution.*

computer science   The field of knowledge embracing all aspects of the design and use of computers.

computer security   The preservation of computing resources against abuse or unauthorized use; especially the protection of data from accidental or deliberate damage, disclosure, or modification.

computer specialist   An individual who provides computer services to computer-using organizations; for example, a systems analyst, a programmer, and so forth.

computer store   A retail store where you can select, from the shelf, a full computer system or just a few accessories. These stores typically sell software, books, supplies, and periodicals. In a com-

Computer system. Courtesy Sperry Corp.

plete computer store, one can examine and operate several types of microcomputer systems.

computer system   A system that includes computer hardware, software, and people. Used to process data into useful information.

ComputerTown   A California organization that promotes "computer literacy" and public access to small computers.

computer user   A person who uses a computer system or its output.

computer users group   A group whose members share the knowledge they have gained and the programs they have developed on a computer or class of computers of a certain manufacturer. Most groups hold meetings and distribute newsletters to exchange information, trade equipment, and share computer programs.

computer utility   A service that provides computational ability. A time-shared computer system. Programs, as well as data, may be made available to the user. The user also may have her or his own programs immediately available in the central processing unit, or have them on call at the computer utility, or load them by transmitting them to the computer prior to using them. Certain data and programs are shared by all users of the service; other data and programs, because of their proprietary nature, have restricted access. Computer utilities are generally accessed by means of data communications subsystems. See *service bureau.*

computer vendor An organization that manufactures, sells, or services computer equipment.

computer word A fixed sequence of bits, bytes, or characters treated as a unit and capable of being stored in one storage location. See *word*.

computing The act of using computing equipment for processing data.

computing system See *computer system*.

COM recorder A device that records computer output on photosensitive film in microscopic form.

COMSAT See *Communications Satellite Corporation*.

concatenate To link together or join two or more character strings into a single character string, or to join one line of a display with the succeeding line.

concatenated data set A collection of logically connected data sets.

concatenated key More than one data item used in conjunction to identify a record.

concentrator A device that allows a number of slow-speed devices to utilize a single high-speed communications line. Also called a *multiplexer*.

concordance An alphabetical list of words and phrases appearing in a document, with an indication of where those words and phrases appear.

concurrent processing The performance of two or more data processing tasks within a specified interval. Contrast with simultaneous processing.

concurrent programming The development of programs that specify the parallel execution of several tasks.

conditional jump instruction An instruction that causes a jump to occur if the criteria specified are met.

condition code Refers to a limited group of program conditions, such as carry, borrow, overflow, and so on, that are pertinent to the execution of instructions.

conditional branching See *conditional transfer*.

conditional statement A statement that is executed only when a certain condition within the routine has been met.

conditional transfer An instruction that may cause a departure from the sequence of instructions being followed depending upon the result of an operation, the contents of a register, or the settings of an indicator. Contrast with *unconditional transfer*.

conditioning The improvement of the data transmission properties of a voiceband transmission line by correction of the amplitude phase characteristics of the line amplifiers.

CONDUIT A nonprofit publisher of educational software. CONDUIT reviews, tests, packages, and distributes instructional computer programs and related printed materials.

configuration An assembly of machines that are interconnected and are programmed to operate as a system.

configuration management The task of accounting for, controlling, and reporting the planned and actual design of a product throughout its production and operational life.

connected graph Moving from a single node in a graph to any other node by traveling via a sequence of edges.

connection matrix See *incidence matrix.*

connector (1) A coupling device that provides an electrical and/or mechanical junction between two cables, or between a cable and a chassis or enclosure. (2) A device that provides rapid connection and disconnection of electrical cable and wire terminations. See *female connector* and *male connector.*

connector symbol A flowcharting symbol used to represent a junction in a line of flow. It connects broken paths in the line of flow and connects several pages of the same flowchart. A small circle containing some identifier is used to represent this symbol:

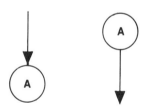

connect time In time-sharing, the length of time you are "on" the computer; that is, the duration of the telephone connection. Connect time is usually measured by the duration between "sign-on" and "sign-off." See *CPU time.*

consistency check A check that ensures the specific input data fall within a predetermined set of criteria.

console The part of a computer system that enables human operators to communicate with the system. See *front panel.*

console operator Same as *computer operator.*

console printer See *console typewriter*.

console typewriter A typewriter on-line to the computer that allows communication between the machine and the *computer operator*.

constant A value that does not change during the execution of the program.

content-addressable memory Same as *associative storage*.

contention A condition on a multipoint communications channel when two or more locations try to transmit at the same time.

contents directory A series of queues that indicate the routines in a given region of internal storage.

contiguous data structure See *sequential data structure*.

contingency plan A plan for recovery of a computer information system following emergencies or disasters.

continuation card A punched card that contains information that was started on a previous punched card.

continuous forms Paper used on printers and accounting machines that can represent checks or any type of preprinted forms as long as the small holes are on the outer edges of the form. Holes are used by equipment to advance the paper line by line.

continuous processing The input of transactions into a system in the order they occur and as soon after they occur as possible.

continuous tone image A color or black-and-white image formed of combinations of separate areas made up of different color tones or gray tones.

contour analysis A technique in optical character recognition that uses a spot of light to search for the outline of the character by moving around its exterior edges.

contouring The visible transition from one graphical intensity level to another.

control The function of performing required operations when certain specific conditions occur or when interpreting and acting upon instructions. See *control section* and *control unit*.

control block A storage area through which a particular type of information required for control of the operating system is communicated among its parts.

control break A point during program processing at which some special processing event takes place.

control cards Punched cards that contain input data required for a specific application of a general routine, such as a generator or operating system; for example, one of a series of cards that directs an operating system to load and initiate the execution of a particular program. See *job control language*.

control character A character inserted into a data stream with the intent of signaling the receiving station to perform some function.

control circuits The electrical circuits within a computer that interpret the program instructions and cause the appropriate operations to be performed.

control clerk A person who has responsibility for performing duties associated with the control over data processing operations.

control console That part of a computer system used for communication between the console operator or service engineer and the computer.

control data One or more items of data used as a control to identify, select, execute, or modify another routine, record, file, operation, or data value.

Control Data Corporation A large manufacturer of computer equipment, including supercomputers.

control field A field in a data record used to identify and classify the record.

control key A special function key on a computer keyboard.

controlled variable A variable that takes on a specific set of values in an iterative structure in a programming language.

controller A device required by the computer in order to operate a peripheral component.

control logic The order in which processing functions will be carried out by a computer.

control panel (1) The part of a computer control console that contains manual controls. (2) A hand-wired plugboard used to control the operations of unit record devices. See *console* and *plugboard*.

control program An operating system program responsible for the overall management of the computer and its resources. See *operating system*.

control punch A specific code that is punched in a card to cause the machine to perform a specific operation.

controls Methods and procedures for ensuring the accuracy, integrity, security, reliability, and completeness of data or processing techniques.

control section The part of the central processing unit responsible for directing the operation of the computer in accordance with the instructions in the program. Same as *control unit*.

control sequence The normal order of selection of instructions by a digital computer wherein it follows one instruction order at a time.

control signal   A computer-generated signal for automatic control of machines and processes.

control statement   An operation that terminates the sequential execution of instructions by transferring control to a statement elsewhere in the program.

control station   The network station that supervises control procedures such as polling, selecting, and recovery. It is also responsible for establishing order on the line in the event of contention or any other abnormal situation.

control structures   The facilities of a programming language that specify a departure from the normal sequential execution of statements.

control total   An accumulation of numeric data fields that are used to check on the accuracy of the input, processed data, or output data.

control unit   The portion of the central processing unit that directs the step-by-step operation of the entire computing system. A basic part of a central processing unit (CPU).

convention   Standard and accepted procedures in computer program development and the abbreviations, symbols, and their meanings as developed for particular programs and systems.

conversational   Pertaining to a program or a system that carries on a dialog with a terminal user, alternately accepting input and then responding to the input quickly enough for the user to maintain his or her train of thought. See *interactive processing*.

conversational language   A programming language that uses a near-English character set that facilitates communication between the user and computer. BASIC is an example of a conversational language.

conversational mode   A mode of operation that implies a dialog between a computer and its user in which the computer program examines the input supplied by the user and formulates questions or comments, which are directed back to the user. See *interactive processing* and *logging-in*.

conversational remote job entry   See *CRJE*.

conversational system   See *interactive system*.

conversion   (1) The process of changing formation from one form of representation to another, such as from the language of one type of computer to that of another or from punch cards to magnetic disk. (2) The process of changing from one data processing method to another or from one type of equipment to another. (3) The process of changing a number written in one base to the base of another numeral system. (See table below.)

conversion table   A table comparing numerals in two different numeral systems.

convert   (1) To change data from radix to radix. (2) To move data from one type of record to another (i.e., floppy disk to magnetic tape).

converter   (1) A device that converts information recorded on one medium to another medium (e.g., a unit that accepts information from punched cards and records the information on magnetic disks). (2) A device that converts information in one form into information in another form (e.g., analog to digital).

cookbook   A step-by-step document describing how to install and use a program.

Conversion Table

Decimal	Binary	Hexadecimal	Octal
0	00000	0	0
1	00001	1	1
2	00010	2	2
3	00011	3	3
4	00100	4	4
5	00101	5	5
6	00110	6	6
7	00111	7	7
8	01000	8	10
9	01001	9	11
10	01010	A	12
11	01011	B	13
12	01100	C	14
13	01101	D	15
14	01110	E	16
15	01111	F	17
16	10000	10	20

coordinate An ordered set of absolute or relative data values that specify a location in a Cartesian coordinate system.

coordinate indexing (1) A system of indexing individual documents by descriptors of equal rank so that a library can be searched for a combination of one or more descriptors. (2) An indexing technique whereby the interrelationships of terms are shown by coupling individual words.

coordinate paper A continuous-feed graph paper that is used for graphs or diagrams produced on a digital plotter.

coprocessor An auxiliary processor that performs time-consuming tasks in order to free the central processing unit, thus resulting in a faster execution time for the overall system.

copy To reproduce data in a new location or other destination, leaving the source data unchanged, although the physical form of the result may differ from that of the source. For example, a copy of a deck of cards onto a magnetic disk. Contrast with *duplicate*.

core storage A form of storage device that utilizes magnetic cores usually strung through wires in the form of an array. See *magnetic core storage*.

corner cut A diagonal cut at the corner of a punched card. It is used as a means of identifying groups of related cards. See *punched card*.

coroutine Instructions used to transfer a set of inputs to a set of outputs.

corrective maintenance The activity of detecting, isolating, and correcting failures after they occur. Contrast with *preventive maintenance*.

cost analysis A technique used to determine the overall cost of a given system and to compare them to cost factors estimated for a new design.

cost-benefit analysis Same as *cost analysis*.

count The successive increase or decrease of a cumulative total of the number of times an event occurs.

counter A device (e.g., a register or computer storage location) used to represent the number of occurrences of an event.

coupling An interaction between systems or between properties of a system.

courseware The name given to computer programs written especially for educational applications.

cpi Characters per inch.

CPM Critical Path Method.

CP/M (Control Program for Microcomputers) The industry standard in operating systems for small computers. A collection of programs on a diskette, CP/M provides specific commands for transferring information among the devices connected to the computer system, for executing programs, and for manipulating files conveniently. See *MP/M* and *UNIX*.

CP/M compatible   Software designed to operate in conjunction with the CP/M operating system.

cps   Characters per second.

CPS   (Conversation Programming System) Refers generally to a computer system in which input and output are handled by a remote terminal; the system employs time-sharing so that the user obtains what appears to be an immediate response. Used more specifically as CPS-PL/I to mean an IBM-devised subset of the PL/I programming language used with remote terminals.

CPU   See *central processing unit*.

CPU time   The amount of time devoted by the central processing unit to the execution of program instructions. See *connect time*.

CR   Carriage Return.

crash   A system shutdown caused by a hardware malfunction or a software mistake. See *head crash*.

Cray Research, Inc.   A manufacturer of supercomputers: Cray 1, Cray X-MP, and Cray 2.

critical path   The path through the network that defines the shortest possible time in which the entire project can be completed. See *critical path method* and *PERT*.

critical path method (CPM)   A management technique for control of large-scale, long-term projects involving the analysis and determination of each critical step necessary for project completion. See *PERT*.

CRJE   (Conversational Remote Job Entry) Refers to a conversational language employed by a terminal user in submitting jobs to a central site and controlling their processing from a remote terminal station.

CROM   (Control ROM) An integral part of most central processing unit (CPU) chips. The CROM is the storage for the microinstructions that CPU assembles into a sequence to form complex macroinstructions (e.g., multiply or branch-on-negative accumulator) that the computer user normally uses.

cross-assembler   Refers to an assembler run on one computer for the purpose of translating instructions for a different computer.

crosscheck   To check the computing by two different methods.

cross-compiler A compiler that runs on a machine other than the one for which it is designed to compile code.

cross-compiling/assembling A technique whereby one uses a minicomputer, large-scale computer, or time-sharing service to write and debug programs for subsequent use on microcomputers.

cross-footing check A process of cross-adding, or subtracting, then zeroing-out the results.

cross-reference dictionary A printed listing that identifies all references of an assembled program to a specific label. In many systems, this listing is provided immediately after a source program has been assembled.

cross talk The unwanted energy transferred from one circuit, called the "disturbing circuit," to another circuit, called the "disturbed circuit." Generally, cross talk occurs when signals from one circuit emerge on another circuit as interference.

crowbar A circuit that protects a computer system from dangerously high voltage surges.

CRT (Cathode-Ray Tube) See *display unit.*

cryoelectronic storage A storage device consisting of materials that become superconductors at extremely low temperatures; for example, Josephson junction.

cryogenics The study and use of devices that utilize the properties assumed by materials at temperatures near absolute zero.

cryosar A two-terminal semiconductor switching device that operates at very low temperatures.

cryoton A current-controlled switching device based on superconductivity that is used primarily in computer circuits.

cryptanalysis The operation of converting encrypted messages to the corresponding plaintext without initial knowledge of the key employed in the encryption. See *plaintext.*

cryptographic techniques Methods of concealing data by representing each character or group of characters by others.

cryptography The various methods for writing in secret code or cipher. As society becomes increasingly dependent upon computers, the vast amounts of data communicated, processed, and stored within computer systems and networks often have to be protected, and cryptography is a means of achieving this protection. It is the only practical method for protecting information transmitted through accessible communications networks, such as telephone lines, satellites, or microwave systems.

crystal A quartz crystal that vibrates at a specific frequency when energy is supplied to it. These vibrations provide an accurate frequency by which to time the clock within a computer system.

CT   A medical application in which a computer records X rays passing through the body in changing directions and generates an image of the body's structures.

CTRL   Control.

CUBE   (Cooperating Users of Burroughs Equipment) The official organization of the users of Burroughs computers.

cue   See *call*.

CUE   (Computer Using Educators) A California organization that promotes computer education to teachers throughout the state.

current   A flow of electrons through a conductor. Current is measured in amperes, where 1 ampere equals 6.25×10^{18} electrons per second.

current awareness system   In this process, a user is notified periodically by a central file or library when selected items of information have been acquired.

current location counter   A counter kept by an assembler to determine the address that has been assigned to either an instruction or constant being assembled.

current loop   A type of serial communication in which the presence or absence of an electrical signal indicates the state of the bit being transmitted.

current mode logic (CML)   A logic circuit that employs the characteristics of a differential amplifier circuit in its design.

cursor   (1) A moving, sliding, or blinking symbol on a video terminal that indicates where the next character will appear. (2) A position indicator used in a display on a video terminal to indicate a character to be corrected or a position in which data is to be entered.

cursor control   The ability to move a video display prompt character to any position on the screen, under either keyboard.

cursor control keys   The keys on the keyboard that are used to position the cursor on the display screen.

cursor tracking   Positioning a cursor on a display screen by moving a stylus on a digitizer connected to the computer.

customer engineer (CE)   An individual responsible for field maintenance of computer hardware and software.

customize   The process of altering a piece of general purpose software or hardware to enhance its performance, usually to fit a specific user's need.

customized form letters   Personalized form letters produced by word processing systems and special form letter programs.

Current mode logic. Courtesy Honeywell, Inc.

custom software Programs that are prepared specifically for an individual and are tailored to his or her needs. Contrast with *canned software*.

cyber A line of supercomputers and large-scale computers manufactured by Control Data Corporation.

cybernetics The branch of learning that seeks to integrate the theories and studies of communication and control in machines and living organisms. See *artificial intelligence*.

cyborg A human with a robot part.

cycle As related to computer storage, a periodic sequence of events occurring when information is transferred to or from the storage device of a computer. It is the time it takes to reference an address, remove the data, and be ready to select it again.

cycle stealing A technique that allows a peripheral device to temporarily disable computer control of the I/O bus, thus allowing the device to access the computer's internal memory.

cycle time (1) The minimum time interval between the starts of successive accesses to a storage location. (2) The time required to change the information in a set of registers.

cyclic code Same as *gray code*.

cyclic redundancy check An error-detection scheme (usually implemented in hardware) that is often used in disk devices. When information is stored, a cyclic redundancy check (CRC) value is computed and stored. Whenever it is reread, the CRC value is computed once again. If the two values are equal, the information is assumed to be error-free.

cyclic shift A shift in which the digits dropped off at one end of a word are returned at the other in a circular fashion; for example, if a register holds eight digits, 23456789, the result of the cyclic shift two columns to the left would be to change the contents of the register to 45678923.

cylinder As related to magnetic disks, a vertical column of tracks on a magnetic disk file unit.

cypher A form of cryptography in which the plaintext is made unintelligible to anyone who intercepts it by a transformation of the information itself, based on some key.

D

D-A converter See *digital-to-analog converter.*

daisy chain Refers to a specific method of propagating signals along a bus. This method permits the assignment of device priorities based on the electrical position of the device along the bus.

daisy wheel The printing element in a daisy wheel printer. Characters are embossed on spokes radiating from a central hub. A character is printed by simply rotating the wheel.

daisy wheel printer A printer that uses a plastic disk, which has printed characters along its edge. The disk rotates until the required character is brought before a hammer, which strikes it against a ribbon. This type of printer is able to produce letter quality printing.

DASD (Direct Access Storage Device) A device such as a magnetic disk storage unit or a magnetic drum storage unit.

DAT See *dynamic address translation.*

Daisy wheel

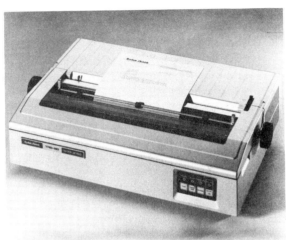

Daisy wheel printer.
Courtesy Radio Shack,
a division of Tandy
Corp.

data acquisition The retrieval of data from remote sites initiated by a central computer system.

data administrator See *data base administrator*.

data aggregate A collection of data items within a record that is given a name and referred to as a whole.

data bank See *data base*.

data base The collection of all data used and produced by a computer program. In large systems, data base analysis is usually concerned with large quantities of data stored in disk and tape files. Smaller microcomputer systems are more frequently concerned with data base allocations of available memory locations between the program and data storage areas. Also called data bank. See *on-line data base*.

data base administrator A person who is responsible for the creation of the information system data base and, once it is established, for maintaining its security and developing procedures for its recovery from disaster.

data base environment That environment resulting from the integration of users, data, and systems by implementing the data base.

data base management A systematic approach to storing, updating, and retrieving information stored as data items, usually in the form of records in a file, by which many users, or even many remote installations, will use common data banks.

data base management system A software system for managing the storage, access, updating, and maintenance of a data base. See *DBMS*.

data base, on-line See *on-line data base*.

data bus A bus system that interconnects the CPU, storage, and all input/output devices of a computer system for the purpose of exchanging data.

data byte The 8-bit binary number that the computer will use in an arithmetic or logical operation, or store in memory.

data capturing Gathering or collecting information for computer handling, the first step in job processing. Also called *data collection*.

data card A punched card that contains one or more data items.

data catalog An organized listing by full name of all data elements used by an organization.

data cell A magnetic storage device developed by the IBM Corporation. A direct access device that handles data recorded on magnetic strips arranged in cells.

data center A computer equipped location. The center processes data and converts the data into a desired form (e.g., reports).

data chaining A process of linking data items together. Each data item contains the location of the next data item.

data channel A communications link between two devices or points.

data clerk A person who does clerical jobs in a computer installation.

data collection (1) The gathering of source data to be entered into a data processing system. (2) The act of bringing data from one or more points to a central point. Also called *data capturing*.

data communications The utilization of communication lines to handle the flow of data between a central computer facility and remote terminals.

data communications analyst A person who specializes in solving the hardware and software problems created by setting up large communications networks.

data communications equipment The equipment associated with the transmission of data from one device to another. Examples are modems, remote terminals, and communications processors. See *input/output channel, Modem*, and *RS-232*.

data communications system A system consisting of computers, terminals, and communications links.

data compression A technique that saves computer storage space by eliminating empty fields, gap redundancies, or unnecesssary data to reduce the size or the length of records.

data concentration Collection of data at an intermediate point from several low- and medium-speed lines for retransmission across high-speed lines.

data control section The organization or group responsible for meeting quality control standards for processing and for collecting inputs from and delivering outputs to computer users.

data conversion The process of changing the form of data representation; for example, punched card to magnetic disks.

data definition In programming, a statement that gives the size, type, and often the content of a field or record.

data definition language See *data description language*.

data description language A language that specifies the manner in which data is to be stored and managed in a data base environment by a data base management system.

data dictionary An ordered collection of data element descriptions containing specific indentification attributes. It describes what the data are.

data directory An ordered collection of data element names and/ or identifiers and their attributes that provides the location of the elements. It describes where the data are located.

data directory/dictionary An ordered collection of data elements that combines the features of a data catalog, data dictionary, and data directory. It describes and locates each data element.

data division One of the four main components of a COBOL program.

data editing A procedure to check for irregularities in input data. See *edit*.

data element A combination of one or more data items that forms a unit or piece of information.

data encryption A coding technique used to secure sensitive data by mixing or jumbling the data according to a predetermined format.

data entry The process of converting data into a form suitable for entry into a computer system.

data entry device The equipment used to prepare data so that the computer can accept it. See *key data entry device*.

data entry operator A person who uses a keyboard device to transcribe data into a form suitable for processing by a computer.

data field The column or consecutive columns used to store a particular piece of information.

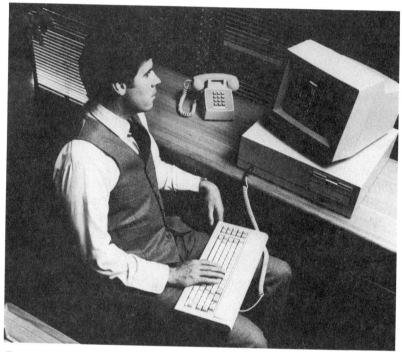

Data entry device. Courtesy Sperry Corp.

data file   A collection of data records usually organized on a logical basis.

data file processing   The updating of data files to reflect the effects of current data.

dataflow   A generic term that pertains to algorithms or machines whose actions are determined by the availability of the data needed for these actions.

dataflow analysis   The study of the movement of data among processing activities.

Data General Corporation   A large manufacturer of minicomputer systems.

data independence   Implies that the data and the application programs that use them are independent, so either may be changed without changing the other.

data integrity   A performance measure based on the rate of undetected errors. See *integrity*.

data item An item of data used to represent a single value. A data item is the smallest unit of named data.

data leakage Illegal removal of data from a computer facility.

data librarian A person who maintains custody and control of disks, tapes, and procedures manuals by cataloging and monitoring the use of these data resources.

data link Equipment that permits the transmission of information in data format. See *channel.*

data logging Recording of data about events that occur in time sequence.

data management (1) A general term that collectively describes those functions of a system that provide access to hardware, enforce data storage conventions, and regulate the use of input/output devcices. (2) A major function of operating systems that involves organizing, cataloging, locating, retrieving, storing, and maintaining data.

data management system (1) A system that provides the necessary procedures and programs to collect, organize, and maintain the data required by the information system. (2) A system that assigns the responsibility for data input and integrity in order to establish and maintain the data bases within an organization.

data manipulating language A language that allows a user to interrogate and access the data base of a computer system using English-like statements.

data medium The material in or on which a specific physical variable may represent data (e.g., magnetic disk or magnetic tape).

data model A formal language for describing data structures and operations on those structures. It is usually divided into a data decription language and a data manipulation language.

data modem See *modem.*

data name The name of the variable used to indicate a data value (e.g., PI for 3.14159).

data origination The translation of information from its original form into machine-sensible form.

dataphone A trademark of the AT&T Company used to identify the data sets manufactured and supplied by the Bell System for use in the transmission of data over the telephone network. See *data set.*

data preparation The process of organizing information and storing it in a form that can be input to the computer.

data preparation device A device that permits data capture in which the source data is collected and transformed into a medium or form capable of being read into a computer.

Datapro A research/publishing company that provides in-depth information about computer hardware and software products.

data processing (1) One or more operations performed on data to achieve a desired objective. (2) The functions of a computer center. (3) A term used in reference to operations performed by data processing equipment.

data processing center A computer center equipped with devices capable of receiving information, processing it according to human-made instructions, and producing the computed results.

data processing cycle The combined functions of input, processing, and output.

data processing management Managing the data processing function, its people, and its equipment. This activity follows the well-recognized principles of planning, control, and operation. The basic prerequisites for data processing management are therefore the same skills that are needed to manage any other enterprise.

Data Processing Management Association See *DPMA*.

Data processing center. Courtesy Honeywell, Inc.

data processing manager A person who runs the information processing center, usually including the operation of the computer. The biggest part of the manager's job is concerned with developing new systems and keeping them running.

data processing system A network of data processing hardware and software capable of accepting information, processing it according to a plan, and producing the desired results.

data processing technology The science of information handling.

data processor Any device capable of performing operations on data (e.g., a desk calculator or a digital computer).

data protection Measures to safeguard data from undesired occurrences that intentionally or unintentionally lead to destruction, modification, or disclosure of data.

data rate The rate at which a channel carries data, measured in bauds (bits per second).

data record A collection of data fields pertaining to a particular subject.

data reduction The process of transforming raw data into useful, condensed, or simplified intelligence. Often adjusting, scaling, smoothing, compacting, editing, and ordering operations are used in the process.

data scope A special display device that monitors a data communications channel and displays the content of the information being transmitted over it.

data security The protection of data from accidental or malicious destruction, disclosure, or modification. See *computer security, disk library*, and *tape library*.

data set (1) A device that permits the transmission of data over communications lines by changing the form of the data at one end so that it can be carried over the lines; another data set at the other end changes the data back to its original form so that it is acceptable to the machine (computer, and so forth) at that end. The dataphone is an example. (2) A collection of related data items.

data sharing The ability of computer processes or of computer users at several nodes to access data at a single node.

data sheet A special form used to record input values in a format convenient for keypunching. See *coding form*.

data storage device A unit for storing large quantities (millions) of characters, typically, a magnetic disk unit, a magnetic tape unit, a magnetic drum, and a magnetic card.

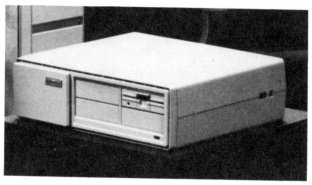

Data storage device. Courtesy Sperry Corp.

data stream   The serial data that is transmitted through a channel from a single input/output operation.

data structure   The relationship among data items.

data tablet   A manual input device for graphic display consoles. Same as *digitizer*.

data terminal   A point in a computer system or data communications network at which data can be entered or retrieved. See *terminal* and *video terminal*.

data transfer rate   The speed of reading or writing data between a storage medium and the computer.

data transmission   The sending of data from one part of a system to another part. See *data communications*.

data type   An interpretation applied to a string of bits.

data value   Any string of symbols that serves as the representative of some item of information.

data word size   Refers to the specific length of data word that a particular computer is designed to handle. See *word* and *word length*.

datum   A unit of information (e.g., a computer word).

daughter board   A circuit board that plugs into a motherboard.

DBMS   (Data Base Management System) A complete collection of computer programs that organizes and processes a particular data base.

DC   An acronym for (1) *data conversion*, (2) *digital computer*, (3) direct current, (4) display console.

DCTL   See *direct coupled transistor logic*.

DDD   (Direct Distance Dialing) The facility used for making long-

Data terminal. Courtesy Sperry Corp.

distance telephone calls without the assistance of a telephone operator. Also used for data commmunications.

DDL   (Data Description Language) A language for declaring data structures in a data base.

dead halt   A halt situation in which the system cannot return to the point at which it halted.

dead letter box   In message switching systems, a file for capturing undeliverable messages.

deadlock   Unresolved contention for the use of a resource.

deallocation   The release of a resource by a program when the probram no longer needs it. The opposite of allocation.

dedicated lines   Telephone-grade communications lines that are used by one organization on a leased basis.

deblocking   Extracting a logical record from a block of group of logical records.

debug   To detect, locate, and remove all mistakes in a computer program and any malfunctions in the computing system itself. Synonymous with troubleshoot. See *bug, debugging aids*, and *test data*.

debugging aids Computer routines that are helpful in debugging programs (e.g., tracing routine, snapshot dump, or post mortem dump).

DEC (Digital Equipment Corporation) A large manufacturer of mini-computer systems.

deceleration time The time required to stop a magnetic tape after reading or recording the last piece of data from a record on that tape.

decimal A characteristic or property involving a selection, condition, or choice in which there are ten possibilities; for example, the numeration system with a radix of 10.

decimal code Describing a form of notation by which each decimal digit is expressed separately in some other number system.

decimal digit A numeral in the decimal numeral system. The radix of the decimal system is 10, and the following symbols are used: 0, 1, 2, 3, 4, 5, 6, 7, 8, and 9.

decimal number A numeral, usually of more than one digit, rep-

Decision Table

Condition/Action	RULES							
	1	2	3	4	5	6	7	8
On hand <20	Y	Y	Y	Y	Y	Y	N	
Weekly usage	>15	>15	8-15	8-15	8-15	<8	-	
Local vendor available	-	-	N	N	Y	-	-	
On order >30	N	Y	N	Y	N	N	Y	
Rush order	X		X					
Regular order		X		X	X	X		
Cancel order							X	
No action								X

resenting a sum, in which the quantity represented by each digit is based on the radix of 10.

decimal system   Base-10 positional notation system.

decimal-to-binary conversion   The process of converting a numeral written to the base 10 to the equivalent numeral written to the base 2. For example:
$$44_{10} = 1 \times 2^5 + 0 \times 2^4 + 1 \times 2^3 + 1 \times 2^2 + 0 \times 2^1 + 0 \times 2^0 = 101100_2$$

decimal-to-hexadecimal conversion   The process of converting a numeral written to the base 10 to the equivalent numeral written to the base 16.

decimal-to-octal conversion   The process of converting a numeral written to the base 10 to the equivalent numeral written to the base 8.

decision   The computer operation of determining if a certain relationship exists between words in storage or registers and of taking alternative courses of action.

decision instruction   An instruction that affects the selection of a branch of a program (e.g., a conditional jump instruction).

decision structure   Same as *selection structure.*

decision symbol   A flowcharting symbol that is used to indicate a choice or a branching in the information processing path. A diamond-shaped figure is used to represent this symbol:

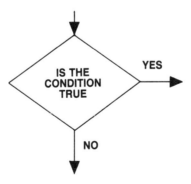

decision table   A table listing all the contingencies to be considered in the description of a problem, together with the corresponding actions to be taken. Decision tables are sometimes used instead of flowcharts to decribe the operations of a program.

decision theory   A broad spectrum of concepts and techniques that have been developed to both describe and rationalize the process of decision making; that is, making a choice among several possible alternatives.

decision tree   A pictorial representation of the alternatives in any situation.

deck   A collection of punched cards. Synonymous with *card deck*.

declaration statement   A part of a computer program that defines the nature of other elements of the program or reserves parts of the hardware for special use.

decode   To translate or determine the meaning of coded information. Contrast with *encode*.

decoder   (1) A device that decodes. (2) A matrix of switching elements that selects one or more output channels according to the combination of input signals present.

decollate   To arrange copies of continuous forms in sets and remove the carbon paper from them.

decrement   The amount by which a value or variable is decreased.

decryption   The process of taking an encrypted message and reconstructing from it the original meaningful message. The opposite of *encryption*.

DECUS   (Digital Equipment Computer Users Society) A user group whose objective is the exchange and dissemination of ideas and information pertinent to computers manufactured by Digital Equipment Corporation.

dedicated   Programs, machines, or procedures that are designed for special use.

dedicated computer   A computer whose use is reserved for a particular task.

dedicated device   A device that is designed to perform only certain functions and cannot be programmed to perform other functions.

dedicated lines   Telephone lines leased for exclusive use by a group or individual for telecommunications. The user pays a set fee rather than per-call or per-minute charges for leased lines.

default   An assumption made by a system or language translator when no specific choice is given by the program or the user.

deferred address   An indirect address. See *deferred entry, deferred exit*, and *indirect addressing*.

deferred entry   An entry into a subroutine that occurs as a result of a deferred exit from the program that passed control to it.

deferred exit   The passing of control to a subroutine at a time determined by an asynchronous event rather than at a predictable time.

definition of a problem The art of compiling logic in the form of algorithms, flowcharts, and program descriptions that clearly explain and define the problem.

degausser A device that is used to erase information from a magnetic device (e.g., magnetic tape). Also called bulk eraser.

degradation A condition in which a system continues to operate, but at a reduced level of service. Unavailability of proper equipment maintenance and computer programs not maintained to accommodate current needs are the two most common causes.

dejagging A computer graphics technique for drawing smooth lines, characters, and polygons.

delay circuit An electronic circuit that deliberately delays the delivery of a signal for a present interval.

deletion record A new record that will replace or remove an existing record of a master file.

delimiter A special character, often a comma or space, used to separate variable names or items in a list or to separate one string of characters from another, as in the separation of data items.

demand paging In virtual storage systems, the transfer of a page from external page storage to real storage at the time it is needed for execution.

demand reports Reports produced only upon request.

demodulation In data communications, the process of retrieving an original signal from a modulated carrier wave. This technique is used in data sets to make communications signals compatible with computer terminal signals.

demodulator A device that receives signals transmitted over a communications link and converts them into electrical pulses, or bits, that can serve as inputs to a data processing machine. Contrast with *modulator*.

demount To remove a magnetic storage medium from a device that reads or writes on it; for example, to demount a disk pack is to remove the disk pack from the disk drive.

demultiplexer A circuit that applies the logic state of a single input to one of several outputs. Contrast with *multiplexer*.

dense binary code A code in which all possible states of the binary pattern are used.

dense list See *sequential list*.

density The ratio of the number of information bits to the total number of bits in a structure.

deque A double-ended queue that allows insertions and deletions at both ends of a list.

Design automation.
Courtesy Radio Shack, a division of Tandy Corp.

descending sort A sort in which the final sequence of records is such that the successive keys compare "less than" or "equal to."

descriptor A significant word that helps to categorize or index information. Sometimes called a *keyword*.

design aids Computer programs or hardware elements that are intended to assist in implementing a computer system. See *debugging aids* and *programming aids*.

design automation The use of computers in the design and production of circuit packages, new computers, and other electronic equipment.

design costs The costs associated with systems design, programming, training, conversion, testing, and documentation.

design cycle (1) In a hardware system, the complete cycle of development of equipment, which includes breadboarding, prototyping, testing, and production. (2) In a software system, the complete plan for producing an operational system, which includes problem description, algorithm development, flowcharting, coding, program debugging, and documentation.

design engineer A person who is involved in the design of a hardware product, such as a disk unit or microprocessor chip.

design phase The process of developing an information system based upon previously established system requirements.

design specifications The result of an analysis of information needs of a specific system within the organization. Included are specifications for input, output, and processing.

desk checking A manual checking process in which representative sample data items, used for detecting errors in program logic, are traced through the program before the latter is executed on the computer. Same as *dry run*.

desktop computer A microcomputer. A small computer containing a microprocessor, input and output devices, and storage, usually in one box or package. See *home computer, microcomputer,* and *personal computer.*

destination The device or address that receives the data during a data transfer operation.

destructive read The process of destroying the information in a location by reading the contents.

detachable keyboard A keyboard that is not built into the same case as the video display. It connects to the video display with a

Desktop computer. Courtesy Sperry Corp.

cable and allows greater flexibility in positioning of the keyboard display.

detail file A file containing relatively transient information; for example, records of individual transactions that occurred during a particular period of time. Synonymous with *transaction file*. Contrast with *master file*.

detail printing An operation in which a line of printing occurs for each card read by an accounting machine.

detection Passive monitoring of an event for the purpose of discovering a problem.

deterministic model A mathematical model for the study of data of known fixed values and direct cause-and-effect relationships.

development time The time used for debugging new programs or hardware.

device A computer peripheral.

device cluster A group of terminals or other devices that share a communications controller.

device code The 8-bit code for a specific input or output device.

device flag A 1-bit register that records the current status of a device.

device independence The ability to command input/output operations without regard to the characteristics of the input/output devices. See *symbolic I/O assignment*.

device name The general name for a kind of device (e.g., model 3330 disk unit or IBM Personal Computer).

diagnosis The process of isolating malfunctions in computing equipment and of detecting mistakes in programs and systems.

diagnostic message A brief explanation issued by a program (compiles, equipment testing routine, and so forth) of an error it has encountered. Sometimes called *error message*.

diagnostic routine A routine designed to locate a malfunction in the central processing unit or a peripheral device.

diagram A schematic representation of a sequence of operations or routines. See *flowchart*.

dialect A version of a particular computer language. For example, TRS-80 BASIC, Apple IIe BASIC, and True BASIC are all dialects of BASIC.

dialog A question-and-answer session between a computer system and a human.

dial-up To use a dial or push-button telephone in data communications to initiate a station-to-station telephone call.

dibit One of the following binary number arrangements: 00, 01, 10, or 11.

dichotomizing search See *binary search*.

dictionary program A spelling check program, often used with word processing systems.

diddle To tamper with data.

die The tiny rectangular pieces of a circular wafer of semiconductor silicon, sawed or sliced during the fabrication of integrated circuits or transistors.

Difference Engine A machine designed by Charles Babbage in 1822 that mechanized a calculating function called the "method of differences." See *Babbage, Charles*.

digit One of the symbols of a numbering system that is used to designate a quantity.

digital Pertaining to data in the form of digits. Contrast with *analog*.

digital communications The transmission of information by coding it into discrete on/off electronic signals.

digital computer A device that manipulates digital data and performs arithmetic and logic operations on these data. See *computer*. Contrast with *analog computer*.

digital control The use of digital technology to maintain conditions in operating systems as close as possible to desired values despite changes in the operating environment.

digital data Data represented in discrete, discontinuous form, as contrasted with *analog data*, which is represented in continuous form.

Digital Equipment Corporation A large manufacturer of minicomputer systems.

digital plotter An output device that uses an ink pen (or pens) to draw graphs, line drawings, and other illustrations.

digital recording A technique for recording information as discrete points onto magnetic recording media.

digital repeater A unit placed in a data communications path to reconstruct digital pulses, which tend to deteriorate as they travel through long conductors.

digital signal A binary process restricted to either the presence or absence of a signal.

digital sorting A sort that uses a technique similar to sorting on tabulation machines. The elapsed time is directly proportional to the number of characters in the sequencing key and the volume of data. Also called *radix sorting*.

Digital computer. Courtesy Sperry Corp.

digital speech Digital speech, like any digital recording of sound, breaks the sound into tiny units. Each of these tiny units has characteristics such as pitch, loudness, and so on that can be represented by numbers. These numbers become the digital code for speech.

digital-to-analog converter (D-A converter) Mechanical or electronic devices used to convert discrete digital numbers to continuous analog signals. Opposite of *analog-to-digital converter*.

digitize The process of converting drawings and pictures to digital form by scanning the drawings and pictures with a device that converts sensed highlights into numbers or horizontal and vertical coordinates.

digitizer An input device that converts graphics and pictorial data into binary inputs for use in a computer.

digitizing tablet A flat input device that can be connected to a computer. By moving a stylus or mouse over the tablet, a user can draw a picture that will be sent to the computer.

digit place In positional notation, the site where a symbol such as a digit is located in a word representing a numeral.

digit punching position The area on a punch card reserved to represent a decimal digit (i.e., a punch in rows 1, 2, ..., 9).

dimension The maximum size or the number and arrangement of the elements of an array.

diode An electronic device used to permit current flow in one direction and to inhibit current flow in the opposite direction.

diode transistor logic See *DTL*.

DIP (Dual In-Line Package) A device on which an integrated circuit is mounted. It provides a protective casing for the integrated circuit and pin connections for plugging the chip into a circuit board.

direct access Pertaining to the process of obtaining data from or placing data into storage when the time required for such access is independent of the location of the data most recently obtained or placed in storage. Also called *random access*. Contrast with *serial access*.

direct access storage device (DASD) A basic type of storage

Digital plotter. Courtesy Radio Shack, a division of Tandy Corp.

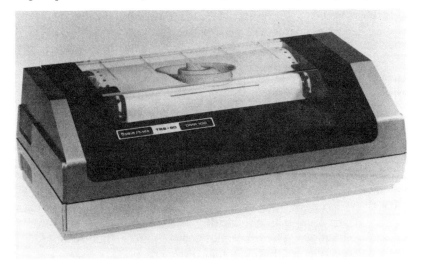

medium that allows information to be accessed by positioning the medium or accessing mechanism directly to the information required, thus permitting direct addressing of data locations.

direct address An address that specifies the storage location of an operand. Contrast with *indirect address*.

direct-connect modem A modulator/demodulator that is connected directly to the phone system for use in data transmission. Contrast with *acoustic coupler*.

direct coupled transistor logic (DCTL) A logic system that uses only transistors as active elements.

direct current The flow of electrons in one direction.

direct data entry Entry of data directly into the computer through machine-readable source documents or through the use of on-line terminals.

direct distance dialing See *DDD*.

direct memory access (DMA) A method by which data can be transferred between peripheral devices and internal memory without intervention by the central processing unit.

directory A partition by software into several distinct files; a directory of these files is maintained on a device to locate the files.

disassembler A program that takes machine language code and generates the assembler language code from which the machine language was produced. See *assembly language*.

disaster dump A computer storage dump that occurs as a result of a nonrecoverable mistake in a program.

disc Alternate spelling for disk. See *magnetic disk*.

discrete Pertaining to distinct elements or to representation by means of distinct elements such as characters.

discrete component An electrical component that contains only one function, as opposed to an integrated circuit.

dish An antenna that receives signals from a satellite.

disk A revolving plate upon which data and programs are stored. See *floppy disk* and *magnetic disk*.

disk access time The time required to locate a specific track on a disk.

disk crash A condition of a disk unit that makes it unusable. It is usually caused by contact between the read/write head of the disk drive and the surface of the disk.

disk drive A device that rotates magnetic disks and accesses its data by means of a read/write head.

disk duplication The process of copying information recorded on one magnetic disk onto another disk.

diskette   A floppy disk. A low-cost bulk-storage medium for micro-computers and minicomputers. See *floppy disk.*

diskette tray   A container that is used to store floppy disks.

disk file   A file that resides on a magnetic disk.

disk library   A special place that houses a file of disk packs or diskettes under secure, environmentally controlled conditions.

disk operating system (DOS)   An operating system in which the programs are stored on magnetic disks. Typically, it keeps track of files, saves and retrieves files, allocates storage space, and manages other control functions associated with disk storage.

disk pack   A removable direct access storage device containing magnetic disks on which information is stored.

disk unit   See *magnetic disk unit.*

disk unit enclosure   A cabinet designed to hold one or more disk drives and a power supply.

dispatch   To select the next job and get it ready for processing.

dispatching priority   A number assigned to tasks and used to determine precedence for use of the central processing unit in a multitask situation.

dispersed data processing   Same as *distributed data processing.*

dispersed intelligence   A network system in which the computing power is scattered or dispersed throughout the computer network.

displacement   The difference between the base address and the actual machine language address.

display   A visual presentation of information (i.e., lights or indicators on computer consoles, a cathode-ray tube, a printed report, or a diagram produced by a plotter).

display console   A device that provides a visual representation of data.

display highlighting   A way of emphasizing information on a display screen using such enhancers as blinking, boldface, high contrast reverse, video underlining, or different colors.

display type   The technology of the display; for example, cathode-ray tube (CRT), light emitting diode (LED), liquid crystal display (LCD), and so forth.

display unit   A device that provides a visual representation of data. See *cathode-ray tube, line printer, plasma display*, and *plotter.*

distortion   Any undesired change in the waveform of an electric signal passing through a circuit, including the transmission medium. In the design of any electronic circuit, one important problem is to modify the input signal in the required way without producing distortion beyond an acceptable degree.

distributed data processing   A concept whereby a company supplements its main computer system (often called the home office computer) with field office terminals. The field office terminals can be used to do local data processing operations without tying down the home office computer. Limited data communications can occur between the home office computer and the field office terminals, thus providing for a company-wide communications system. Contrast with *centralized data processing*.

distributed design   An information structure that identifies the existence of independent operating units but recognizes the benefits of central coordination and control.

distributed network   A network configuration in which all node pairs are connected either directly or by redundant paths through intermediate nodes.

distributed processing   Same as *distributed data processing*.

distributive sort   A sort formed by separating the list into parts and then rearranging the parts in order.

disturbance   An irregular phenomenon that interferes with the interchange of intelligence during transmission of a signal.

dithering   The intermingling of dots of various colors to produce what appears to be a new color. The dots must be so small and closely spaced that the eye fuses them together.

dividend   In the division operation a/b, *a* is the dividend and *b* is the divisor. The result is the quotient and remainder.

division check   A multiplication check in which a zero-balancing result is compared against the original dividend.

divisor   The quantity that is used to divide another quantity.

DMA   See *direct memory access*.

DML   See *data manipulating language*.

DNC   (Direct Numerical Control) Computer control of automatic machine tools. Control is applied at discrete points in the process rather than applied continuously. See *APT* and *numerical control*.

DOA   (Dead On Arrival) Used to describe a product that does not work when you take it out of the box.

documentation   During systems analysis and subsequent programming, the preparation of documents that describe such things as the system, and programs prepared, and the changes made at later dates.

documentation aids   Aids that help automate the documentation process; for example, program description write-ups, flowcharts, programs, program runs, and so forth.

documentor   A program designed to use data processing methods in the production and maintenance of program flowcharts, text material, and other types of tabular or graphic information.

document reader A general term referring to OCR or OMR equipment that reads a limited amount of information.

document retrieval Acquiring data from storage devices and, possibly, manipulating the data and subsequently preparing a report.

domain A set of data values from which a relational attribute may draw its values.

domain tip A type of storage device that uses thin films to create magnetic domains for storing digital data. See *thin film.*

dope vector A vector wherein an atom of a linked list describes the contents of the other atoms in the list.

doping The process of introducing impurity elements into the crystalline structure of pure silicon during semiconductor fabrication.

DOS See *disk operating system* and *operating system.*

dot matrix A technique for representing characters by composing them out of selected dots from within a rectangular matrix of dots.

dot matrix printer An inexpensive printer that uses a matrix of wire pens to form characters on paper.

double buffering A software or hardware technique to transfer information between the computer and peripheral devices. Information in one buffer is acted on by the computer while information in the other is transferred in or out.

double-dabble The process of converting binary numbers into their decimal equivalents.

double density A diskette that holds twice as much data as a single-density diskette.

double precision Pertaining to the use of two computer words to represent a number in order to gain increased precision.

double punch More than one numeric punch in any one column of a card.

double-sided disk A magnetic disk capable of storing information on both of its surfaces.

doublestriking See *overstriking.*

double word An entity of storage that is two words in length.

doubly linked list List in which each atom contains one pointer that relates to the successor atom.

down A term that means the hardware circuits of a computer are inoperable or that there is a failure in the software system. When a computer is "down," it is simply not functioning.

download The transfer of information from a remote computer system to the user's system. Opposite of *upload.*

downtime The length of time a computer system is inoperative due to a malfunction. Contrast with *available time*.

downward compatible Refers to a computer that is compatible with a smaller or previous generation computer.

DPMA (Data Processing Management Association) A professional data processing organization whose primary purpose is to develop and promote business methods and education in data processing and data processing management.

DPMA certificate A certificate given by the Data Processing Management Association indicating that a person has attained a certain level of competence in the field of data processing. The certificate is obtained by passing an examination that is offered yearly.

dragging A technique of making a displayed graphics object follow the cursor.

drain One of the three connecting terminals of a field effect transistor, the other two being the *source* and the *gate*. If the charge carriers are positive, the conventional current flows from the source to the drain.

drift A change in the output of an electric circuit. This change slowly occurs over a period of time.

drive A short name for a disk drive.

driver A software driver consists of a series of instructions the computer follows to reformat data for transfer to and from a particular peripheral device. The electrical and mechanical requirements are different from one kind of device to another, and the software drivers are used to standardize the format of data between them and the central processor.

DRO (Destructive ReadOut) See *destructive read*.

droid A humanlike robot; contraction of android (male) or gynoid (female).

drop In a network, a remote terminal location.

drop dead halt A halt from which there is no recovery.

drop out In data transmission, a momentary loss in signal, usually due to the effect of noise or system malfunction.

drum See *magnetic drum*.

drum plotter An output device that draws schematics, graphs, pictures, and so forth on paper with an automatically controlled pen. The paper is wrapped around a cylindrical drum. This drum turns forward and backward at various speeds under a pen that slides to and fro, marking the paper.

drum printer A printing device that uses a drum embossed with alphabetic and numeric characters. A type of *line printer*, a drum printer can print several thousand lines per minute.

drum sorting A sort program that uses magnetic drums for auxiliary storage during sorting.

drum storage See *magnetic drum.*

dry plasma etching A method for developing a mask on a wafer.

dry run A program-checking technique. The process of examining the logic and coding of a program from a flowchart and written instructions and recording the results of each step of the operation before running the program on the computer. Same as *desk checking.*

DTL (Diode Transistor Logic) Microelectronic logic based on connections between semiconductor diodes and the transistor.

dual channel controller A controller that enables reading from, and writing to, a device to occur simultaneously.

dual density (1) Refers to tapes or disks on which data are densely recorded. (2) A floppy disk with dual-side recording capability.

dual disk drive A floppy disk system that contains two disk drives, thus providing an increased storage capacity.

dual in-line package (DIP) A popular type of integrated circuit package on which a chip is mounted.

dual-intensity Indicates the ability of a terminal or printer to produce characters in regular as well as highlighted or bold formats.

dumb terminal A visual display terminal with minimal capabilities. It has no processing capability. See *intelligent terminal* and *smart terminal.*

dummy Used as an adjective to indicate an artificial instruction, address, or record of information inserted solely to fulfill prescribed conditions.

dummy argument Variables, used as function arguments, that do not have any values.

dummy instruction (1) An artificial instruction or address inserted in a list to serve a purpose other than its execution as an instruction. (2) An instruction in a routine that, in itself, does not perform any functions. Often used to provide a point at which to terminate a program loop.

dump The data that results from a "dumping" process. See *post mortem dump* and *snapshot dump.*

dumping Copying all or part of the contents of a storage unit, usually from the computer's internal storage, into an auxiliary storage unit or onto a line printer. See *dump, post mortem dump,* and *snapshot dump.*

duplex Relates to a communications system or equipment capable of transmission in both directions. See *full duplex* and *half duplex*.

duplex channel A channel that allows simultaneous transmission in both directions. See *full duplex, half duplex*, and *simplex*.

duplexing The use of duplicate computers, peripheral equipment, or circuitry so that, in the event of a component failure, an alternate component can enable the system to continue.

duplicate To copy so that the result remains in the same physical form as the source; for example, to make a new diskette with the same information as an original diskette. Contrast with *copy*.

duplication check A check requiring that the results of two independent performances of the same operation be identical. The check may be made concurrently on duplicate equipment or at a later time on the same equipment.

Dvorak keyboard A keyboard arrangement that is easier and faster to use than the standard QWERTY keyboard.

dyadic Referring to an operation that uses two operands.

dyadic operation An operation on two operands.

dynamic address translation (DAT) In virtual storage systems, the change of a virtual storage address to a real storage address during execution of an instruction.

dynamic dump A dump taken during the execution of a program.

dynamic memory A type of storage that requires continual refreshing (internal regeneration) of its contents.

dynamic RAM Storage that the computer must refresh at frequent intervals. Contrast with *static RAM*.

dynamic relocation The movement of part or all of an active (i.e., currently operating) program from one region of storage to another. All necessary address references are adjusted to enable proper execution of the program to continue in its new location.

dynamic scheduling Job scheduling that is determined by the computer on a moment-to-moment basis, depending upon the circumstances.

dynamic storage A memory device that must constantly be recharged or "refreshed" at frequent intervals to avoid loss of data. A very volatile memory.

dynamic storage allocation Automatic storage allocation. See *storage allocation*.

E

E A symbol that stands for exponent. Used in floating-point numbers to mean "to the power."

EAM (Electronic Accounting Machine) Usually refers to unit record equipment.

EAROM (Electrically Alternable ROM) ROM memory that can be selectively altered without erasing all stored data, as is done with EPROM devices.

easywriter A software package used for word processing.

EBAM (Electron Beam Addressed Memory) An electronic storage device that uses electrical circuits to control a beam that reads from or writes on a metal oxide semiconductor surface.

EBCDIC (Extended Binary Coded Decimal Interchange Code) An 8-bit code used to represent data. EBCDIC can represent up to 256 distinct characters and is the principal code used in many current computers. *See page 94.*

echo check A check on the accuracy of a data transfer operation in which the data received is transmitted back to the source and compared with the original data.

Eckert, J. Presper Coinventor of the ENIAC, an early electronic computer. See *ENIAC* and *Mauchly, John.*

ECL (Emitter Coupled Logic) Also called Current Mode Logic (CML). ECL is faster than TTL, but much less popular.

ECOM (Electronic Computer Oriented Mail) A process of sending and receiving messages in digital form over telecommunications facilities.

edge A connection between two nodes in a graph.

edge card A circuit board (or card) with contact strips along one edge, designed to mate with an edge connector.

edge connector A slot-shaped electrical socket that connects a circuit card to a motherboard or chassis.

edge cutter/trimmer A device for removing the sprocketed margin from continuous line printer paper.

edge-punched card A card into which data may be recorded by punching holes along one edge in a pattern similar to that used for punched tape. Hole positions are arranged to form coded patterns in five, six, seven, or eight channels and usually represent data in a binary code decimal system.

edit (1) To check the correctness of data. (2) To change as necessary

Character	EBCDIC
0	1111 0000
1	1111 0001
2	1111 0010
3	1111 0011
4	1111 0100
5	1111 0101
6	1111 0110
7	1111 0111
8	1111 1000
9	1111 1001
A	1100 0001
B	1100 0010
C	1100 0011
D	1100 0100
E	1100 0101
F	1100 0110
G	1100 0111
H	1100 1000
I	1100 1001
J	1101 0001
K	1101 0010
L	1101 0011
M	1101 0100
N	1101 0101
O	1101 0110
P	1101 0111
Q	1101 1000
R	1101 1001
S	1110 0010
T	1110 0011
U	1110 0100
V	1110 0101
W	1110 0110
X	1110 0111
Y	1110 1000
Z	1110 1001

the form of data by adding or deleting certain characters. For example, part of the program can edit data for printing, adding special symbols, spacing, deleting, nonsignificant zeros, and so on.

editing Making the corrections or changes in a program or data. See *data editing*

editing run In batch processing, the editing program will check the data for ostensible validity (e.g., test to assure that dates and numbers fall within the expected ranges, compare totals with separately entered batch or hash totals, and prove check digits) and identify any errors for correction and resubmission.

editor Computer program designed to make it easy to review and alter a file or program interactively. For example, one editing command might locate and display the first occurrence of a given string of characters; a second command might delete or change those characters wherever they occur.

EDP (Electronic Data Processing) Data processing performed largely by electronic digital computers.

EDP auditor A person who performs evaluations of systems and operational procedures.

EDS Exchangeable Disk Store.

EEROM (Electronically Erasable Read-Only Memory) A device that can be erased electrically and reprogrammed.

effective address The address that is derived by performing any specified address modification operations upon a specified address.

effectiveness The degree to which the output produced achieves the desired purpose.

efficiency The ratio of resources consumed to produce a given amount of output; the time and other resources used to produce computer output.

EFT (Electronic Funds Transfer) An EFT network transfers funds from one account to another with electronic equipment rather than with paper media, such as checks.

ego-less programming The concept of arranging the programming tasks so that credit for success or blame for failure must be shared by several programmers rather than just one person.

EIA Electronic Industries Association.

EIA interface A standard interface between peripherals and microcomputers, and modems and terminals. Another name for RS-232 interface.

eight-bit chip A CPU chip that processes data eight bits at a time.

electrical communications The science and technology by which information is collected from an originating source, transformed into electric currents or fields, transmitted over electrical networks or through space to another point, and reconverted into a form suitable for interpretation by a receiving entity.

electromagnetic delay line   A delay line whose operation is based on the time of propagation of electromagnetic waves through distributed or lumped capacitance and inductance. Used in early computers.

electromechanical   Referring to a system for processing data that uses both electrical and mechanical principles.

electron beam deflection system   A narrow stream of electrons moving in the same direction under the influence of an electric or magnetic field.

electronic   Pertaining to the flow of electricity through semiconductors, valves, and filters, in contrast with the free flow of current through simple conductors. The essence of computer technology is the selective use and combination of electronic apparatus whereby current can be allowed to flow or can be halted by electronic switches working at a very high speed.

electronic accounting machine   Data processing equipment that is predominantly electromechanical; for example, keypunch, mechanical sorter, tabulator, or collator.

electronically programmable   A programmable ROM (read-only memory) or any other digital device in which the data 1s and 0s in binary code can be entered electrically, usually by the user with a piece of equipment called a *PROM programmer.*

electronic bulletin board   A computer system that maintains a list of messages so that people can call up (with their microcomputer systems) and either post a message or read those that are already there.

electronic cottage   The concept of permitting workers to remain at home to perform work using computer terminals connected to a central office.

electronic data processing   Data processing performed largely by electronic equipment.

electronic data processing system   A system for data processing by means of machines using electronic circuitry at electronic speed, as opposed to electromechanical equipment.

electronic fund transfer (EFT)   A cashless approach to paying for goods and services. Electronic signals between computers are often used to adjust the accounts of the parties involved in a transaction.

electronic journal   A log file summarizing, in chronological sequence, the processing activities performed by a system.

electronic magazine A magazine published in a videotape or videodisk format. A type of electronic publishing.

electronic mail The process of sending, receiving, storing, and forwarding messages in digital form over telecommunications facilities.

electronic music Music in which the sounds are produced by electronic means. See *computer music* and *synthesizer.*

electronic office An office that relies on word processing and computer and data communications technologies.

electronic pen A penlike stylus that is commonly used in conjunction with a cathode-ray tube for inputting or changing information under program control. Often called a *light pen.*

electronic power supply A source of electric energy employed to furnish the tubes and semiconductor devices of an electronic circuit with the proper electric voltages and currents for their operation.

electronic publishing A technology encompassing a variety of activities that contain or convey information with a high editorial and value added content in a form other than print. Included in the list of presently practiced electronic publishing activities are: educational software disks, educational software cassettes, on-line data bases, electronic mail videotext, teletext, videotape cassettes, and videodisks.

electronics The branch of science and technology relating to the conduction and control of electricity flowing through semiconducting materials or through vacuum or gases.

electronic spreadsheet A computer program that turns a computer terminal into a huge ledger sheet. The program allows large columns and rows of numbers to change according to parameters determined by the user. A whole range of numbers can be changed when a single entry is varied, allowing complex projections and numerical forecasts to be performed without tedious manual calculations. Examples are VisiCalc and Lotus 1-2-3.

electronic tube The dominant electronic element found in computers prior to the advent of the transistor.

electrosensitive paper Printer paper with a thin coating of conductive material, such as aluminum. Print becomes visible because it darkens where a matrix-type print head allows electric current to flow onto the conductive surface.

electrosensitive printer A printer that uses electricity to form characters on specially treated paper.

electrostatic printer A high-speed printer that forms characters on chemically treated paper.

electrothermal printer A high-speed printer that uses heated elements to create characters as matrices of small dots on heat-sensitive paper.

element An item of data within an array.

elements of a microcomputer A microcomputer usually consists of a microprocessor, program memory (usually ROM), data storage (usually RAM), input/output circuitry, and clock generators.

eleven-punch A punch in the second row from the top of a Hollerith punched card. Synonymous with X-punch.

elite type A size of type that fits twelve characters into each inch of type.

embedded command In word processing, one or more characters inserted into the text that do not print but direct the word processing program or printer to perform some task, such as end a page or skip a line.

embedded systems Computer systems that cannot be programmed by the user because they are preprogrammed for a specific task and are buried within the equipment they serve.

emitter An electrode within a transistor.

empty string A string containing no characters. Also called a *null string*.

emulate To imitate one system with another such that the imitating system accepts the same data, executes the same programs, and achieves the same results as the imitated system.

emulator A type of program or device that allows user programs written for one kind of computer system to be run on another system.

emulsion laser storage See *laser storage*.

enable To switch a computer device or facility so that it can operate.

encipher To alter data (scramble) so that they are not readily usable unless the changes are first undone.

enciphering See *encryption*.

enclosure A housing for any electrical or electronic device.

encode To convert data into a code form that is acceptable to some piece of computer equipment.

encoder A device that produces machine-readable output (e.g., diskette) either from manual keyboard depressions or from data already recorded in some other code.

encryption The coding of information or data in such a way as to make them unintelligible without the key to decryption.

end-around carry A carry from the most significant digit place to the least significant digit place.

end-around shift   See *circular shift.*

endless loop   The endless repetition of a series of instructions with no exit from the loop possible.

end mark   A code or signal that indicates termination of a unit of data.

end-of-block (EOB)   Termination of a block.

end-of-file (EOF)   Termination or point of completion of a quantity of data. End-of-file marks are used to indicate this point on magnetic files. See *end-of-tape marker.*

end-of-message (EOM)   Termination of a message.

end-of-page halt   A feature that stops the printer at the end of each completed page of output.

end-of-tape marker   A marker on a magnetic tape used to indicate the end of the permissible recording area.

end-user   Anyone who uses a computer system or its output.

engine   Another name for a processor.

engineering units   Units of measure as applied to a process variable.

ENIAC   (Electronic Numerical Integrator And Calculator) An early all-electronic digital computer. It was built by J. Mauchly and J. Eckert at the Moore School of Electrical Engineering, University of Pennsylvania, in 1946. See *Eckert, J. Presper* and *Mauchly, John.*

E notation   A format for the representation of very large or very small numbers. The notation consists of two parts: a mantissa and an exponent. Also called scientific notation.

ENTER key   A special key on some keyboards that means "execute a command." Same as "return" on some keyboards. Often used interchangeably with carriage return.

entry point   Any location in a routine to which control can be passed by another routine. Entry is also referred to as the *transfer address.* It is often the first instruction to be executed in a program.

environment   In a computing context, this is more likely to refer to the mode of operation (e.g., "in a time-sharing environment") than to physical conditions of temperature, humidity, and so forth. But either kind of environment may affect operational efficiency.

environment division   One of the four main component parts of a COBOL program.

EOB   See *end-of-block.*

EOF   See *end-of-file.*

EOJ   End-Of-Job.

EOLN or EOL   (End-Of-Line) A flag indicating the end of a line of data.

EOM See *end-of message*.

EOT End-of-Transmission.

EPO (Emergency Power Off) The circuit, and the buttons activating it, that can turn an entire computer off in an emergency. There may be as many as twenty EPO buttons in a large installation.

EPROM (Erasable Programmable Read-Only Memory) A special PROM that can be erased under high-intensity ultraviolet light and reprogrammed. EPROMs can be reprogrammed repeatedly.

EPROM programmer A special machine that is used to program EPROM chips.

equality The idea expressed by the equal sign, written =. In many programming languages and program designs, the = sign is also used as a "replacement symbol."

equation A mathematical sentence with an = sign between two expressions that name the same number; $y = x^2 + 4x - 36$, for example, is an equation.

equipment bay A cabinet or case into which electronic equipment is installed.

erasable programmable read-only memory See *EPROM*.

erasable storage A storage medium that can be erased and reused. Magnetic disk, drum, or tape are mediums that can be erased and reused; punched cards or punched paper tape cannot.

erase To remove data from storage without replacing it.

erase head In a domestic tape recorder, the erase head is the device that cleans the tape of the earlier signals immediately before new matter is recorded. In a computer storage device based on magnetization of ferric-oxide surfaces (e.g., tape, card or disk, but not core), the erase head operates immediately before the write head to perform a precisely similar function.

ergonomics Adapting machines to the convenience of operators, with the general aim of maximum efficiency. For example, adding a numeric keypad to a standard keyboard.

EROM (Erasable ROM) Same as *EPROM*.

error The general term referring to any deviation of a computed or a measured quantity from the theoretically correct or true value. Contrast with *fault, malfunction*, and *mistake*. See *intermittent error* and *round-off error*.

error analysis The branch of numerical analysis concerned with studying the error aspects of numerical analysis procedures. It includes the study of errors that arise in a computation because of the peculiarities of computer arithmetic.

error checking   Refers to various techniques that test for the valid condition of data.

error control   A plan, implemented by software, hardware, or procedures, to detect and/or correct errors introduced into a data communications system.

error-correcting code   (1) A code in which each acceptable expression conforms to specific rules of construction. Nonacceptable expressions are also defined. If certain types of errors occur in an acceptable expression, an equivalent will result and the error can be corrected. (2) A code in which the forbidden pulse combination produced by the gain or loss of a bit will indicate which bit is wrong. Same as *self-correcting code*.

error correction   A system that detects and inherently provides correction for errors caused by transmission equipment or facilities.

error-detection code   (1) A code in which each expression conforms to specific rules of construction. When expressions occur that do not conform to the rules of these constructions, an error is indicated. (2) A code in which errors produce forbidden combinations. A single error-detecting code produces a forbidden combination if a digit gains or loses a single bit. A double error-detecting code produces a forbidden combination if a digit gains or loses either one or two bits, and so on. Also called a *self-checking code*.

error file   A file generated during data processing to retain erroneous information sensed by the computer, often printed as an error report.

error guessing   A test data selection technique. The selection criterion is to pick values that seem likely to cause errors.

error message   A printed statement indicating the computer has detected a mistake or malfunction.

error rate   In data communications, a measure of quality of circuit or equipment; the number of erroneous bits of characters in a sample.

error ratio   The ratio of the number of data units in error to the total number of data units.

error transmission   A change in data resulting from the transmission process.

escape key (ESC or ESCAPE)   A standard control key that is available on most computer keyboards. It is usually used to take control of the computer away from a program, or to escape from that program.

ethernet A type of network system that allows audio and video information to be carried as well as computer data.

ETX End-Of-Text.

evaluation The process of determining if a newly created computer system is actually doing what it was designed to do.

exception reporting A technique for screening large amounts of computerized data in order to display or print reports containing only specific information.

excess-three code A binary coded decimal notation in which each decimal digit X is represented by the binary numeral of X plus 3.

exchangeable disk See *disk pack*.

exchange buffering A technique using data chaining for eliminating the need to move data in internal storage.

exclusive OR (XOR) The Boolean operator that gives a truth table value of true if only one of the two variables it connects is true. If both variables it connects are true, this value is false.

executable A program statement that gives an instruction of some computational operation to be performed then (e.g., assignment statements are executable). Contrast with *nonexecutable*.

execute To run a program on a computer or to carry out an instruction. Same as *run*.

execute cycle The period of time during which a machine instruction is interpreted and the indicated operation is performed on the specified operand.

execution The operating cycle during which a program is actually being processed, or run.

execution time The time it takes for a program to run from start to finish.

executive A master program that controls the execution of other programs. Often used synonymously with *monitor, supervisory system*, and *operating system*.

exerciser A device that enables users to create and debug programs and hardware interfaces by manual means.

exit The point in an algorithm or program from which control is transferred elsewhere.

expandability The ability to increase the capability of a computer system by adding modules or devices.

expansion card A card added to a system for the purpose of mounting additional chips or circuits to expand the system capability.

expansion interface A circuit board that allows one to add disk drives, additional memory, and other peripherals to a basic computer.

expansion slots Extra slots in a computer circuit board that are used for adding new expansion boards to the basic computer.

expert system Methods and techniques for constructing human-machine systems with specialized problem-solving expertise. The pursuit of this area of artificial intelligence research has emphasized the knowledge that underlies human expertise and has simultaneously decreased the apparent significance of domain-independent problem-solving theory.

explicit address A storage address explicitly stated (rather than an address symbolically represented) in a source language program.

exponent A symbol or number written above and to the right of another symbol or number that denotes the number of times the latter is used as a factor.

exponential notation A notation in which members are written as a "significant digits" part times an appropriate power of 10; for example, 0.26418×10^7 or 0.26418E7 to mean 2,641,800.

exponential smoothing A forecasting technique.

exponentiation The mathematical process of raising a number to a power of a base (e.g., 2^4).

expression An arithmetic formula coded in a programming language.

extended addressing Refers to an addressing mode that can reach any place in memory and requires more than one byte to locate the date in memory.

Extended Binary Coded Decimal Interchange Code See *EBCDIC*.

extender board A debugging aid that allows one to monitor circuit boards more conveniently.

extensible language A concept whereby the user adds new features to a programming language by modifying existing ones.

extension Additional features that are added to a programming language or computer system.

extent A collection of physical records that are contiguous in auxiliary storage.

external data file Data that is stored separately from the program that processes it.

external reference A reference to a symbol defined in another routine.

external sort The second phase of a multipass sort program, wherein strings of data are continually merged until one string of sequenced data is formed.

external storage See *auxiliary storage*.

external symbol (1) A control section name, entry point name, or external reference. (2) A symbol contained in the external symbol dictionary.

external symbol dictionary Control information associated with an object program that identifies the external symbols in the program.

extract To remove specific information from a computer word as determined by a mask or filter.

F

f See *frequency*.

fabricated language See *symbolic language*.

FACE See *field alterable control element*.

facility See *channel*.

facsimile (FAX) (1)Transmission of pictures, maps, diagrams, and so on. The image is scanned at the transmitter, reconstructed at the receiving station, and duplicated on some form of paper. (2) A hard copy reproduction.

facsimile transceiver A unit used to transmit and receive electronic transmissions of images.

factor analysis A mathematical technique for studying the interaction of many factors in order to determine the most significant factors and the degree of significance.

factorial A product of factors, computed by multiplying together all the integers from 1 to a specified number. The exclamation point (!) is used to represent factorial. For example:

$$4! = 1 \cdot 2 \cdot 3 \cdot 4$$
$$6! = 1 \cdot 2 \cdot 3 \cdot 4 \cdot 5 \cdot 6$$
$$n! = 1 \cdot 2 \cdot 3 \cdot 4 \ldots (n-1) \cdot n$$

fail-safe system A system designed to avoid catastrophe but possibly at the expense of convenience. For example, when a fault is detected in a computer-controlled traffic light system, a fail-safe arrangement might be to set all the traffic lights to red rather than turn them off. Similarly, in a power plant operation, overheating might simply disconnect the power supply. See *fail-soft system*.

fail-soft system A system that continues to process data despite the failure of parts of the system. Usually accompanied by a deterioration in performance. Using the two examples described under fail-safe system, the traffic lights might turn to flashing amber rather than red, and the overheat system might maintain battery power for emergency equipment while the main source of power was turned off. See *fail-safe system*.

failure prediction A technique that attempts to determine the failure schedule of specific parts or equipment so that they may be discarded and replaced before failure occurs.

fairness Fairness holds when every action requested in a system is guaranteed to execute after a finite amount of time.

fallback A backup system brought into use in an emergency situation, especially the reserve data base and programs that would be switched in quickly, or even automatically, in the event of a detected fault in a real-time system.

fallout The failure of electronic components sometimes experienced during the burn-in of a new piece of equipment.

family of computers Series of central processing units allegedly of the same logical design but of different speeds. This philosophy is supposed to enable the user to start with a slower, less expensive CPU and grow to a faster, more expensive one as the workload builds up, without having to change the rest of the computer system.

FAMOS (Floating gate Avalanche injection MOS) A fabrication technology for charge storage devices such as PROMs.

fanfold paper One long continuous sheet of paper perforated at regular intervals to mark page boundaries and folded fan-style into a stack.

fan-in The number of signal inputs to a digital component.

fan-out The number of TTL unit loads a given TTL device output can supply or drive under the worst case conditions.

farad A unit of measure of capacitance. A capacitor has a capacitance of 1 farad if it will store a charge of 1 coulomb when a 1-volt potential is applied across it.

fatal error An unexpected failure or other problem that occurs while the program is executing. A fatal error prevents the computer from continuing to execute the program. If the error is nonfatal, the program will proceed, but not correctly.

father file A system of updating records that retains a copy of the original record as well as provides an amended version. When a file update program is run, the old master file is termed the "father file." The updated file is termed the "son file." The file that was used to create the father file is termed the "grandfather file." The technique is particularly applicable to files held on magnetic media, such as disk or tape.

fault A condition that causes a component, a computer, or a peripheral device to not perform to its design specifications (e.g., a broken wire or a short circuit). Contrast with *error, malfunction,* and *mistake.*

fault tolerant computing The art of building computing systems that continue to operate satisfactorily in the presence of faults.

FAX See *facsimile.*

FCC (Federal Communications Commission) An organization of the U.S. government responsible for regulating interstate communications, communications common carriers, and the broadcast media.

FE See *field engineer.*

feasibility study Concerned with a definition of the data processing problem, together with alternative solutions, a recommended course of action, and a working plan for designing and installing the system.

feature Something special that is accomplished in a program or hardware device.

feature extraction The selection of dominant characteristics for pattern recognition. This enables a computer-controlled video camera to recognize objects by such features as shapes and edges.

feed The mechanical process whereby lengthy materials (e.g., paper or magnetic tape, line printer paper, printer ribbon, and so on) are moved along the required operating position.

feedback (1) A means of automatic control in which the actual state of a process is measured and used to obtain a quantity that modifies the input in order to initiate the activity of the control system. (2) In data processing, information arising from a particular stage of processing could provide a feedback to affect the processing of subsequent data; for example, the fact that an area of storage was nearly full might either delay the acceptance of more data or divert it to some other storage area.

feedback circuit A circuit that returns a portion of the output signal of an electronic circuit or control system to the input of the circuit of the system.

feed holes Holes punched in a paper tape to enable it to be driven by a sprocket wheel.

feep Another name for the beep that terminals make to get your attention.

female connector Pertaining to the recessed portion of a device into which another part fits. See *connector* and *male connector*.

femto One quadrillionth, or a millionth of a billionth, 10^{-15}.

ferrous oxide The substance that coats recording disks and tapes. It can be magnetized, thereby permitting information to be recorded on it magnetically.

FET (Field Effect Transistor) A semiconductor device used as a storage element.

fetch To locate and load a quantity of instructions or data from storage.

FF *form feed.*

fiber optics A data transmission medium made of tiny threads of a glass or plastic that transmits huge amounts of information at the speed of light.

fiche Microfiche. A sheet of photographic film containing multiple microimages. See *COM*.

field A group of related characters treated as a unit; for example, a group of adjacent card columns used to represent an hourly wage rate. An item in a record.

field alterable control element (FACE) A chip used in some systems to allow the user to write microprograms.

fielddata code The U.S. military code used in data processing as a compromise between conflicting manufacturers' codes.

field effect transistor (FET) A three-terminal semiconductor device that acts as a variable charge storage element. The most commonly used type in microcomputers is the metallic oxide semiconductor (MOS) transistor.

field emission The emission of electrons from a metal or semiconductor into a vacuum under the influence of a strong electric field.

field engineer (FE) An individual responsible for field maintenance of computer hardware and software.

field upgradable Hardware that is capable of being enhanced in the field (in one's office or at a local repair center or computer store).

FIFO (First In-First Out) A method of storing and retrieving items from a list, table, or stack, such that the first element stored is the first one retrieved. Contrast with *LIFO*.

FIFO-LIFO Refers to two techniques for the collection of items to which additions and deletions are to be made. See *FIFO* and *LIFO*.

fifth generation computer plan A plan, proposed by the Japan Information Processing Development Center, to develop an advanced computer by the year 1990. Other countries, including the United States and Great Britain, are also conducting development work on fifth generation computers.

figure shift A keyboard key (or the code generated by the key) signifying that the following characters are to be read as figures until a letter shift appears in the message. Same as *letter shift*.

file conversion Changing the file medium or structure.

file gap A space at the end of the file that signifies to the system where the file terminates.

file handling routine The part of a computer program that reads data from, and data to, a file.

file layout The arrangement and structure of data in a file, including the sequence and size of its components.

file level model A model concerned with defining data structures for optimum performance of data base application programs or queries.

file librarian A person who has responsibility for the safekeeping of all computer files; for example, programs and data files on disk packs, magnetic tapes, punched cards, microfilm, and so forth.

file maintenance The updating of a file to reflect the effects of nonperiodic changes by adding, altering, or deleting data; for example, the addition of new programs to a program library on magnetic disks.

file name Alphanumeric characters used to identify a particular file.

file name extension A code that forms the second part of a file name and that is separated from the file name by a period. It identifies the kind of data in the file.

file organization The manner in which the applications programmers views the data.

file processing The periodic updating of master files to reflect the effects of current data, often transaction data contained in detail files; for example, a monthly inventory run updating the master inventory file.

file protection A technique or device used to prevent accidental erasure of data from a file; for example, a magnetic tape file protect ring or a gummed tab over the write protect notch of a floppy disk. See *file protect ring* and *write protect notch*.

file protect ring   Used to protect data on magnetic tape. Accidental writing on the tape is prevented by removing the ring from the tape reel.

file size   The number of records in a file.

file storage   Devices that can hold a reservoir of mass data within the computer system. Magnetic disk units, magnetic tape units, and magnetic card units are examples of file storage devices.

file transfer   The movement of a file from one place to another, or from one storage medium to another.

filling   In computer graphics, a software function that allows the interior of a closed polygon to be filled with a color of the operator's choosing.

FILO   (First In-Last Out) A method of storing and retrieving items from a list, table, or stack, such that the first element stored is the last one retrieved. Same as *LIFO*. Contrast with *FIFO*.

filter   See *mask*.

finite element method   An approximation technique used to solve field problems in various engineering fields.

firmware   A program permanently held in a ROM (Read-Only Memory), as compared to a software program held outside a computer (e.g., on a disk or tape). See *ROM*.

first generation computers   The first commercially available computers, introduced with UNIVAC I in 1951 and terminated with the development of the transistor in 1959. First generation computers are characterized by their use of vacuum tubes. They are now museum pieces.

first in-first out   See *FIFO*.

fixed area   The portion of internal storage that has been assigned to specific programs or data areas.

fixed-head disk unit   A storage device consisting of one or more magnetically coded disks on the surface of which data are stored in the form of magnetic spots arranged in a manner to represent binary data. These data are arranged in circular tracks around the disks and are accessible to reading and writing by read-write heads assigned one per track. Data from a given track are read or written sequentially as the disk rotates under the read-write head.

fixed-length record   A record that always contains the same number of characters. Contrast with *variable-length record*.

fixed point   Pertaining to a number system in which each number is represented by a single set of digits and the position of the radix point is implied by the manner in which the numbers are used. Contrast with *floating point*.

fixed point arithmetic (1) A method of calculation in which the operations take place in an invariant manner and the computer does not consider the location of the radix point. This is illustrated by desk calculators with which the operator must keep track of the decimal point. This occurs similarly with many automatic computers, in which the location of the radix point is the computer user's responsibility. (2) A type of arithmetic in which the operands and results of all arithmetic operations must be properly scaled to have a magnitude between certain fixed values.

fixed program computer See *wired program computer*.

fixed size records File elements, each of which has the same number of words, characters, bytes, bits, fields, and so on.

fixed spacing The printing of characters at fixed horizontal intervals on a page.

fixed storage Storage whose contents are not alterable by computer instructions (e.g., *read-only storage*).

fixed word length Pertaining to a machine word or operand that always has the same number of bits, bytes, or characters. Contrast with *variable word length*.

flag (1) An indicator used frequently to tell some later part of a program that some condition occurred earlier, such as an overflow or carry. (2) A symbol used to mark a record for special attention. For example, on a listing of a program, all statements that contain errors may be flagged for the attention of the program writer. (3) An indicator of special conditions, such as interrupts.

flat-bed plotter A digital plotter using plotting heads that move over a flat surface in both vertical and horizontal directions.

flat pack A small, low-profile (flat), integrated circuit package that can be spot-welded or soldered to a terminal or a printed circuit board. The pins extend outward rather than pointing down, as on a DIP.

flat screen A thin panel screen such as that found on a notebook or portable computer display.

flexible disk A *floppy disk*.

flexowriter A form of typewriter accepting paper tape input. Used as an input/output device with many older computers.

flicker An unsteady lighting of the display due to inadequate refresh rate and/or fast persistence.

flight computer A computer resident in a spacecraft, airplane, or missile.

flight simulator A computer-controlled simulator that is used by airline companies to train pilots on new aircraft.

flip-flop A device or circuit containing active elements capable of assuming either one of two stable states at a given time. Synonymous with *toggle*.

flippy Synonymous with *floppy disk*.

floating point A form of number representation in which quantities are represented by a number called the mantissa multiplied by a power of the number base. Contrast with *fixed point*. See *characteristic* and *mantissa*.

floating point arithmetic A method of calculation that automatically accounts for the location of the radix point.

floating point BASIC A type of BASIC language that allows the use of decimal numbers.

floating point constant A number, usually consisting of two parts. One part contains the fractional component of the number; the other part is expressed as a power of the radix (base) of the number.

floating point operation A method of calculation that automatically accounts for the location of the radix point.

floating point routine A set of subroutines that cause a computer to execute floating point operations on a computer with no built-in floating point hardware.

FLOP Floating Point Operation.

floppy disk A flexible disk (*diskette*) of oxide-coated mylar that is stored in proper or plastic envelopes. The entire envelope is inserted in the disk unit. Floppy disks provide low-cost storage that is used widely with minicomputers and microcomputers. Floppy disks were originally developed for low-capacity storage, low cost, and relatively low data transfer rates. Regular floppy disks have a diameter of 20.32 centimeters (8 inches), mini floppy disks have a diameter of 13.3 centimeters (5¼ inches), and micro floppy disks have a diameter of less than 9 centimeters (3½ inches). See *magnetic disk*.

floppy disk case A container, usually made of plastic, for storing and protecting floppy disks.

floppy disk controller The circuit board or chip that controls a floppy disk unit.

floppy disk unit A peripheral storage device in which data are recorded on magnetizable floppy disks (diskettes).

flow A general term to indicate a sequence of events.

flowchart A diagram that uses symbols and interconnecting lines to show (1) the logic and sequence of specific program operations

Floppy disk unit. Courtesy Radio Shack, a division of Tandy Corp.

(program flowchart) or (2) a system of processing to achieve objectives (system flowchart). See *program flowchart* and *system flowchart*.

flowchart symbol A symbol used to represent operations, data, flow, or equipment on a flowchart. See *annotation symbol, connector symbol, decision symbol, input/output symbol, processing symbol*, and *terminal symbol*.

flowchart template A plastic guide that contains cutouts of the flowchart symbols and is used in the preparation of a flowchart.

flowchart text The descriptive information that is associated with flowchart symbols.

flow diagram See *flowchart*.

flowline On a flowchart, a line representing a connecting path between flowchart symbols.

flush (1) To empty a portion of storage of its contents. (2) Type set in alignment with the left (flush left) or right (flush right) edges of the line measure.

FM (Frequency Modulation) The process of changing the value represented by a signal by varying the frequency of the signal.

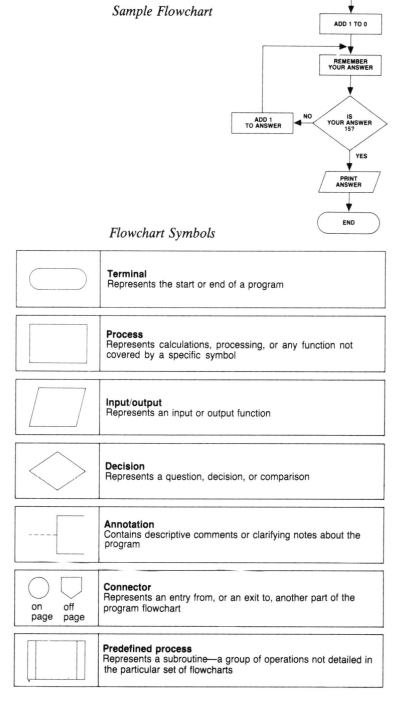

Sample Flowchart

START

ADD 1 TO 0

REMEMBER
YOUR ANSWER

ADD 1
TO ANSWER

NO

IS
YOUR ANSWER
15?

YES

PRINT
ANSWER

END

Flowchart Symbols

	Terminal Represents the start or end of a program
	Process Represents calculations, processing, or any function not covered by a specific symbol
	Input/output Represents an input or output function
	Decision Represents a question, decision, or comparison
	Annotation Contains descriptive comments or clarifying notes about the program
on page off page	**Connector** Represents an entry from, or an exit to, another part of the program flowchart
	Predefined process Represents a subroutine—a group of operations not detailed in the particular set of flowcharts

font A group of characters of one size and style.

footer Information printed at the bottom of a page; for example, page numbers. Most word processors can automatically print footers on each page of a document.

footprint The shape and area of floor space required for a piece of equipment.

force To intervene manually in a program and cause the computer to execute a jump instruction.

foreground job See *foreground program.*

foreground processing The automatic execution of the computer programs that have been designed to preempt the use of the computing facilities.

foreground program A program that has a high priority and therefore takes precedence over other concurrently operating programs in a computer system using multiprogramming techniques. Contrast with *background program.*

foreground task See *foreground program.*

forest A collection of trees. See *tree.*

form The format of the program output.

formal language Abstract mathematical objects used to model the syntax of programming languages, such as COBOL or BASIC, or of natural languages, such as English or French.

formal logic The study of the structure and form of valid argument without regard to the meaning of the terms of the argument.

format (1) The specific arrangement of data. (2) The programming associated with setting up text arrangements for output.

formatter The section of a word processing program that formats the text.

form feed (FF) (1) The physical transport of continuous paper to the beginning of a new line or page. (2) The standard ASCII character that causes a form feed to occur. See *line feed.*

form letter program A program that produces form letters. Also called a *merge-print program.*

forms design The creation of data input forms and source documents.

formula A rule expressed as an equation; for example, $C = 2\pi r$ is the formula for finding the circumference of a circle. It is a way of showing the equal relationship between certain quantities.

FORTH A programming language for use in functional programming that has a specific orientation toward productivity, reliability, and efficiency. Capabilities include structured programming, top-down development, and virtual memory. It has been described as a macrolanguage for a virtual stack machine. It is implemented by a series of "primitives" generated in machine language, and the remainder of the language is compiled from either source files on disk or input from a terminal. FORTH was developed primarily for use on microcomputer systems.

FORTRAN (FORmula TRANslator) A high-level programming language that is widely used to perform mathematical, scientific, and engineering computations. FORTRAN has been approved as an American Standard programming language in two versions (FORTRAN and Basic FORTRAN).

FORTRAN-77 A version of the FORTRAN language that conforms to the ANSI X3.9–1978 standard, with added features for use in microcomputer environments.

FORTRAN translation process The process of translating a program written in FORTRAN into a usable form for computer manipulation.

forward pointer A pointer that tells the location of the next item in a data structure.

FOSDIC (Film Optical Sensing Device for Input to Computers) An input device used by the Census Bureau to read completed census questionnaire data into a computer.

four-address instruction A machine instruction that usually consists of the address of two operands, the address for storing the result, the address of the next instruction, the command to be executed, and miscellaneous indices.

four-out-of-eight code A code for error detection.

fourth generation computer A modern digital computer that uses very large scale integrated (VLSI) circuitry.

FPLA (Field Programmable Logic Array) A FPLA can be programmed by the user in the field, whereas an ordinary PLA is programmable only by asking at the semiconductor manufacturer's factory.

fragmentation The presence of small increments of unused main memory space spread throughout main storage.

frame (1) The video image produced by one complete scan of the screen of a raster-scan display unit. (2) An area, one recording position long, extending across the width of a paper or magnetic tape perpendicular to its movement. Several bit or punch positions may be included in a single frame through the use of different recording positions across the width of the tape.

free form A type of *optical scanning* in which the scanning operation is controlled by symbols that are entered by the input device at the time of data entry.

freeware Software provided by a vendor at no charge.

frequency The number of times that sound pressure, electrical intensity, or other quantities specifying a wave vary from their equilibrium value through a complete cycle in unit time. The most common unit of frequency is the hertz (Hz); 1 Hz is equal to 1 cycle per second.

frequency counter An electronic device capable of counting the number of cycles in an electrical signal during a preselected time interval.

frequency shift keying (FSK) A method of data transmission in which the state of the bit being transmitted is indicated by an audible tone.

friction-feed A paper-feed system that operates by clamping a sheet of paper between two rollers. As the rollers rotate, the paper is drawn into the printer.

friendliness How easy a computer or program is to work with. A "user-friendly" program is one that takes little time to learn and is easy to use.

friendly interface A term applied to a combination of terminal equipment and computer program that is designed to be easy to operate by casual users of computers.

frob To fiddle with a picking device, such as a joystick or mouse.

front end processor A dedicated communications computer at the front end of a host computer. It may perform communications line assignment, data conversion, error analysis, message handling, and other data communications functions.

front panel The collection of switches and indicators by which the computer operator may control a computer system. Same as *control panel.*

FSK See *frequency shift keying.*

full adder A computer circuit capable of adding three binary bits, one of which is a "carry" from a previous addition.

full duplex Pertaining to the simultaneous, independent transmission of data in both directions over a communications link. Contrast with *half duplex* and *simplex.*

full page display A terminal, used in word processing systems, that displays a standard 21 × 28 centimeter (8½ × 11 inch) page of text on the screen at one time.

full screen Used to imply that the entire face of the video screen is used for display.

full screen editing The ability to move the cursor over the entire screen to alter text.

full text searching The retrieval of certain information by searching the full text of an article or book stored in a computer's auxiliary storage.

fully formed characters Refers to printing mechanisms that print characters such as those of a typewriter, as opposed to dot matrix characters.

function (1) A process that is performed on a number or character string; for example, squaring is the mathematical function of multiplying a number by itself. (2) A precoded routine.

functional design The specification of the working relationships between the parts of a system in terms of their characteristic actions.

functional programming Programming that uses function application as the only control structure.

functional specification A set of input, output, processing, and storage requirements detailing what a new system should be able to do. It is the output of the *systems analysis function* and presents a detailed, logical description of a new system.

functional units of a computer The organization of digital computers into five functional units: *arithmetic-logic unit, storage device, control unit, input device,* and *output device.*

function codes Special codes that help control functions of peripheral devices. For example, "clear display screen" would be a function code.

function key A specially designed key that, when pressed, initiates some function on a computer keyboard, word processor, or graphics terminal.

function subprogram A subprogram that returns a single value result.

funware Game programs in firmware.

fuse A safety protective device that opens an electric circuit if overloaded. A current above the rating of the fuse will melt a fusible link and open the circuit. Most computer devices use fuses to protect the equipment from current overloads.

fusible link A widely used PROM programming technique. An excessive current is used to destroy a metallized connection in a storage device, creating a zero, for instance, if a conducting element is interpreted as a one.

gain A general term used to denote an increase in signal power or voltage produced by an amplifier in transmitting a signal from one point to another. The amount of gain is usually expressed in decibels above a reference level. Opposite of *attenuation*.

gallium arsenide A crystalline material used to make high-grade semiconductors. It is superior to silicon but far more costly.

game playing See *computerized game playing*.

game theory A branch of mathematics concerned with probability, among other things. The term was first used by John von Neumann in 1928 to describe the strategy of winning at poker. A mathematical process of selecting an optimum strategy in the face of an opponent who has a strategy of her or his own.

gamut The total range of colors that can be displayed on a computer display.

gang punch To punch identical or constant information into all of a group of punch cards.

Gantt chart A bar chart used for scheduling time sequences.

gap Magnetic memory space between two records (interrecord gap) or two blocks of data (interblock gap). See *interblock gap* and *interrecord gap*.

garbage (1) A term often used to describe incorrect answers from a computer program that usually result from equipment malfunction or a mistake in a computer program. (2) Unwanted and meaningless data carried in storage. (3) Incorrect input to a computer. See *GIGO*.

garbage collection Loosely, a term for cleaning dead storage locations out of a file.

gas display A flat panel display screen filled with an inert gas that glows when current is applied. Character images are formed in a dot matrix fashion by applying power at the appropriate points to make "dots" of glowing gas.

gate This term has two distinct meanings in computer technology, the controlling element of certain transistors, or a logic circuit that has two or more inputs that control one output.

gateway A computer that connects two distinctly different communications networks together. Used so that one local area network computer system can communicate and share its data with another local area network computer system.

gating circuit Refers to a circuit that operates as a selective switch, allowing conduction only during selected time intervals or when the signal magnitude is within certain limits.

gb (gigabyte) One billion bites. One thousand megabytes (mb).

geek An unsophisticated computer user.

GEMISCH A programming language developed for medical record applications.

generalized routine A routine designed to process a large range of specific jobs within a given type of application.

general-purpose computer A computer that is designed to solve a wide class of problems. The majority of digital computers are of this type. Contrast with *special-purpose computer*. See *digital computer*.

general-purpose register A CPU register used for indexing, addressing, and arithmetic and logical operations.

general register A storage device that holds the inputs and outputs of the various functional units of a computing system. Also used for temporary storage of intermediate results.

generate The creation of new data from some given information.

generation (of computers) A term usually applied to the progression of computers from those using vacuum tubes (*first generation*) to those using transistors (*second generation*), to those using integrated circuits (*third generation*), and to those using *LSI* and *VLSI* circuits (*fourth generation*).

generator A computer program that instructs other programs to perform a particular type of operation (e.g., a report program generator, I/O generator).

generic Pertaining to the next (generally improved) type of an item or device.

geocoding A method of providing a graphic display of data in relation to a geographic area.

germanium A chemical element (atomic number 32) used in the manufacture of chips.

GERT (Graphical Evaluation and Review Technique) A procedure for the formulation and evaluation of systems using a network approach.

get To obtain a record from an input file. Another name for load.

gibberish Unnecessary data.

giga (G) A prefix indicating 1 billion. More accurately, 2^{30}, or 1 073 741 824.

gigabyte One billion bytes. More accurately, 1 073 741 824, or 2^{30} bytes.

gigahertz (GHz) A frequency of a billion times a second.

GIGO (Garbage In-Garbage Out) A term used to describe the incorrect data put into and taken out of a computer system; that is, if the input data is bad (Garbage In), then the output data will also be bad (Garbage Out).

glare A reflection from the surface of a display screen.

glitch A popular term for a temporary or random malfunction in hardware.

global A term that refers to a variable whose name is accessible by a main program and all its *subroutines*.

global operation In word processing, an operation performed throughout an entire file.

global search and replace In word processing, the ability to find a string anywhere it appears in a document and to substitute another string for it.

global variable A variable that has the same value regardless of where or in what program it is used.

gnomon An object representing direction and dimension that facilitates interpretation of a two-dimensional image of a three-dimensional solid.

go down To crash.

GP General Purpose.

GPSS (General Purpose Systems Simulation) A problem-oriented language used to develop simulation systems.

grabber A fixture on the end of a test equipment lead wire with a spring actuated hook and claw designed to connect the measuring instrument to a pin of an integrated circuit, socket, transistor, and so forth.

graceful degradation The process of undergoing failure in such a way that limited operation can continue. See *fail-soft system*.

grade The range or width of the frequencies available for transmission on a given channel.

gram A metric unit of mass weight equal to 1/1000 kilogram.

grammar Rules prescribing how various elements of a language may be combined. See *syntax*.

grammatical mistake A violation of the rules of use of a given programming language.

grandfather file See *father file*.

graph A set containing two elements: edges (lines) and nodes (points). It provides a mathematical model for data structures in which the nodes correspond to data items and the edges to pointer fields. A cross-referenced model for program planning.

Graphic output device. Courtesy Radio Shack, a division of Tandy Corp.

graphical terminal   A visual display terminal that has a screen to display a drawing as well as textual information.

graphic data structure   The logical arrangement of digital data representing graphic data for graphic display.

graphic digitizer   See *digitizer.*

graphic display   A computer terminal that displays information on a screen, usually a cathode-ray tube, TV terminal, or video monitor.

graphic display resolution   The number of lines and characters per line able to be shown on a video screen.

graphic input device   A device such as a digitizer that gives the computer the points that make up an image in such a way that the image can be stored, reconstructed, displayed, or manipulated.

graphic output   Computer-generated output in the form of visual displays, printouts, or plots.

graphic output device   A device used to display or record an image. A display screen is an output device for soft copy; hard copy output devices produce paper, film, or transparencies of the image.

graphics   Any computer-generated picture produced on a screen or paper. Graphics range from simple line or bar graphs to colorful and detailed images.

graphics, business A computer-generated chart or graph that represents business-related tasks, such as sales, inventory, profits, losses, forecasts, and so on. Common business graphics include bar graphs, pie charts, and scatter graphs.

graphics program A computer program that lets the computer produce graphics.

graphics tablet An input device that converts graphic and pictorial data into binary inputs for use in a computer. The tablet provides an efficient method of converting object shapes into computer storable information. The device utilizes a flat tablet and a stylus for graphic input.

graphics terminal An output device that displays pictures and drawings.

graph theory A branch of mathematics that belongs partly to combinatorial analysis and partly to topology. Its applications occur in electrical network theory, operations research, statistical mechanics, and sociological and behavorial research.

gray code A code in which successive integers differ from one another by only one digit. This is advantageous in analog-to-digital conversion equipment. Gray code is used only for input/output purposes. The coded values must be converted to binary before

Graphics tablet. Courtesy Apple Computer, Inc.

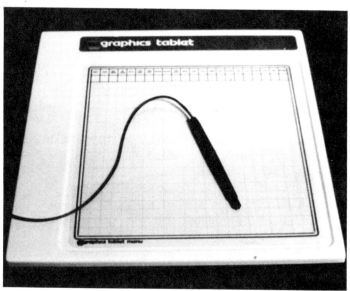

arithmetic calculations can be performed. Also called *cyclic code* and *reflected code*.

gray code-to-binary conversion A binary equivalent of a gray code number can be obtained by applying the following rule: the most significant binary digit equals the corresponding gray code digit, while the following binary digits change if the gray code digit is a 1 and remain the same if the gray code digit is a 0. For example, the gray code value 110100110 equals the binary number 100111011.

grid A surface divided into squares, such as graph paper.

grid chart A table that relates the input data to its applications program.

gridding A graphic image construction constraint that requires all line endpoints to fall on grid points.

Gray Code

Decimal	Natural Binary	Gray Code
0	0000	0000
1	0001	0001
2	0010	0011
3	0011	0010
4	0100	0110
5	0101	0111
6	0110	0101
7	0111	0100
8	1000	1100
9	1001	1101
10	1010	1111
11	1011	1110
12	1100	1010
13	1101	1011
14	1110	1001
15	1111	1000

grouping   Arranging data into groups having common characteristics.

group mark   Any indicator signaling the end of a word or other unit of data.

group printing   An operation during which information prints from only the first card of each group passing through an accounting machine.

guest computer   A computer operating under the control of another computer (host computer).

GUIDE   (Guidance of Users of Integrated Data Processing Equipment) An international association of users of large-scale IBM computers.

gulp   A small group of bytes.

gun   The group of electrodes constituting the electron beam emitter in a cathode-ray tube.

gynoid   A humanlike female robot.

H

hacker   A computer enthusiast. One who is experienced in using computers and enjoys solving complex or unusual problems on a computer. Often produces programs with little advance planning. Sometimes called a "computer junkie." A hacker is intensely interested in and/or very knowledgeable about computer hardware and software.

half adder   A computer circuit capable of adding two binary bits.

half duplex   A communications path that can carry a message in either direction but only one way at a time.

halftoning   Using dot patterns of variable density to simulate gray levels on a display that is strictly black and white.

halfword   A contiguous sequence of bits, bytes, or characters that comprises half a computer word and is capable of being addressed as a unit. See *word*.

halting problem   A problem for which there is no *algorithm*.

halt instruction   A machine instruction that stops the execution of the program.

hamming code   A 7-bit error-correcting data code capable of being corrected automatically.

hand-held computer   A portable, battery-operated, hand-held computer that can be programmed in BASIC to perform a wide variety of tasks. Also called a *pocket computer.*

handler   A program with the sole function of controlling a particular input, output, or storage device, a file, or the interrupt facility.

handshaking   The exchange of predetermined signals when a connection is established between the central processing unit and a peripheral device.

hands-on   The process of physically using a computer system.

handwriting recognition   Scanning handwritten material with a computer-controlled visual scanning device to determine information content or to verify a signature.

hang-up   A nonprogrammed stop in a routine. It is usually an unforeseen or unwanted halt in a machine run. It is often caused by improper coding of a problem, by equipment malfunction, or by the attempted use of a nonexistent or illegal operation code.

hard copy   A printed copy of machine output in readable form; for example, reports, listings, documents, or summaries. See *soft copy.*

hard disk   Same as *Winchester disk.*

hard error   An error caused by a malfunction in the hardware.

hard failure   The failure of a piece of equipment. It generally requires repair before the unit can be used again.

hard sector   Magnetic floppy disks are divided into wedges called sectors that are physically marked by holes punched through the disk to indicate the various sectors. Contrast with *soft sector.*

hardware   Physical equipment, such as electronic, magnetic, and mechanical devices. Contrast with *software.*

hardware configuration   The relationships and arrangement of the various pieces of equipment that make up a computer system, including the cables and communications paths that connect them.

hardware description languages (HDL)   Languages and notations that facilitate the documentation, design, simulation, and manufacturing of digital computer systems.

hardware resources   CPU time, internal storage space, direct access storage space, and input/output devices, all of which are required to do the work of processing data automatically and efficiently.

hardware specialist   A person whose job it is to diagnose, repair, and maintain the equipment of a computer system. See *customer engineer.*

Hard disk. Courtesy Radio Shack, a division of Tandy Corp.

hardwired The physical connection of two pieces of electronic equipment by means of a cable.

harness A group of separate cables that are bound together.

HASCI (Human Applications Standard Computer Interface) A keyboard layout.

hash Visual static on the screen.

hashing A key-to-address transformation in which the keys determine the location of the data. Sometimes called hash coding.

hash totals The totals of the numbers of identifying fields.

head (1) A device that reads, records, or erases data on a storage medium; for example, a small electromagnet used to read, write, or erase data on a magnetic disk. (2) A special data item that points to the beginning of a list.

head cleaning device A material containing a dirt solvent that is used to clean the read/write head of a floppy disk drive or a tape drive.

head crash Occurs when the read/write head collides with the recording surface of a hard disk.

header The first part of a message containing all the necessary information for directing the message to its destination(s).

header card A card that contains information about the data in cards that follow.

header record A record containing constant, common, or identifying information for a group of records that follows.

head slot An opening in a diskette jacket that exposes the disk surface to read/write heads.

Heath/Zenith A manufacturer of microcomputer equipment and electronic kits and products.

heap sort See *tree sort*.

helical wave guide A metal tube containing thin glass fibers and wires capable of transmitting thousands of messages over communications lines.

HELLO A common sign-on message used with terminals in a time-sharing system.

help A handy function available on many systems. It supplies the user with additional information on how the system or program works.

henry A unit of measure of *inductance*. One henry is the inductance of a circuit in which an electromotive force of 1 volt is produced by a current in the circuit that varies at the rate of 1 ampere per second.

Hertz (Hz) Cycles per second.

heuristic Descriptive of an exploratory method of attacking a problem. The solution is obtained by successive evaluations of the progress toward the final results (e.g., guided trial and error). Contrast with *algorithm*. See *artificial intelligence* and *machine learning*.

hex See *hexadecimal*.

hexadecimal Pertaining to a numeral system with a radix of 16. Digits greater than 9 are represented by letters of the alphabet. For example, the binary numeral 1110001011010011 can be represented as hexadecimal E2D3.

hexadecimal number A numeral, usually of more than one digit, representing a sum in which the quantity represented by each digit is based on a radix of 16. The digits used are 0,1,2,3,4,5,6,7,8,9,A,B,C,D,E, and F.

hexadecimal point The radix point in a hexadecimal numeral system. The point that separates the integer part of a mixed hexadecimal numeral from the fractional part. In the numeral 3F.6A7, the hexadecimal point is between the digits F and 6.

hidden line When displaying a three-dimensional object, the line (hidden line) that would be obscured from the viewer's sight by the mass of the object itself is visible as a result of the projection. Additional programs are required to remove these hidden lines.

hierarchical model   A data base model in which each object is of a particular hierarchy in a tree structure.

hierarchical network   A computer network in which processing and control functions are performed at several levels by computers specially designed for the functions performed.

hierarchy   (1) Order in which the arithmetic operations, within a formula or statement, will be executed. (2) Arrangement into a graded series.

high-level language   A programming language that allows its users to write instructions in an English-like notation rather than in a machine code. Each statement in a high-level language corresponds to several machine code instructions. Contrast with *low-level language*.

highlighting   The process of making a display segment more luminous; flickering, blinking, brightening, or reversing the background and the character images (e.g., black characters on a white background). Most video displays have software controls to accomplish this on a selective basis.

high order   Pertaining to the digit or digits of a number that have the greatest weight or significance; for example, in the number 7643215, the high order digit is 7. Contrast with *low order*. See *most significant digit*.

high order column   The leftmost column of a punch card field.

high-persistence phosphor   A phosphor coating used on display monitor screens. It holds an image much longer than the coating used on standard TV screens.

high-punch   Same as *twelve-punch* and *Y-punch*.

high resolution   Refers to the quality and accuracy of detail that can be represented by a graphics display. Resolution quality depends upon the number of basic image-forming units (called *pixels*) within a picture image—the greater the number, the higher the resolution.

high-speed printer   See *line printer*.

high storage   The upper address range of a computer. In most machines, it is occupied by the operating system.

HIPO   (Hierarchy plus Input-Process-Output) An IBM flowcharting technique that provides a graphical method for designing and documenting programs logic.

hi-res graphics   (high-resolution graphics) A smooth and realistic picture on a display screen produced by a large number of pixels. Contrast with *low-res graphics*.

HIS   Hospital Information System.

histogram A horizontal bar chart often used to graph statistical information.

hit A successful comparison of two items of data. Contrast with *match*.

hobby computer See *home computer, microcomputer*, and *personal computer*.

Hoff, Ted An engineer with Intel Corporation, he designed the first microprocessor (the 4004). The chip contained 2,250 transistors and all of the components of a full-size central processing unit. This small chip caused the computer industry and its suppliers to rethink the future role of the computer.

holding time In data communications the length of time a communications channel is in use for each transmission. Includes both message time and operating time.

Hollerith card A punched card consisting of eighty columns, each of which is divided from top to bottom in twelve punching positions.

Hollerith code A particular type of code used to represent alphanumeric data on punched cards. Named after Herman Hollerith, the originator of punched card tabulating. Each card column holds one character, and each decimal digit, letter, and special character is represented by one, two, or three holes punched into designated row positions of the column.

Hollerith, Herman (1860–1929) As a statistician and employee of the Census Bureau, he proposed using punched cards in conjunction with electromechanical relays to accomplish simple additions and sortings needed in the 1890 census. He set up a company to manufacture his punched card tabulator, and it became one of the parents of the IBM Corporation.

hologram A three-dimensional image produced in thin air by lasers interacting with one another.

holography A method of storing data by making a multidimensional photograph on a storage medium.

home The starting position for the cursor on a terminal screen. It is usually in the top left-hand corner of the screen.

homebrew Refers to early microcomputer systems made by hobbyists that gave rise to the popularity of the personal computer.

home computer A microcomputer used in the home. It may be used to play games, to control household appliances, to aid students with homework, to perform business computations, and for a wide variety of other tasks. See *microcomputer* and *personal computer*.

home grown software Programs written by the users of a computer system.

home key A keyboard function that directs the cursor to the top left portion of the display screen.

home record The first record in a chain of records in the chaining method of file organization.

home row The row of keys on the keyboard where keyboard users rest their fingers between keystrokes.

Honeywell A large manufacturer of computer equipment.

hopper See *card hopper*.

horizontal scrolling Refers to the moving of horizontal blocks of data on text, thus allowing one to view more data than can fit on the screen at one time.

host computer The *central processing unit* (CPU) that provides the computing power for terminals and peripheral devices connected to it.

host language A programming language in which another language is included or embedded.

hot zone On some word processors, a user-defined region beginning at the right margin of a page and extending about seven spaces to the left. If a word ends in the hot zone, the system automatically places the character entered at the beginning of the next line.

housekeeping Computer operations that do not directly contribute toward the desired results; in general, initialization, set-up, and clean-up operations. Sometimes called *bookkeeping*.

HSP See *high-speed printer*.

huffman tree Tree with minimum values. See *minimal tree* and *optimal merge tree*.

human engineering Concerned with designing a product so that it is easier and more comfortable for humans to use. Also called *ergonomics*.

human-machine interface The boundary at which people interact with machines.

hybrid computer system A system that uses both analog and digital equipment.

hybrids Circuits fabricated by interconnecting smaller circuits of different technologies mounted on a single *substrate*.

hypertape A magnetic tape unit that uses a cartridge rather than a reel of tape. Cartridge consists of a reel of tape and the take-up reel.

hysteresis The lagging of an effect behind the cause that is producing it; for example, the lagging of the polarization of a magnetic material behind the magnetizing force that is producing it.

Hz Hertz; cycles per second.

I

IBI (Intergovernmental Bureau of Informatics) An organization consisting of members of the United Nations, UNESCO, or other UN agencies. The goal is to promote scientific research, computer education and training, and the exchange of information between developed and developing countries. The main focus of IBI is to promote *informatics*, particularly in developing countries.

IBM Corporation The world's largest manufacturer of data processing equipment.

IBM PCjr An inexpensive microcomputer developed by the IBM Corporation.

IBM Personal Computer A popular microcomputer system manufactured by the IBM Corporation.

IC (Integrated Circuit) A complex electronic circuit fabricated on a simple piece of material, usually a silicon chip.

ICCE (International Council for Computers in Education) A professional organization for those interested in instructional computing at the precollege level.

ICCP (Institute for Certification of Computer Professionals) ICCP is a nonprofit organization established for the purpose of testing and certifying knowledge and skills of computing personnel. ICCP sponsors the CCP and CDP examinations.

ICES (Integrated Civil Engineering System) A system developed to aid civil engineers in solving engineering problems. ICES consists of several engineering systems and programming languages.

ICON A graphic image used to refer to some object.

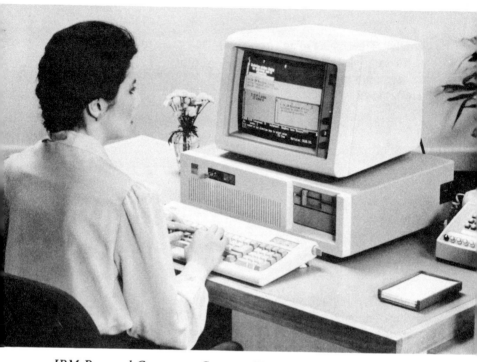

IBM Personal Computer. Courtesy IBM Corp.

identification division   One of the four main component parts of a COBOL program.

identifier   A symbol whose purpose is to identify, indicate, or name a body of data.

idle characters   Characters used in data communications to synchronize the transmission.

idle time   The time that a computer system is available for use but is not in actual operation.

IDP   See *integrated data processing.*

IEEE   (Institute of Electrical and Electronics Engineers) A professional engineering organization with a strong interest in computer systems and their uses.

IEEE-CS   The IEEE Computer Society. A group formed to advance the theory and practice of computer and information processing technology. See IEEE.

IEEE-488   An interface standard mainly used to connect laboratory instruments and other scientific equipment to computers, either for control purposes or to allow the computer to collect data.

IEEE 696/S-100   The identification of a standard, developed by the

Institute of Electrical and Electronic Engineers. It ensures the compatibility of all computing products designed to this standard.

IFAC (International Federation of Automatic Control) A multinational organization concerned with advancing the science and technology of control.

IFIPS (International Federation of Information Processing Societies) A multinational organization representing professional and educational societies actively engaged in the field of information processing. Meets every three years.

IIR International Institute for Robotics.

I²L (Integrated Injection Logic) I²L chips are used in electronic wristwatches and as control devices for industrial products, automobiles, and computer systems. This is a developing technology that will be used in future microprocessors and semiconductor memories.

illegal character A character or combination of bits that is not accepted as a valid or known representation by the computer.

IMACS (International Association for Mathematics and Computers in Simulation) A professional organization to facilitate the exchange of scientific information among specialists, builders, or users interested in analog and hybrid computations methods.

image An exact logical duplicate stored in a different medium. If the computer user displays the contents of memory on a display screen, he or she will see an image of memory.

image processing A method for processing pictorial information by computer. Includes enhancement of drawings and photographs for analysis and animation.

immediate access Ability of a computer to put data in (or remove it from) storage without delay.

immediate access storage See *internal storage.*

immediate address Pertaining to an instruction whose address part contains the value of an operand rather than its address. It is not an address at all but rather an operand supplied as part of an instruction.

impact printer A data printout device that imprints by momentary pressure of raised type against paper, using ink or ribbon as a color medium. See *daisy wheel printer, line printer, thimble printer.*

impedance The total opposition (resistance) a circuit offers to the flow of alternating current at a given frequency.

implementation (1) The process of installing a computer system. It involves choosing the equipment, installing the equipment, training the personnel, and establishing the computing center operating policies. (2) The representation of a programming language on a specific computer system. (3) The act of installing a program.

IMS (Information Management System) A data base management system software package that provides the facilities for storing and retrieving information from hierarchically structured files and data bases.

Inactive A transaction that has been loaded into the computer's memory but has not yet been executed.

Incidence matrix A two-dimensional array that describes the edges in a graph. Also called a *connection matrix*.

Inclusive OR (OR) The Boolean operator that gives a *truth table* value of true if either or both of the two variables it connects is true. If neither is true, the value is false.

Increment An amount added to or subtracted from a value of a variable.

Incremental plotter See *plotter*.

Incremental spacing A synonym for *microspacing*.

Indegree The number of directed edges that point to a node.

Index (1) A symbol or number used to identify a particular quantity in an array of similar quantities; for example, $X(5)$ is the fifth item in an array of Xs. (2) A table of references, held in storage in some sequence, which may be addressed to obtain the addresses

Impact printer. Courtesy Radio Shack, a division of Tandy Corp.

of other items of data; for example, items in a file. See *index register*.

Indexed address An address that is modified by the content of an index register prior to or during the execution of a computer instruction.

Indexed sequential access method A means of organizing data on a direct access device. A directory or index is created to show where the data records are stored. Any desired data record can thus be retrieved from the device by consulting the index(es).

Indexer A program that generates an index for a document.

Index hole A hole punched through a floppy disk medium that can be read by the electrooptical system in the disk drive to locate accurately the beginning of sector zero on the disk.

Indexing A programming technique whereby an instruction can be modified by a factor called an index. See *index*.

Index register A register whose contents can be added to or subtracted from an address prior to or during the execution of an instruction.

Indicator A device that registers a condition in the computer.

Indirect addressing Using an address that specifies a storage location that contains either a direct address or another indirect address. Also called *multilevel addressing*.

Induce To produce an electrical charge, current, or voltage by *induction*. A charge on the gate of a *field effect transistor* (FET) induces an equal charge in the channel.

Inductance In a circuit, the property that opposes any change in the existing current.

Induction The process by which a body having electric and magnetic properties produces an electrical charge, a voltage, or a magnetic field in an adjacent body, without physical contact.

Industrial robot A computer-controlled machine used in assembly and production work that performs certain predetermined operations.

Inference program A program that derives a conclusion from certain facts.

Infix notation A notation in which operators are embedded within operands.

Informatics A word used more or less synonymously with *information technology*.

Information Meaningful and useful facts that are extracted from data fed to a computer. The meaning assigned to data by known conventions.

Information processing center. Courtesy Burroughs Corp.

information banks Large data bases that store information pertaining to a specific application.

information bits In telecommunications, those bits that are generated by the data source and do not include error control bits.

information management system A system designed to organize, catalog, locate, store, retrieve, and maintain information.

information networks The interconnection, through telecommunications, of a geographically dispersed group of libraries and information centers for the purpose of sharing their total information resources among more people.

information processing The totality of operations performed by a computer. It involves evaluating, analyzing, and processing data to produce usable information.

information processing center A computer center equipped with devices capable of receiving information, processing it according to human-made instructions, and producing the computed results.

information processing machine A computer.

information providers The large businesses that supply information to a computer network, such as the Source or CompuServe, for a fee.

information retrieval (1) That branch of computer technology concerned with techniques for storing and searching large quantities of data and making selected data available. (2) The methods used to recover specific information from stored data.

information revolution The name given to the present era because of the impact of computer technology on society. Sometimes called the *computer revolution.*

information storage and retrieval See *information retrieval.*

information system A collection of people, procedures, and equipment that is designed, built, operated, and maintained to collect, record, process, store, retrieve, and display information.

information technology The merging of computing and high-speed communications links carrying data, sound, and video.

information theory The branch of learning concerned with the likelihood of accurate transmission or communication of messages subject to transmission failure, noise, and distortion.

information utility See *computer utility.*

initialize To preset a variable or counter to proper starting values before commencing a calculation. See *preset.*

ink-jet printer A high-speed, nonimpact printer that directs droplets of ink at the paper to form the desired characters.

in-line coding Coding that is located in the main part of a routine.

in-line processing The processing of data in random order, not subject to preliminary editing or sorting.

in-line subroutine A subroutine that is inserted into the main routine as many times as it is needed.

input The introduction of data from an external storage medium into a computer's internal storage unit. Contrast with *output.*

input area An area of internal storage reserved for input data (data transferred from an input device or an auxiliary storage device). Contrast with *output area.*

input data Data to be processed. Synonymous with *input.* Contrast with *output data.*

input device A unit that is used to get data from the human user into the *central processing unit.* Card readers, typewriters, MICR units, and acoustic character recognition (voice input) units are examples of input devices. Contrast with *output device.*

input job stream See *job stream.*

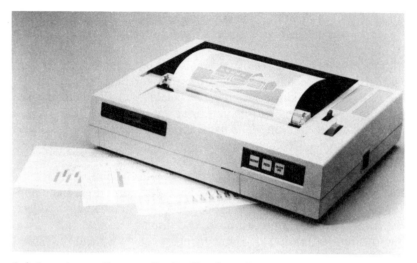

Ink-jet printer. Courtesy Radio Shack, a division of Tandy Corp.

input media The physical substance upon which input data is recorded; for example, diskettes, punched cards, MICR documents, and OCR documents.

input/output (I/O) Pertaining to the techniques, media, and devices used to achieve human/machine communication.

input/output channel A channel that transmits input data to, or output data from, a computer. See *multiplexer channel, RS-232,* and *selector channel.*

input/output control system (IOCS) A set of routines for handling the many detailed aspects of input and output operations.

input/output device A unit that is used to get data from the human user into the central processing unit and to transfer data from the computer's internal storage to some storage or output device. See *input device, output device,* and *peripheral equipment.*

input/output instructions Directions for the transfer of data between peripheral devices and main storage that enable the central processing unit to control the peripheral devices connected to it.

input/output ports The sockets on a computer where the peripherals interface. See *peripheral equipment.*

input/output processor An auxiliary processor, dedicated to controlling input/output transfers, that frees the central processing unit for non-I/O tasks.

input/output symbol A flowcharting symbol used to indicate an

Input/output device. Courtesy Honeywell, Inc.

input operation to the procedure or an output operation from the procedure. A parallelogram figure is used to represent this symbol:

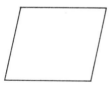

Input stream   The sequence of control statements and data submitted to the operating system on an input unit especially activated for that purpose by the operator. Same as *job stream*.

Inputting   The process of entering data into a computer system.

Inquiry   A request for data from storage; for example, a request for the number of available airline seats in an airline reservation system.

Inquiry processing   The process of selecting a record from a file and immediately displaying its contents.

Inquiry station   The device from which any inquiry is made. The inquiry station or terminal can be geographically remote from the computer or at the computer console.

Insertion method See *sifting*.

Installation A general term for a particular computing system in the context of the overall function it serves and the individuals who manage it, operate it, apply it to problems, service it, and use the results it produces.

Installation time The time spent installing, testing, and accepting equipment.

Instant print A feature of some word processing programs that lets one use the system as a typewriter.

Instruction A group of characters, bytes, or bits that defines an operation to be performed by the computer. An instruction is usually made up of an operation code and one or more operands. See *machine instruction*.

Instructional computing The educational process of teaching individuals the various phases of computer science and data processing.

Instruction code Same as *operation code*.

Instruction counter A counter that indicates the location of the next computer instruction to be interpreted. Same as *program counter*.

Instruction cycle The time required to process an instruction. This includes fetching the instruction from internal storage, interpreting or decoding the instruction, and executing the instruction.

Instruction format The makeup and arrangement of computer instruction.

Instruction register A hardware register that stores an instruction for execution.

Instruction set A set of vendor-supplied operation codes for a particular computer or family of computers. Synonymous with *repertoire*.

Instruction time The time it takes for an instruction to be retrieved from internal storage by the control unit and interpreted.

Instruction word A computer word that contains an instruction.

Instrument A document designed as a form, report, questionnaire, or guide to be used in a planned, systematic data-gathering procedure for the purpose of providing information to the individual, group, or organization initiating the request.

Instrumental input Data captured by machines and placed directly into the computer.

Integer A whole number that may be positive, negative, or zero. It does not have a fractional part.

Integer BASIC A type of BASIC language that can process whole numbers (integers) only.

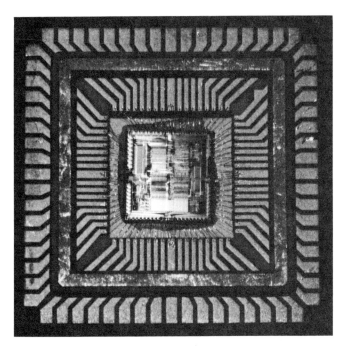

Integrated circuit. Courtesy NCR Company.

integer constant   A number that does not contain a decimal point. Also called a fixed-point number.

integrate   The process of putting various components together to form a harmonious computer system.

integrated circuit   A combination of interconnected circuit elements and amplifying devices that are inseparably associated on or within a continuous layer of semiconductor material, called a *substrate.* See *large scale integration, linear IC, medium scale integration, small scale integration,* and *very large scale integration.*

integrated data processing (IDP)   A system that coordinates a number of previously unconnected processes in order to improve overall efficiency by reducing or eliminating redundant data entry or processing operations.

integrated injection logic   See *I²L.*

integration   Combining diverse elements of hardware and software, often acquired from different vendors, into a unified system.

integrity   The preservation of programs or data for their intended purpose. See *data integrity.*

Intel Corporation The company that produced the first microprocessor, the 4-bit 4004. This was superseded by 8-bit microprocessors, the 8008, the 8080, and the 8080A. More recent microprocessors include 16- and 32-bit microprocessors.

Intelligence See *artificial intelligence.*

Intelligent terminal An input/output device in which a number of computer processing characteristics are physically built into, or attached to, the terminal unit. See *point-of-scale terminal.*

Intensity The amount of light in a graphics display unit.

Interactive An immediate response to input. The user is in direct and continual two-way communication with the computer.

Interactive graphics The general term applied to any graphics system in which the user and the computer are in active communication.

Interactive processing A type of real-time processing involving a continuing dialog between user and computer; the user is allowed to modify data and/or instructions. See *conversational mode.*

Interactive program A system in which the human user or device serviced by the computer can communicate directly with the operating program. For human users, this is termed a *conversational system.*

Interblock gap The space between blocks of records on magnetic tape and disk. The gap is used to signal that the end of a block has been reached.

Interconnection The physical and electrical connection of equipment furnished by different vendors.

Interface A connecting point between two pieces of hardware or between two systems.

Interlace To assign successive addresses to physically separated storage locations on a magnetic disk or drum in such a way as to reduce the access time.

Interleaving A multiprogramming technique in which parts of one program are inserted into another program so that if there are processing delays in one of the programs, parts of the other program can be processed.

Interlock A protective facility that prevents one device or operation from interfering with another; for example, the locking of the switches on the control console to prevent manual movement of the switches while the computer is executing a program.

Interlude Preliminary *housekeeping.*

Intermittent error An error that occurs intermittently, constantly, and is extremely difficult to reproduce.

Internal data representation   Data representation in registers, storage, and other devices inside the computer.

Internal memory   Same as *internal storage.*

Internal sort   The sequencing of two or more records within the central processing unit. The first phase of a *multipass sort* program.

Internal storage   Addressable storage directly controlled by the central processing unit. The central processing unit uses internal storage to store programs while they are being executed and data while they are being processed. Also called *immediate access storage, internal memory, main storage,* and *primary storage.*

Interpreter   A language translator that converts each source language statement into machine code and executes it immediately, statement by statement.

Interpreting   The process of printing on punched cards with the meaning of the holes punched in the same card.

Interrecord gap   The space between records on magnetic disk and tape. The gap is used to signal that the end of a record has been reached.

Interrupt   A signal that, when activated, causes the hardware to transfer program control to some specific location in internal storage, thus breaking the normal flow of the program being executed. After the interrupt has been processed, program control is again returned to the interrupted program. An interrupt can be generated as the result of a program action by an operator activating switches on the computer console or by a peripheral device causing the interrupting signal. Often called *trapping.*

Interrupt driven   A computer system that makes extensive use of interrupts.

Interval timer   A mechanism whereby elapsed time can be monitored by a computer system.

Inventory control   The use of a computer system to monitor an inventory.

Inverted file   A file organized so that it can be accessed by character rather than by record key.

Inverter   A circuit in which a binary 1 input produces a binary 0 output, and vice versa.

Inverting circuit   A circuit for changing direct current to alternating current.

Invisible refresh   A scheme that refreshes dynamic memories without disturbing the rest of the system.

I/O   See *Input/output.*

I/O board A circuit board that controls the input and output of information between the computer and peripheral devices.

I/O bound The term applied to programs that require a large number of input/output operations, resulting in much central processing unit wait time. Contrast with *compute-bound*.

I/O channel Part of the input/output system of a computer. Under the control of I/O commands, the channel transfers blocks of data between the internal storage and peripheral equipment.

IOCS (Input/Output Control System) A standard set of input/output routines designed to initiate and control the input and output processes of a computer system.

I/O port A connection to a *central processing unit* (CPU) that provides data paths between the CPU and peripheral devices, such as display terminals, typewriters, line printers, magnetic disk units, and so on.

I/O processor A circuit board or chip that is used only to handle input/output operations between the computer and peripherals.

IPL (Information Processing Language) See *list processing languages*.

IPL-V (Information Processing Language Five) A list processing language primarily used for working with heuristic problems.

IRG (InterRecord Gap) See *interrecord gap*.

IRM (Information Resources Manager) The person responsible for operating the company's main computer and for keeping an eye on the numerous employees using it.

ISAM (Indexed Sequential Access Method) A procedure for storing and retrieving data. The procedure uses a set of indexes that describes where the records are located on the disk file.

ISO (International Standards Organization) An international agency that is responsible for developing standards for information exchange. This agency has a function similar to that of ANSI in the United States.

Isolation In a computer security system, information is compartmentalized so that access to it is on a "need to know" basis.

ISR (Information Storage and Retrieval) See *information retrieval*.

Item A group of related characters treated as a unit. (A record is a group of related items, and a file is a group of related records.)

Iterate To repeat automatically, under program control, the same series of processing steps until a predetermined stop or branch condition is reached. See *loop* and *Newton-Raphson*.

Iterative Repetitive. Often used when each succeeding "iteration," or repetition, of a procedure comes closer to the desired result.

J

jack A connecting device to which a wire or wires of a circuit may be attached and that is arranged for the insertion of a plug.

jacket The stiff paper container that holds a diskette.

jaggies In a computer graphics display, the stairstepped effect of diagonals, circles, and curves.

JCL (Job Control Language) A special language used to give instructions to the operating system of a large computer.

JES (Job Entry System) A portion of the operating system that accepts and schedules jobs for execution.

jitter Brief instability of a signal, applied particularly to signals on a video display.

job A collection of specified tasks constituting a unit of work for a computer; for example, a program or related group of programs used as a unit.

job control language A language that defines a job and the resources it requires from the computer system, including constraints on the job, such as time limits. The language is more often interpreted than compiled.

job control statement One statement, written in a job control language, that defines one aspect of a job.

job number An identification number assigned to a job.

job queue The set of programs and data currently making its way through the computer. In most operating systems, each job is brought into the queue and is processed (given control of the computer) when it is the "oldest" job within its own priority. An exception to this is a job of higher priority that has not yet obtained sufficient resources to be processed.

job scheduler A person who aids computer operators in the running of a large computer installation.

job stream The input to the operating system; it may consist of one or more jobs. Same as *input stream*.

job-to-job transition The process of locating a program and the files associated with the program and of preparing the computer for the execution of a particular job.

job turnaround The elapsed time from when a job is given to the computer system until its printed output reaches the person who submitted the job.

Josephson junction A potentially high-capacity data storage system based upon the properties of super-cold circuits.

JOVIAL (Jules's Own Version of the International Algorithmic Language) A programming language used primarily for working with scientific and command and control problems. The language has wide usage in systems implemented by the United States Air Force.

joystick A type of input device. It has a stick that is manipulated by the user to produce different inputs. Joysticks are often used in conjunction with graphics terminals.

joyswitch A joystick-type input device that can be moved in any of eight directions: up, down, right, left, and in four diagonal directions.

JUG (Joint Users Group) An organization of digital computer user groups. See *users group*.

Julian number A form of calendar representation within a computer system. The Julian date indicates the year and number of elapsed days in the year; for example, 84–131 was May 10, 1984, the 131st day of 1984.

jump A departure from the normal sequence of executing instructions in a computer. Synonymous with *branch* and *transfer*. See *conditional transfer* and *unconditional transfer*.

junction The part of a diode or transistor where two opposite types of semiconductor material meet.

junk Usually refers to garbled data received over a communications line.

justification The act of adjusting, arranging, or shifting digits to the left or right in order to make them fit a prescribed pattern.

justify To align the characters in a field. For example, to left justify, the first character (e.g., the *most significant digit*) is written in the last or rightmost character position in the field. See *normalize*.

K

K (1) An abbreviation for kilo, or 1000 in decimal notation. For example, "100K ch/s" means "a reading speed of 100,000 characters per second." (2) Loosely, when referring to storage capacity,

2^{10}; in decimal notation, 1024. The expression 8K represents 8192 (8 × 1024).

Kansas City Standard A low-speed cassette storage format.

Karnaugh map A two-dimensional plot of *truth table*.

kb (kilobyte) A kb is 1024 bytes.

kc One thousand characters per second. Used to express the rate of data transfer operations.

Kelvin The unit of temperature measurement of the SI metric system; for normal use, expressed in degrees Celsius.

kernel The set of programs in an operating system that implement the most primitive of that system's functions. See *primitive*.

key (1) The field or fields that identify a record. (2) The field that determines the position of a record in a sorted sequence. (3) A lever on a manually operated machine, such as a typewriter or keyboard.

keyboard An input device used to key programs and data into the computer's storage. See *Dvorak keyboard* and *QWERTY keyboard*.

keyboarding The process of entering programs and data onto input media or directly into the computer by typing on a keyboard. For example, using the keyboard of a word processor or computer terminal.

keyboard-to-disk system A data entry system in which data can be entered directly onto a disk by typing the data at a keyboard.

keyboard-to-tape system A data entry system in which data can be entered directly onto a tape by typing the data at a keyboard.

key bounce A characteristic of some poorly designed keyboards— a character registers twice for each time the user presses the key.

key data entry device The equipment—including keypunch machines, key-to-disk units, and key-to-tape units—used to prepare data so that computer equipment can accept it.

keypad An input device that uses a set of decimal digit keys (0–9) and two special function keys. Used as a separate device or sometimes located on devices to the right of a *QWERTY keyboard*.

keypunch A keyboard operated device used to punch holes in punch cards to represent data.

keypunching The process by which the original or source data are recorded on punch cards. The operator reads source documents and, by depressing keys on a keypunch machine, converts source document information into punched holes.

key stations Terminals used for data input on a multiuser system.

key switch The switch part of the input key on a keyboard.

key-to-address See *hashing*.

key-to-disk unit A keyboard unit used to store data directly on a magnetic disk.

key-to-tape unit A keyboard unit used to store data directly on magnetic tape.

key verification See *card verification*.

key-verify The use of the punch card machine known as a verifier, which has a keyboard, to make sure that the information supposed to be punched in a punch card has actually been properly punched. The machine indicates when the punched hole and the depressed key disagree. See *verifier machine*.

keyword A primary element in a programming language statement (e.g., words such as LET, GOTO, and INPUT in the BASIC programming language).

key-word-in-context See *KWIC*.

kHz Kilohertz.

Kilby, Jack An inventor with Texas Instruments, he introduced the integrated circuit. He also developed an early handheld electronic calculator.

kill To delete. To terminate a process before it reaches its natural conclusion.

kilo A metric prefix meaning 1000 times.

kilobaud A thousand bits per second. Used to measure data communications speeds.

kilobit A thousand bits.

kilobyte A kilobyte is 2^{10}, or 1024 bytes. It is commonly abbreviated K and used as a suffix when describing memory size. Thus, 24K really means a $24 \times 1024 = 24,576$ byte memory system.

kilocycle One thousand cycles per second.

kilohertz (kHz) One thousand hertz.

kilomegacycle A billion cycles per second.

kludge Makeshift. A collection of mismatched components that have been assembled into a system.

knowledge base A data base of knowledge about a particular subject.

knowledge engineering The engineering discipline whereby knowledge is integrated into computer systems to solve complex problems normally requiring a high level of human expertise.

knowledge industries The industries that perform data processing and provide information products and services.

KSR (Keyboard Send/Receive) A teletypewriter unit with keyboard and printer.

KWIC   (Key-Word-In-Context) A method of indexing information by preselected words or phrases that takes into consideration the context in which the words are used.

L

label   An identifier or name that is used in a computer program to identify or describe an instruction, statement, message, data value, record, item, or file. Same as *name*.

LAN   (Local Area Network) Hardware and software systems that undertake the job of interdevice communications within limited distances.

land   The area of a printed circuit board available for mounting electronic components.

language processor   A program that translates human-written source language programs into a form that can be executed on a computer. There are three general types of language processors: *assemblers, compilers,* and *interpreters.*

language statement   A statement coded by a user of a computing system that conveys information to a processing program such as a *language translator program, service program,* or *control program.* A statement may signify that an operation be performed or may simply contain data that is to be passed to the processing program.

language subset   A part of a language that can be used independently of the rest of the language.

language translation   The process of changing information from one language to another; for example, BASIC to FORTRAN, or FORTRAN to Pascal.

language translator program   A program that transforms statements from one language to another without significantly changing their meaning (e.g., a *compiler* or *assembler*).

large scale integration (LSI)   The process of placing a large number (usually over 100) of integrated circuits on one silicon chip. See *very large scale integration.*

laser A device that uses the principle of amplification of electromagnetic waves by simulated emission of radiation and operates in the infrared, visible, or ultraviolet region. The term "laser" is an acronym for Light Amplification by Stimulated Emission of Radiation.

laser disk A high-density storage medium that holds promise as a means for archivally storing large amounts of computer data. Information is inscribed on the disk by a laser, which burns a pattern of holes into a tellurium film on the disk's surface.

laser-holographic storage A potentially high-capacity data storage system that uses a laser beam to create images on film.

laser printer A high-speed printing device that can print in excess of 20,000 lines per minute. It combines laser beams and electrophotographic technology to form images on paper.

laser storage A storage system that uses a controlled laser beam to expose small sections of a photosensitive area. See *holography*.

last in-first out See *LIFO*.

last in-last out See *LILO*.

latency The rotational delay in reading or writing a record to a direct access auxiliary storage device such as a disk or drum.

layout The overall design or plan, such as system flowcharts, schematics, diagrams, format for printer output, format for card columns, makeup of a document (book), and so forth.

LCD (Liquid Crystal Display) A way to make letters and numbers appear by reflecting light on a special crystalline substance. It features high visibility in high illumination levels but no visibility in low illumination levels. Because of its thin profile, LCD technology is often used in pocket calculators, pocket computers, briefcase computers, keyboards, watches, and other devices.

LDL (Language Description Language) A metalanguage—a language that describes a language.

leader A blank section of tape at the beginning of a reel of paper tape or magnetic tape.

leading edge (1) The edge of a punched card that first enters the card reader. (2) In optical scanning, the edge of the document or page that enters the read position first.

leaf A terminal node of a *tree*.

lease A method of acquiring the use of a computer system. A lease contract requires no financing and is less expensive than renting the system.

leased line Generally refers to a dedicated communications channel that is leased from a common carrier.

Laser printer. Courtesy Burroughs Corp.

leasing companies   Companies that specialize in leasing computer equipment, which they purchase from a computer manufacturer.

least significant digit (LSD)   Pertaining to the digit of a number that has the least weight or significance (e.g., in the number 54321, the least significant digit is 1). See *justify* and *low order*.

LED   (Light Emitting Diode) A commonly used alphanumeric display unit that glows when supplied with a specified voltage.

left justify   See *justify*.

Leibniz's calculator   A calculating machine, called a "stepped reckoner," designed by Baron von Leibniz. The machine performed addition and subtraction in the same manner as *Pascal's calculator*; however, additional gears were included in the machine that enabled it to multiply directly.

Leibniz, Gottfried (1646–1716) A German mathematician who invented a calculating machine called a "stepped reckoner" (1672) that could add, subtract, and multiply.

length The number of characters, bytes, or bits in a computer word. A variable word is made up of several characters ending with a special end character. A fixed word is composed of the same number of bits, bytes, or characters in each word. See *fixed word length* and *variable word length*.

letter quality printer A printer that uses a daisy wheel, thimble, or ball element to produce a print image similar to that produced by an office typewriter. The most desired type of printer for use with microcomputers.

letter shift A keyboard key (or the code generated by the key) that signifies that the characters that follow are to be read as letters until a figure shift appears in the message. Same as *figure shift*.

level A measure of the distance from a node to the root of a tree.

LF See *line feed*.

librarian (1) A person who is responsible for an organization's library of technical documentation, including manuals used by programmers, operators, and other employees. (2) A person who has responsibility for the safekeeping of all computer files; for example, disk packs, magnetic tapes, and so forth. Also called a *file librarian* and *tape librarian*.

library A published collection of programs, routines, and subroutines available to every user of the computer. Same as *program library*. See *disk library* and *tape library*.

library automation Application of computers and other technology to library operations and services.

library manager The program that maintains the programs stored in an operating system.

library routine A tested routine that is maintained in a program library.

license contract A piece of paper that authorizes the purchaser of a software product to run the product on his or her computer.

LIFO (Last In-First Out) The way most microprocessor program stacks operate. The last data or instruction word placed on the stack is the first to be retrieved. See *FIFO* and *push down stack*.

light emitting diode See *LED*.

light guide   A channel designed for the transmission of light, such as a cable of optical fibers.

light pen   An electrical device that resembles a pen and can be used to write or sketch on the screen of a cathode-ray tube; that is, to provide input to the computer through its use. A tool for display terminal operators.

LILO   (Last In-Last Out) A method of starting and retrieving items from a list, table, or stack, such that the last item placed on the stack is the last to be retrieved. Same as *FIFO*. Contrast with *FILO*.

limit check   An input control technique that tests the value of a data field to determine whether values fall within set limits or a given range.

limiting operation   The capacity of a total system with no alternative routing can be no greater than the operation with the least capacity. The total system can be effectively scheduled by simply scheduling the limiting operation. Synonymous with *bottleneck*.

line   See *channel*.

linear IC   An analog integrated circuit, as opposed to a digital integrated circuit. See *integrated circuit*.

linear list   See *sequential list*.

linear programming (LP)   A technique for finding an optimum combination when there may be no single best one. For example, linear programming could be used to solve the problem, What combination of foods would give the most calories and best nutrition for the least money?

linear search   A search that begins with the first element and compares until a matching key is found or the end of the list is reached.

line chart   A method of charting business data.

line circuit   A physical circuit path, such as a data communications line.

line feed (LF)   The printer operation that advances the paper by one line. See *form feed*.

line filter   A device used to correct electromagnetic interference that comes in over the power line.

line height   The height of one line of type. It is measured by the number of lines per vertical inch.

line number   In programming languages such as BASIC, a number that begins a line of the source program for purposes of identification; a numerical label.

line of code A statement in a programming language usually occupying one line of code.

line printer An output peripheral device that prints data one line at a time. See *electrostatic printer*.

line printer controller A device that provides character print buffers and automatic control and timing for a specific printer.

line printing The printing of an entire line of characters as a unit.

line speed The maximum rate at which signals may be transmitted over a given channel usually in bauds or bits per second.

lines per minute (LPM) Usually used to describe the speed of a line printer.

line surge A sudden, high voltage condition. Short surges of high voltage can cause misregistration, false logic, lost data, and even destruction of delicate circuits in computers, data entry terminals, and data communications equipment. These spikes can be a result of inductive load switching of transformers and other types of equipment—even from lightning and static. Equipment can be

Line printer. Courtesy Honeywell, Inc.

protected from voltage surges by using surge protectors. See *surge protector*.

line voltage The AC voltage that comes out of a standard wall socket.

link In data communications, a physical connection between one location and another whose function is to transmit data. See *communications channel*.

linkage Coding that connects two separately coded routines; for example, the coding that links a subroutine to the program with which it is to be used. See *calling sequence*.

linker A program that links other programs or sections of programs.

linking loader An executive program that connects different program segments so that they may be run in the computer as one unit. A useful piece of software that makes subtasks easily available to a main task.

link register A register of one bit that acts as an extension of the *accumulator* during rotation or carry operations. Also called *carry register*.

links Data communications channels in a computer network.

liquid crystal display (LCD) A visual display that is made of two glass plates sandwiched together with a nematic liquid crystal solution between them.

Lisa A business microcomputer system manufactured by Apple Computer, Inc.

LISP (LISt Processing) A high-level programming primarily designed to process data consisting of lists. It is especially suited for text manipulation and analysis. See *list processing languages*.

list (1) Organization of data using indexes and pointers to allow for nonsequential retrieval. (2) To print every relevant item of input data. (3) A system command to print program statements; for example, the LIST command in the BASIC language will cause the system to print a listing of the program. (4) An ordered collection of *atoms*.

listing Generally, any report produced on a printing device (printer or typewriter). For example, a source listing is a printout of the source program processed by the compiler; an error listing is a report showing all input data found to be invalid by the processing program. See *assembly listing*.

list processing A method of processing data in the form of lists. Usually, chained lists are used so that the logical order of items can be changed without altering their physical locations.

list processing languages Languages designed especially to process data that are in list form. Examples include *IPL, LISP*, and *POP-2*.

literal Another name for *constant*. A symbol that defines itself.

live data The actual data that are to be processed by the computer program.

load (1) To read information into the storage of a computer. (2) To put cards into a card reader, or to put a disk back onto a disk drive unit.

load-and-go An operating technique in which the loading and execution phases of a program are performed in one continuous run. See *compile-and-go*.

loader A service routine designed to read programs into internal storage in preparation for their execution.

load point A spot at the beginning of a tape.

load sharing The technique of using two or more computers in order to handle excess volume during peak periods. It is desirable to have one computer handle less than peak loads and the other act as the fallback equipment.

local (1) A term that refers to computer equipment at one's own location. (2) Pertaining to items used only in one defined part of a program. Contrast with *global*.

local area network A network of computer equipment confined to a small area (room, building, site) and interconnected by dedicated communications channels. These computers can not only intercommunicate but can also share resources such as disk storage and printers.

local intelligence Processing power and storage capacity built into a terminal so that it does not need to be connected to a computer to perform certain tasks. A *dumb terminal* has no local intelligence. See *smart terminal*.

local store A relatively small number of high-speed storage elements that may be directly referred to by the instructions.

location A place in the computer's memory where information is to be stored.

lock To permit exclusive use of a computer resource.

lock code A sequence of letters and/or numbers provided by the operators of a time-sharing system to prevent unauthorized tampering with a user's program. The lock code serves as a secret password in that the computer will refuse any changes to the program unless the user supplies the correct lock code. Also called *password*.

lockout (1) Suppression of an *interrupt*. (2) A programming technique used in a multiprocessing environment, to prevent access to critical data by both CPUs at the same time.

lock-up   A situation in which no further action may occur.

log   A record of the operations of data processing equipment, listing each job or run, the time it required, operator actions, and other pertinent data.

logarithm   The exponent of the power to which a fixed number is to be raised to produce a given number. The fixed number is called the *base* and is usually 10 or *E*. In the example $2^3 = 8$, 3 is the logarithm of 8 to the base 2; this means that 2 must be raised to the third power to produce 8.

logging-in   The process of establishing communication with and verifying the authority to use the computer during conversational programming. See *conversational mode*.

logging-off   The process of terminating communication between the computer and the user.

logic   (1) The science dealing with the formal principles of reasoning and thought. (2) The basic principles and application of *truth tables* and the interconnection among logical elements required for arithmetic computation in an automatic data processing system.

logical design   The specification of the working relationships among the parts of a system in terms of *symbolic logic* and without primary regard for hardware implementation.

logical error   A programming mistake that causes the wrong processing to take place even though the program is syntactically correct.

logical file   A collection of one or more logical records. See *logical record*.

logical instruction   An instruction that executes an operation that is defined in symbolic logic such as AND, OR, or NOR.

logical multiply   The AND operator.

logical operations   The computer operations that are logical in nature, such as logical tests and decisions. This is in contrast with the arithmetic and data transfer operations, which involve no decision.

logical product   The AND function of several terms. The product is 1 only when all of the terms are 1; otherwise it is 0.

logical record   A complete unit of information describing something, for example, an invoice, a payroll roster, or an inventory. In an inventory file containing 2000 different product items, there are 2000 logical records, one for each item. Contrast with *physical record*.

logical sum The inclusive *OR* function of several terms. The sum is 1 when any or all of the terms are 1; it is 0 only when all are 0.

logical symbol A symbol used to represent a *logical operator*.

logical value A value that may be either "true" or "false" depending on the result of a particular logical decision.

logic card A circuit board that contains components and wiring that perform one or more logic functions or operations.

logic circuits The basic building blocks used to realize consumer and industrial products that incorporate digital electronics. Such products include digital computers, voice synthesizers, robot controls, pocket calculators, and video games.

logic diagram A diagram that represents a *logical design* and sometimes the hardware implementation.

logic element A device that performs a logic function.

logic gates Components in electrical digital circuitry.

logic operator Any of the Boolean operators such as *AND, OR, NAND, exclusive OR*, and *NOR*.

logic seeking The ability of a printer that works bidirectionally to seek out the shortest printing path.

logic symbol A symbol used to represent a logic element graphically:

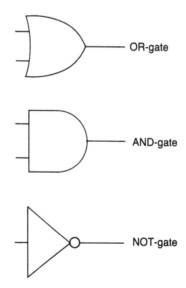

logic theory The science that deals with logic operations, which are the basis of computer operations.

log in To sign in on a computer. Same as *log on*.

log in name   The name by which the computer system knows a user.

LOGO   A high-level programming language that assumes the user has access to some type of graphics terminal. The language was designed for school students and seems particularly suited to those in the younger age groups. It is highly interactive, permitting children to learn quickly how to draw geometric patterns and pictures on the screen. It was developed at the Massachusetts Institute of Technology by Seymour Papert.

log on   The action by which a user begins a terminal session. Same as *log in*.

log off   To terminate your connection with the computer. Same as *log out*.

log out   To stop using the computer. The process of signing off the system. Same as *log off*.

look alike   A program that imitates another program so closely that users of the original program can use the look alike program without learning any new operating instructions.

look-up   See *table look-up*.

loop   A sequence of instructions in a program that can be executed repetitively until certain specified conditions are satisfied. See *closed loop*.

loop code   The repetition of a sequence of instructions by using a program *loop*. Loop coding requires more execution time than straight line coding but will result in a savings of storage. Contrast with *straight line code*.

loophole   A mistake or omission in software or hardware that allows the system's access controls to be circumvented.

looping   Executing the same instruction or series of instructions over and over again.

loop structure   One of the three primary structures of a structured flowchart. It provides for repetitive execution of a function until a condition is reached.

loop technology   A method of connecting communicating machines in a computer network.

Lovelace, Ada Augusta   (1815–1852) Ada Augusta, the Countess of Lovelace, developed the essential ideas of programming. She was a skilled mathematician and close friend of Charles Babbage, and wrote about his proposed machine: "The Analytical Engine weaves algebraical patterns just as the Jacquard loom weaves flowers and leaves." See *Ada, analytical engine*, and *Babbage, Charles*.

low-level language   A machine-dependent programming language translated by an assembler into instructions and data formats for a given machine. Same as *assembly language*. Contrast with *high-level language*.

low order   Pertaining to the digit or digits of a number that have the least weight or significance; for example, in the number 7643215, the low order digit is 5. Contrast with *high order*. See *least significant digit*.

low order column   The rightmost (highest numbered) column of a punch card field.

low-res graphics   (low-resolution graphics) A blocky and jagged picture on a display screen produced by a small number of *pixels*. Contrast with *hi-res graphics*.

LP   (Linear Programming and Line Printer) Linear programming is a technique for finding an optimum combination when there may be no single best one. A line printer is a high-speed output device that prints a line at a time and several hundred or thousand lines per minute.

LPM   See *lines per minute*.

LSC   (Least Significant Character) See *least significant digit*.

LSD   See *least significant digit*.

LSI   See *large scale integration*.

Lukasiewicz notation   See *Polish notation*.

luminance   Amount of radiant energy per unit area as objectively measurable. The subjective synonym is brightness.

luminosity   Same as luminance.

M

M   Abbreviation for mega, meaning 1 million. Used to represent 1,048,576. Often used to label the capacity of storage devices (i.e., disks).

M68000   A 16-bit microprocessor chip manufactured by Motorola. It was developed especially for use in microcomputers.

machine address   Same as *absolute address*.

machine code   An operation code that a machine is designed to recognize.

machine cycle The time period it takes for a computer to perform a given number of internal operations.

machine dependent A machine-dependent program works on only one particular type of computer.

machine error A deviation from correctness in data resulting from an equipment failure.

machine independent (1) A term used to indicate that a program is developed in terms of the problem rather than in terms of the characteristics of the computer system. (2) The ability to run a program on computers made by different manufacturers or on various machines made by the same manufacturer.

machine instruction An instruction that a computer can directly recognize and execute. See *instruction*.

machine intelligence See *artificial intelligence*.

machine language The basic language of a computer. Programs written in machine language require no further interpretation by a computer.

machine learning Refers to a heuristic process whereby a device improves its performance based on past actions. See *artificial intelligence* and *heuristic*.

machine operator See *computer operator*.

machine-oriented language A programming language that is more like a machine language than a human language.

machine-readable information Information recorded on any medium in such a way that it can be sensed or read by a machine. Also called *machine-sensible*.

machine run See *run*.

machine-sensible See *machine-readable information*.

Macintosh A popular microcomputer system manufactured by Apple Computer, Inc.

macro A single, symbolic programming language statement that when translated results in a series of machine language statements.

macro assembler An assembler that allows the user to create and define new computer instructions (called macro instructions). See *macro instruction*.

macro instruction (1) A source language instruction that is equivalent to a specified number of machine language instructions. (2) A machine language instruction that is composed of several micro instructions. See *micro instruction*.

macroprogramming Programming with macro instructions; for example, writing control programs for a microprocessor using macro instructions. See *macro instruction* and *micro instruction*.

mag   An abbreviation for magnetic.

mag card   A magnetic card developed by the IBM Corporation that is coated with a magnetic substance on which information is recorded. Magcards are frequently used in word processing systems.

magnetic   Of, producing, caused by, or operated by magnetism.

magnetic bubble memory   A memory that uses magnetic "bubbles" that move. The bubbles are locally magnetized areas that can move about in a magnetic material, such as a plate of orthoferrite. It is possible to control the reading in and out of this "bubble" within the magnetic material, and as a result, a very high-capacity memory can be built.

magnetic card   A storage device consisting of a tray or cartridge of magnetically coated cards. These cards are made of material similar to magnetic tape (although considerably thicker) and have specific areas allocated for storing information. A magnetic card may be visualized as a magnetic tape cut into strips; several strips are placed side by side on a plastic card and mounted on a cartridge. See *data cell*.

magnetic characters   A set of characters, used for checks, insur-

Macintosh. Courtesy Apple Computer, Inc.

ance billings, utility bills, invoices, and so forth, that permit special character-reading devices (MICR readers) to be employed to read the characters automatically. See *magnetic ink character recognition.*

magnetic core A tiny, doughnut-shaped piece of magnetizable material that is capable of storing one binary digit.

magnetic core plane A network of magnetic cores, each of which represents one core common to each storage location. A number of core planes are stacked together to form a magnetic core storage unit.

magnetic core storage A system of storage in which data are represented in binary form by means of the directional flow of magnetic fields in tiny, doughut-shaped arrays of magnetic cores.

magnetic disk A disk made of rigid material (hard disk) or heavy mylar (floppy disk). The disk surface is used to hold magnetized information. Information is written on the disk and retrieved from the disk by a disk drive.

magnetic disk unit A peripheral storage device in which data are recorded on a magnetizable disk surface. See *direct access, disk pack, fixed-head disk unit, floppy disk,* and *moveable-head disk unit.*

magnetic drum A peripheral storage device consisting of a cylinder with a magnetizable surface on which data are recorded. See *direct access.*

magnetic film storage A storage device that uses 35-millimeter magnetic film, which is contained on a spool. The spool may be loaded onto a film handler unit.

magnetic head A device that is used for reading and writing information on devices such as magnetic tapes, disks, or drums.

magnetic ink An ink that contains particles of a magnetic substance whose presence can be detected by magnetic sensors.

magnetic ink character reader An input device that reads documents imprinted with magnetic ink characters.

magnetic ink character recognition (MICR) The recognition, by machines of characters printed with a special magnetic ink.

magnetic media A generic name for floppy disks, tapes, and any other devices that store data in the form of magnetic impulses.

magnetic resonance The phenomenon in which a movement of a particle or system of particles is coupled resonantly to an external magnetic field.

magnetic storage Utilizing the magnetic properties of materials

Magnetic disk unit. Courtesy Honeywell, Inc.

to store data on such devices and media as disks, tapes, cards, drums, cores, and film.

magnetic strip card   A small card resembling a credit card to which a strip of magnetizable material is affixed. Information can be read from or written on this magnetic strip.

magnetic tape   A plastic tape having a magnetic surface for storing data in a code of magnetized spots. Information may be represented on tape using an 8-bit coding structure. A reel of tape is about 750 meters (2400 feet) in length. Information is written on the tape and retrieved from the tape by a tape drive.

magnetic tape cartridge   A magnetic tape contained in a cartridge. The cartridge consists of a reel of tape and the take-up reel. It is similar to a cassette but of slightly different design.

magnetic tape cassette A magnetic tape storage device. A cassette consists of a ⅛-inch magnetic tape housed in a plastic container.

magnetic tape cassette recorder An input/output and storage device that reads and writes cassette tapes. Used widely with microcomputer systems.

magnetic tape code The system of coding that is used to record magnetized patterns on magnetic tape. The magnetized patterns represent alphanumeric data. See *BCD* and *EBCDIC*.

magnetic tape deck Same as *magnetic tape unit*.

magnetic tape density The number of characters that can be recorded on 2.54 centimeters (1 inch) of magnetic tape.

magnetic tape drive A device that moves tape past a head. Synonymous with magnetic tape transport.

magnetic tape reel A reel used to preserve the physical characteristics of magnetic tape. The tape is usually 1.27 centimeters (½ inch) wide and 751.52 meters (2400 feet) in length.

magnetic tape sorting A sort program that uses magnetic tapes for auxiliary storage during a *sort*.

magnetic tape transport Same as *magnetic tape drive*.

magnetic tape unit A device containing a magnetic tape drive together with reading and writing heads and associated controls. Synonymous with magnetic tape deck. See *magnetic tape cartridge* and *magnetic tape cassette*.

magnetic thin film See *thin film*.

magnitude The absolute value of a number.

mag tape Magnetic tape.

mailbox A set of locations in a storage area. An area reserved for data addressed to specific peripheral devices or other processors.

mailing list program A program that maintains names, addresses, and related data, and produces mailing labels of them.

mail-merging The process of automatically printing form letters with names and addresses from a mailing list file.

mainframe A large computer that typically offers high-speed operation and extensive storage facilities.

main-line program The section of a program that controls the order of execution of other modules in the program.

main memory Same as *internal storage*.

main storage Addressable storage directly controlled by the central processing unit (CPU). The CPU uses main storage to store programs while they are being executed and data while they are being processed. Same as *internal storage* and *primary storage*.

Magnetic tape unit. Courtesy Honeywell, Inc.

maintainability The characteristic associated with the isolation and repair of a failure.

maintenance programmer An individual who works with programs that have already been implemented into an information system, making changes as needed from time to time.

maintenance routine A routine designed to help a customer engineer carry out routine preventive maintenance on a computer system.

male connector A plug adapted so as to fit into a matching hollow part. See *connector* and *female connector*.

malfunction A failure in the operation of the central processing unit

Mainframe. Courtesy Honeywell, Inc.

or peripheral device. The effect of a *fault*. Contrast with *error* and *mistake*. See *crash*.

Maltron keyboard A keyboard layout that allows potentially much faster speeds, and is easier to learn, than the traditional QWERTY layout.

management graphics Charts, graphs, and other visual representations of the operational or strategic aspects of a business. They are intended to aid management in assimilating and presenting business data.

management information system (MIS) An information system designed to supply organizational managers with the necessary information needed to plan, organize, staff, direct, and control the operations of the organization.

management science A mathematical or quantitative study of the management of a business's resources, usually with the aid of a computer.

mantissa That part of a floating point number that specifies the significant digits of the number. For example, in $.64321 \times 10^3$, $.64321$ is the mantissa.

manual input   Data entered manually by the computer user to modify, continue, or resume processing of a computer program.

manual operation   Processing of data in a system by direct manual techniques.

manufacturer's software   A set of programming aids that the computer manufacturer supplies or makes available with a computer. See *systems programs*.

map   A list that indicates the area of storage occupied by various elements of a program and its data. Also called *storage map*.

mapping   A transformation from one set to another set; a correspondence.

marginal checking   A preventive maintenance procedure in which the unit under test is varied from its normal value in an effort to detect and locate components that are operating in a marginal condition.

mark   A sign or symbol used to signify or indicate an event in time or space.

mark sensing   The ability to mark cards or pages with a pencil to be read directly into the computer via a mark sense reader. This is a very useful technique for acquiring data by hand and for avoiding the time lag and inaccuracy of keypunching. See *optical mark reader*.

maser   (Microwave Amplification by the Stimulated Emission of Radiation) A device capable of amplifying or generating radio frequency radiation. Maser amplifiers are used in satellite communications ground stations to amplify the extremely weak signals received from communications satellites.

mask   (1) A machine word containing a pattern of bits, bytes, or characters that is used to extract or select parts of other machine words by controlling an instruction that retains or eliminates selected bits, bytes, or characters. (2) A glass photographic plate that contains the circuit pattern used in the silicon-chip fabrication process.

massage   To process data.

mass storage device   A device used to supply relatively inexpensive storage for large amounts of information. Examples are mass storage cartridge systems, Winchester disks, videodisks, and large magnetic disk systems.

master clear   A switch on some computer consoles that will clear certain operational registers and prepare for a new mode of operation.

master clock The device that controls the basic timing pulses of a computer.

master data A set of data that is altered infrequently and supplies basic data for processing operations.

master file A file containing relatively permanent information that is used as a source of reference and is generally updated periodically. Contrast with *detail file*.

master-slave computer system A computer system consisting of a master computer connected to one or more slave computers. The master computer provides the scheduling function and jobs to the slave computer(s).

match To check for identity between two or more items of data. Contrast with *hit*.

matching A data processing operation in which two files are checked to determine whether there is a corresponding item or group of items in each file.

mathematical functions A set of mathematical routines that are available in most programming languages. They are usually supplied as part of the language.

FUNCTION	*MEANING*
SQR(X)	- square root of X
SIN(X)	- trigonometric sine of X
COS(X)	- trigonometric cosine of X
TAN(X)	- trigonometric tangent of X
ATN(X)	- angle whose tangent is X
ABS(X)	- absolute value of X
INT(X)	- integer part of X
EXP(X)	- exponential of X
LOG(X)	- logarithm of X
RND	- random number

mathematical logic The use of mathematical symbols to represent language and its processes. These symbols are manipulated in accord with mathematical rules to determine whether or not a statement or a series of statements is true or false. See *logic*.

mathematical model A group of mathematical expressions that represents a process, a system, or the operation of a device. See *simulation*.

mathematical software The set of computer algorithms in the area of mathematics.

mathematical symbols   Symbols used in formulas, equations, and flowcharts.

mathematics   The study of the relationships among objects or quantities, organized so that certain facts can be proved or derived from others by using logic.

matrix   A group of elements (numbers, symbols, or characters) organized on a rectangular grid. See *array*.

matrix display   A display in which characters are represented as patterns of tiny lighted dots.

matrix notation   Introduced by the English mathematician Arthur Cayley in 1858. He used an abbreviated notation, such as ax = b, for expressing systems of linear equations.

matrix printer   A printer that uses a matrix of dots to form an image of the character being printed. A type of *line printer*.

mature system   A system that is fully operational and performing all the functions it was designed to accomplish.

Mauchly, John   (1907–1980) Co-inventor of the ENIAC, an early electronic computer. See *Eckert, J. Presper* and *ENIAC*.

maxi-minicomputer   A designation of the largest type of minicomputers that uses 16-bit words.

mb (megabyte)   One million bytes.   1000 kb.

mechanical data processing   A method of data processing that

Mathematical Symbols

× or •	multiplied by	>	is greater than
÷ or /	divided by	<	is less than
+	positive; add	≥	is greater than or equal to
−	negative; subtract	≤	is less than or equal to
±	plus or minus	∴	therefore
=	is equal to	∠	angle
≡	identity	△	increment or decrement
≃	is similar to	⊥	is perpendicular to
≠	does not equal	‖	is parallel to

involves the use of relatively small and simple (usually nonpro-grammable) mechanical machines.

mechanical translation A generic term for language translation by computers or similar equipment.

media The plural form of "medium." Media can be classified as source, input, and output. Checks are an example of source media. Punched cards and diskettes are examples of input media. Output media can be magnetic tape and paper printouts.

media eraser A device designed to demagnetize magnetic tapes and diskettes.

medium The physical substance upon which data are recorded; for example, magnetic disk, floppy disk, magnetic tape, punch cards, and paper.

medium scale integration (MSI) The class of integrated circuits having a density between those of *large scale integration* (LSI) and *small scale integration* (SSI). See *TTL*.

mega (M) A prefix indicating million; more accurately, 1,048,576, or 2^{20}.

megabit A megabit is 1024 kilobits; 1,048,576 bits.

megabyte A megabyte is 1024 kilobytes; 1,048,576 bytes. Roughly, 1 million bytes of storage.

megacycle A million cycles per second.

megaflop A million floating point operations per second.

megahertz (MHz) A unit of electrical frequency equal to a million cycles per second.

membrane keyboard A keyboard constructed of two thin plastic sheets (called membranes) that are coated with a circuit made of electrically conductive ink. It is an economical, flat keyboard that is used in several low-priced microcomputers.

memory The storage facilities of the computer, capable of storing vast amounts of data. See *auxiliary storage, floppy disk, internal storage, magnetic bubble memory, magnetic core storage, magnetic disk, magnetic drum, magnetic tape, PROM, RAM, ROM, semiconductor storage, storage,* and *virtual storage.*

memory allocatiion See *storage allocation.*

memory chip A semiconductor device that stores information in the form of electrical charges.

memory cycle The amount of time required to move one byte or word of information into or out of memory.

memory dump A printout showing the contents of memory.

memory management The technique of efficiently controlling and allocating memory resources.

memory map An image in memory of information appearing somewhere else. For example, in a display unit there is a memory map of the screen display, with one memory location corresponding to each character position on the display.

memory protection See *storage protection*.

memory sniffing Refers to the continuous testing of storage during processing.

menu A list of options within a program that allows the user to choose which part to interact with. Menus allow computer users a facility for using programs without knowing any technical methods.

menu-driven software Computer programs that make extensive use of menus. Software of this type is designed so that it may be used easily by people with minimal computer experience.

merge To combine items into one sequenced file from two or more similarly sequenced files without changing the order of the items. Same as *collate*.

merge-print program A program that lets you produce personalized form letters.

MESFET (MEtal Semiconductor Field Effect Transistor) The main active device used in gallium arsenide integrated circuits to provide current gain and inversion.

mesh A set of branches forming a closed path in a network.

message A group of characters having meaning as a whole and always handled as a group.

message format Rules for the placement of such portions of a message as message heading, address text, and end of message.

message header The leading part of a message that contains information concerning the message, such as the source or destination code of the message, the message priority, and the type of message.

message queuing In a data communications system, a technique for controlling the handling of messages, allowing them to be accepted by a computer and stored until they have been processed or routed to another destination.

message retrieval The capability to retrieve a message sometime after it has entered an information system.

message switching The switching technique of receiving a message, storing it until the proper outgoing circuit and station are available, and then retransmitting it toward its destination. Computers are often used to perform the switching function.

message switching center A center in which messages are routed according to information contained within the messages themselves.

metacharacter In programming language systems, these characters have some controlling role in respect to the other characters with which they are associated.

metacompiler A compiler for a language that is used primarily for written compilers, usually syntax-oriented compilers. A special-purpose metacompiler language is not very useful for writing general programs.

metalanguage A language that is used to describe a language.

metallic oxide semiconductor (MOS) (1) A field-effect transistor in which the gate electrode is isolated from the channel by an oxide film. (2) A *capacitor* in which semiconductor material forms one plate, aluminum forms the other plate, and an oxide forms the dielectric. See *CMOS*.

meta-metalanguage A language that is used to decribe a meta-language.

meter Base unit of length in the SI metric system, approximately equal to 1.1 yards.

metric system Systeme International d'Unites or SI. The modern version of the metric system currently in use world-wide. It is based on seven base units; meter, kilogram, second, ampere, Kelvin (degrees Celsius), candela, and mole.

metric ton Measure of weight equal to 1000 kilograms, or about 2200 pounds.

MFT An acronym for Multiprogramming with a Fixed number of Tasks, the tasks being programs. Sometimes called (jokingly, of course) Multiprogramming with a Finite amount of Trouble.

MHz An abbreviation for megahertz, a million cycles per second.

MICR See *magnetic ink character recognition*.

micro (1) One millionth, used as a prefix; for example, a microsecond is a millionth of a second. (2) Computerese for "quite small"; for example, as in microcomputer.

microchart A chart showing the ultimate details of the program's or system's design.

micro code Software that defines the instruction set of a micro-programmable computer. See *microprogrammable computer* and *microprogramming*.

microcode A term used to mean firmware, a computer program permanently "burned" into a ROM (Read-Only Memory).

microcoding Composing computer instructions by combining basic, elementary operations to form higher-level instructions such as

MICR (Magnetic Ink Character Reader). Courtesy NCR Corp.

addition or multiplication. See *micro instruction, microprogrammable computer*, and *microprogramming*.

microcoding device A circuit board with fixed instructions for performing standard functions through miniature logic circuits, thus avoiding the need to code these instructions during programming.

microcomputer A small, low-cost computer that performs input, processing, storage, and output operations following a set of instructions. See *home computer* and *personal computer*.

microcomputer applications Microcomputers are finding applications in business, technology, industry, and the home. They are used in video game machines, traffic control systems, point-of-sale terminals, scientific instruments, blood analyzers, credit card verification, pinball machines, automotive ignition control, and inventory control systems. Industry is using microcomputers and

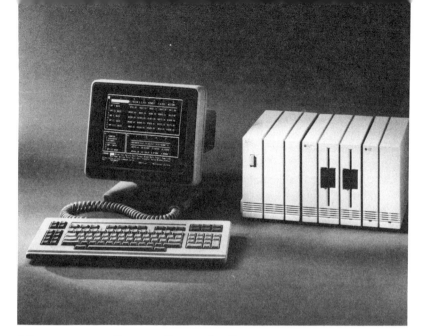

Microcomputer. Courtesy Burroughs Corp.

microprocessors in microwave ovens, sewing machines, flow meters, gas station pumps, paint mixing machines, process monitoring, pollution monitoring, and as control units for hundreds of other devices.

microcomputer chip A microcomputer on a chip. Differs from a microprocessor in that it not only contains the central processing unit (CPU) but also includes on the same piece of silicon a RAM, a ROM, and input/output circuitry. Often called a "computer-on-a-chip." See *microcomputer* and *microprocessor*.

microcomputer components The major components of a microcomputer are a microprocessor, a memory (ROM, PROM, EPROM, RAM), and input/output circuitry.

microcomputer development system A complete microcomputer system used to test and develop both the hardware and software of other microcomputer-based systems from initial development through debugging of final prototypes. A typical microcomputer system includes assembler, facilities, a text editor, debugging facilities, hardware emulation capabilities, PROM programmer, monitor, and disk/tape I/O system.

microcomputer kit See *computer kit.*

microcomputer system A system that includes a microcomputer, peripherals, operating system, and applications programs.

microcontroller A device or instrument that controls a process with high resolution, usually over a narrow region. A microprogrammed machine (microcomputer or microprocessor) used in a control operation; that is, to direct or make changes in a process of operation. For example, the Singer Company uses a microcontroller and a ROM to operate sewing machines. See *microcomputer* and *microprocessor*.

microelectronics   The field that deals with techniques for producing miniature circuits; for example, integrated circuits, thin film techniques, and solid logic modules.

microfiche   A sheet of film about 10 centimeters by 15 centimeters (4 inches by 6 inches) upon which the images of computer output may be recorded. Up to 270 pages of output may be recorded on one sheet of microfiche. See *computer output microfilm recorder* and *ultrafiche*.

microfilm   Photographic film used for recording graphic information in a reduced size. See *computer output microfilm (COM) recorder*.

micro floppy disk   A floppy disk with a diameter less than 9 centimeters (3½ inches). See *floppy disk*.

microform   A medium that contains miniaturized images; for example, *microfiche* and *microfilm*.

micrographics   The use of miniature photography to condense, store, and retrieve graphics information. Involves the usage of all types of microforms and microimages such as microfilm, microfiche, and computer output microfilm.

micro instruction   A low-level instruction used to obtain a macro, or machine language instruction. See *microprogramming*.

microjustification   In some word processing programs, the ability to add small slivers of blank space between words and between letters within words.

micrologic   The use of a permanent stored program to interpret instructions in a microprogram.

microminiature chip   A *large scale integration* or *very large scale integration* chip used for computer storage (memory chip) or control (microprocessor chip).

microminiaturization   A term implying very small size, one step smaller than miniaturization.

micron   One millionth of a meter, or approximately ½₅,₀₀₀ of an inch.

microphone   An electroacoustic device containing a transducer that is actuated by sound waves and delivers essentially equivalent electric waves.

microprocessor   The basic arithmetic, logic, and control elements required for processing (generally contained on one integrated circuit chip). Microprocessors are widely used as the control devices for household appliances, business machines, calculating devices, toys, video game machines, and thousands of other devices.

microprogrammable computer   A term referring to any computer whose instruction set is not fixed but can be tailored to individual needs by the programming of ROMs or other memory devices. Consequently, whether the computer is a large scale machine, minicomputer, or microprocessor, theoretically it can be microprogrammed. See *microprogramming*.

microprogramming   A method of operating the control part of a computer in which each instruction is broken into several small steps (microsteps) that form part of a microprogram. Some systems allow users to microprogram, and hence determine the instruction set of their own machine. See *micro code* and *microprogrammable computer*.

microsecond   One millionth of a second (0.000001), abbreviated μs or μsec.

microspacing   A feature of some printers that allows them to move extremely small distances. Used to do microjustification and shadow printing.

microwave   An electromagnetic wave that has a wavelength in the centimeter range. Microwaves occupy a region in the electromagnetic spectrum that is bounded by radio waves on the side of longer wave lengths and by infrared waves on the side of shorter wavelengths.

microwave hop   A microwave radio channel between two dish antennas aimed at each other.

microwave transmission lines   Structures used for transmission of electromagnetic energy at microwave frequencies from one point to another.

MICR (Magnetic Ink Character Reader)   An input device that reads documents imprinted with magnetic ink characters.

midi-minicomputer   A designation of a medium-size minicomputer that uses a 16-bit word.

milli   One thousandth, used as a prefix; for example, a millisecond is a thousandth of a second.

millimicrosecond   Same as *nanosecond*, one billionth of a second.

millisecond   (ms or msec) One thousandth of a second (0.001).

mini   Minicomputer.

minicomputer   A digital computer that is distinguished from a mi-

Minicomputer. Courtesy Honeywell, Inc.

crocomputer by higher performance, more powerful instruction sets, a higher price, and a wide selection of available programming languages and operating systems. Minicomputer systems are divided into four operational classes: mini-, midi-, maxi-, and super-minicomputers.

mini floppy disk A 13.3 centimeter (5¼ inch) diameter disk used in microcomputer systems. See *floppy disk, magnetic disk,* and *micro floppy disk.*

minimal tree Tree whose terminal nodes are ordered to make the tree operate at optimum.

minimax A technique for minimizing the maximal error of a process.

mini-minicomputer The smallest classification of minicomputer systems. It possesses a limited set of operational features.

minuend A number from which another number, called the subtrahend, is to be subtracted. In the subtraction 7 − 3 = 4, 7 is the minuend, 3 is the subtrahend, and 4 is the difference.

mips Millions of instructions per second. Refers to the average number of machine language instructions that a large computer performs in 1 second. For example, a Cray 1 supercomputer is a 125-MIPS machine because it executes about 125 million instructions per second.

MIS See *management information system.*

mistake A human failing that produces an unintended result; for example, faulty arithmetic, use of incorrect computer instructions, incorrect keypunching, or use of incorrect formula. Contrast with *error, fault,* and *malfunction.* See *bug.*

mixed number A number having a fractional part (e.g., 63.71, -18.006, 298.413).

ML (Manipulator Language) An IBM Corporation programming language for controlling robots.

mnemonic code An easy-to-remember assembly language code; for example, a code that uses an abbreviation such as MPY for "multiply."

mnemonic language A programming language that is based on easily remembered symbols and can be assembled into machine language by the computer.

mode (1) The form of a number, name, or expression. (2) The most common or frequent value in a group of values.

model See *mathematical model.*

modeling The process of accurately describing or representing certain parts of a system. See *simulation.*

modem (MOdulator DEModulator) A device that provides the appropriate interface between a communications link and a data processing machine or system by serving as a modulator and/or demodulator. Same as *data set.*

modify (1) To alter a portion of an instruction so that its interpretation and execution will be other than normal. The modification may permanently change the instruction or leave it unchanged and affect only the current execution. (2) To alter a program according to a defined parameter.

modular coding Refers to the technique of programming in which the logical parts of a program are divided into a series of individual modules or routines so that each routine may be programmed independently.

modular constraint In computer graphics, a limitation on the placement of images such that some or all points of an image are forced to lie on the intersections of an invisible grid.

modularity The concept of designing computers in a "building-block" format to promote efficient and economical upgrading of the equipment.

modular programming A technique for designing a system or program as a number of self-contained modules. See *module*.

modulation In data communications, the process by which some characteristic of a high frequency carrier signal is varied in accordance with another, lower frequency "information" signal. This technique is used in data sets to make computer terminal signals compatible with communications facilities.

modulator A device that receives electrical pulses, or bits, from a data processing machine and converts them into signals suitable for transmission over a communications link. Contrast with *demodulator*.

module (1) Specifically, one logical part of a program. A major program may be broken down into a number of logically self-contained modules. These modules may be written (and possibly tested separately) by a number of programmers. The modules can then be put together to form the complete program. This is called *modular programming*. (2) An interchangeable plug-in item containing components.

modulo A mathematical function that yields the remainder of division. A number x evaluated modulo n gives the integer remainder of x/n. For example, 100 modulo 84 equals the remainder of 100/84, or 16.

Modem. Courtesy Radio Shack, a division of Tandy Corp.

monadic   An operation that uses only one operand.

monadic Boolean operator   A Boolean operator with only one operand, such as the *NOT* operator.

monitor   (1) A control program. (2) A video display. See *operating system* and *video monitor*.

monochrome display   A display capable of producing only one color against the background; for example, white on black or green on black.

monolithic   (1) The single silicon substrate upon which an integrated circuit is constructed. (2) Complete and all in one piece. For example, a linkage editor combines several fragmentary program modules into a single monolithic program.

monolithic integrated circuit   A class of integrated circuits wherein the substrate is an active material, such as the semiconductor silicon. See *integrated circuit*.

monte carlo (method)   A trial-and-error method of repeated calculations to discover the best solution of a problem. Often used when a great number of variables are present with interrelationships so extremely complex as to eliminate straightforward analytical handling.

MOS   (Metallic Oxide Semiconductor) A semiconductor structure that is used in many *FET*s and integrated circuits.

MOSFET   (Metallic Oxide Semiconductor Field Effect Transistor) A semiconductor characterized by an extremely high input impedance, a fairly high active impedance, and low switching speeds. When a voltage (negative with respect to the substrate) is applied to the gate, then the MOSFET is a conductor; and, if a potential difference is applied between source and drain, there will be current flow.

MOS/LSI   See *metallic oxide semiconductor* and *large scale integration*.

most significant digit (MSD)   Pertaining to the digit of a number that has the greatest weight or significance (e.g., in the number 54321, the most significant digit is 5). See *high order* and *justify*.

motherboard   An interconnecting assembly into which printed circuit cards, boards, or modules are connected. Synonym for *backplane*.

Motorola   A manufacturer of electronic equipment, including microprocessors.

mouse   A type of input device. Rolling the mouse around on a flat surface produces X and Y coordinate motion of a cursor on the display screen.

move   To transfer from one location of storage to another location.

moveable-head disk unit A storage device or system consisting of magnetically coated disks, on the surface of which data are stored in the form of magnetic spots arranged in a manner to represent binary data. These data are arranged in circular tracks around the disks and are accessible to reading and writing heads on an arm that can be moved mechanically to the desired disk and then to the desired track on that disk. Data from a given track are read or written sequentially as the disk rotates. See *magnetic disk*.

MP/M (Multiprogramming Control Program for Microcomputers) A multiuser operating system for small computers. See *operating system*.

MPU (MicroProcessing Unit) See *microprocessor*.

MPX See *multiplexer*.

ms An abbreviation of millisecond.

MSD See *most significant digit*.

MSI See *medium scale integration*.

MSSG An abbreviation of message.

MTBF (Mean Time Between Failure) The average length of time a system or component is expected to work without failure.

MTTF (Mean Time To Failure) The average length of time in which the system, or a component of the system, works without fault.

MTTR (Mean Time to Repair) The average time expected to be required to detect and correct a fault in a computer system.

mu The name of the Greek letter μ. The symbol is used to denote the prefix micro. For example, μs means microsecond.

MUG (MUMPS Users Group) See *MUMPS*.

multiaccess computer A computer system in which computational and data resources are made available simultaneously to a number of users. Users access the system through terminal devices, normally on an interactive or conversational basis. A multiaccess computer system may consist of only a single central processor connected directly to a number of terminals (star configuration), or it may consist of a number of processing systems that are distributed and interconnected with one another (ring configuration) as well as with other terminals.

multiaddress Pertaining to an instruction format containing more than one address part.

multicomputer system A computer system consisting of two or more central processing units.

multidrop line A communications system configuration using a single channel or line to serve multiple terminals.

multifile sorting The automatic sequencing of more than one file, based upon separate parameters for each file, without operator intervention.

multijob operation A term that describes concurrent execution of job steps from two or more jobs.

multilayer A type of printed circuit board that has several circuit layers connected by electroplated holes.

multilevel addressing See *indirect addressing*.

multilinked list List with each atom having at least two pointers.

multipass Refers to running through the same data more than once in order to accomplish a task too complicated to be accomplished in one pass.

multipass sort A sort program that is designed to sort more data than can be contained within the internal memory of a central computer. Intermediate storage, such as disk, tape, or drum, is required.

multiple access A system with a number of on-line communications channels providing concurrent access to the common system.

multiple-address instruction An instruction consisting of an operation code and two or more addresses. Usually specified as a two-address, three-address, or four-address instruction.

multiple-address message A message to be delivered to more than one destination.

multiple connector A connector to indicate the merging of several lines of flow into one line, or the dispersal of one line of flow into several lines.

multiple-job processing Controlling the performance of more than one data processing job at a time.

multiple pass printing A technique used on some dot matrix printers to obtain higher quality characters. The print head makes one pass, the paper is moved slightly, and another pass is made. The end product is a printed character that is easier to read.

multiple punching The punching of two or more holes in a card column.

multiple user system A computer system designed to allow more than one user on the system at a time.

multiplex To interleave or sumultaneously transmit two or more messages over a single channel or other communications facility. See *interleaving*.

multiplexer (MPX or MUX) A device that allows several communications lines to share one computer data channel.

multiplexer channel   A special type of input/output channel that can transmit data between a computer and a number of simultaneously operating peripheral devices.

multiplexor   An alternate spelling of *multiplexer*.

multiplicand   The quantity that is multiplied by another quantity.

multiplication time   The time required to perform a multiplication. For a binary number, it will be equal to the total of all the addition times and all the shift time involved in the multiplication.

multiplier   The quantity that is used to multiply another quantity.

multiprecision arithmetic   A form of arithmetic in which two or more computer words are used to represent each number.

multiprocessing   The simultaneous execution of two or more sequences of instructions by multiple central processing units under common control. See *multiprogramming*.

multiprocessor   A computer network consisting of two or more central processors under a common control.

multiprogramming   Running two or more programs at the same time in the same computer. Each program is allotted its own place in memory and its own peripherals, but all share the central processing unit. It is made economical by the fact that peripherals are slower than the central processing unit, so most programs spend most of their time waiting for input or output to finish. While one program is waiting, another can use the central processing unit.

multireel sorting   The automatic sequencing of a file having more than one input tape, without operator intervention.

multisystem network   A communications network with two or more host computers. It enables a terminal to select the computer with which it wishes to communicate.

multitask operation   Two or more segments within a program running in one computer at the same time.

multiuser   A computer system that contains two or more user terminals that can be used concurrently.

multiviewports   A screen display that shows two or more viewing screens that are adjacent but independent.

multivolume file   A file so large that it requires more than one disk pack, diskette, or reel of magnetic tape to hold it.

MUMPS   (Massachusetts General Hospital Utility Multi-Programming System) A programming language designed specifically for handling medical records. The language is strong in data management and text manipulation features.

μs   See *microsecond*.

musical language A method by which musical notation may be represented in code suitable for computer input. See *computer music.*

musicomp A compositional programming language that provides techniques for generating original musical scores as well as for synthesizing music.

music synthesizer A device that can be linked to a computer for recording music, playing music, and so on.

MUX (MUltipleXer) A channel used to connect low-speed devices to a computer.

MVT An acronym for Multiprogramming with a Variable number of Tasks, the tasks being programs. (Also jokingly called Multiprogramming with a Vast amount of Trouble.)

mylar A DuPont trademark for polyester film, often used as a base for magnetically coated or perforated information media.

N

naive user A person who wants to do something with a computer but does not have the experience needed to program the computer.

NAK An international transmission control code returned by a receiving terminal to signify that a frame of information has been received but the frame is incorreect. Contrast with *ACK.*

name An alphanumeric term that identifies a program, a control statement, data areas, or a cataloged procedure. Same as *label.*

nand A logical operator having the property that, if P is a statement, Q is a statement, . . . then the nand of P, Q, . . . is true if at least one statement is false and false if all statements are true.

nanosecond (ns) One billionth of a second (0.000000001), one thousand-millionth of a second. Same as *millimicrosecond.* Light travels approximately 1 foot per nanosecond, electricity slightly less.

narrowband Pertains to a data communications system that handles low volumes of data.

NASA National Aeronautics and Space Administration.

National Computer Conference (NCC) An annual meeting of computer users, computer science educators, software developers, and computer equipment manufacturers.

native compiler A compiler that produces code usable only for a particular computer.

native language A computer language that is peculiar to the machines of one manufacturer. See *machine language*.

natural language A language that allows users to prepare programs in an English-like or other natural language.

NBS (National Bureau of Standards) A government agency that has the responsibility of establishing standards for the computer industry.

NCC (National Computer Conference) A large computer trade show held annually.

N-channel MOS (NMOS) A circuit that uses a current made up of negative charges. It has a higher speed but lower density than *PMOS*.

NCIC An acronym for the FBI's computerized National Crime Information Center, the heart of a large law enforcement network.

NCR Corporation A large manufacturer of computer equipment.

NDRO (Non-Destructive ReadOut) See *nondestructive read*.

near letter quality An output produced by some printers (dot matrix) that does not look as readable or as good as that produced by letter quality printers.

negate To perform the logical operator *NOT*.

negative true logic A system of logic in which a high voltage represents the bit value 0 and a low voltage represents the bit value 1.

NELIAC (Naval Electronics Laboratory International Algorithmic Compiler) A high-level programming language used primarily for solving scientific and real-time control problems.

nested loop A loop that is contained within another loop. See *loop*.

nesting Embedding program segments or blocks of data within other program segments or blocks of data. Algebraic nesting involves grouping expressions within parentheses; for example, (W * X * (A − B)).

network (1) A system of interconnected computer systems and terminals. (2) A series of points connected by communications channels.

network chart A chart that depicts time estimates and activity relationships.

networking   A technique for distributing data processing functions through communications facilities. The design of networks.

network, local area   See *local area network*.

network, ring   See *ring network*.

network, star   See *star network*.

network theory   The systematizing and generalizing of the relationships among the elements of an electrical network.

Newton-Raphson   A term applied to an iterative procedure used for solving equations. See *iterate*.

nibble   One half of a byte; namely, a 4-bit data element. Sometimes spelled nybble.

niladic   An operation for which no operands are specified.

nil pointer   A pointer used to denote the end of a linked list.

nine's complement   A numeral used to represent the negative of a given value. A nine's complement numeral is obtained by subtracting each digit from a numeral containing all nines; for example, 567 is the nine's complement of 432 and is obtained by subtracting 432 from 999.

ninety column card   A punched card used with early UNIVAC card handling equipment. The card contains ninety columns and one character can be punched in each column.

ninety-six column card   A punched card used with card handling equipment. The card physically contains eighteen rows and thirty-six columns, and three characters can be punched in each column.

nixie tube   A vacuum tube used to display legible numbers.

NMOS   (N-channel MOS) Circuits that use currents made up of negative charges and produce devices at least twice as fast as PMOS. See *PMOS*.

node   (1) Any terminal, station, or communications computer in a computer network. (2) A point in a *tree structure* where two or more branches come together.

noise   (1) Loosely, any disturbance tending to interfere with the normal operation of a device or system, including those attributable to equipment components, natural disturbance, or manual interference. (2) Spurious signals that can introduce errors. (3) An unwanted signal.

noise immunity   A device's ability to accept valid signals while rejecting unwanted signals.

nonconductor   A substance through which electricity cannot pass.

nondestructive read   A read operation that does not alter the information content of the storage media.

nonerasable storage   A storage device whose information cannot be erased during the course of computation; for example, punched paper tape, punched cards, and certain nondestructible readout magnetic memories.

nonexecutable A program statement that sets up a program but does not call for any specific action on the part of the program in which it appears. Contrast with *executable*.

nongraphic character A character that when sent for a printer or display unit, does not produce a printable character image; for example, carriage control, uppercase, and so forth.

nonimpact printer A printer that uses heat, laser technology, or photographic techniques to print output.

nonlinear programming An area of applied mathematics concerned with finding the values of the variables that give the smallest or largest value of a specified function in the class of all variables satisfying prescribed conditions.

nonnumeric programming Programming that deals with symbols rather than numbers. Usually refers to the manipulation of symbolic objects, such as words, rather than the performance of numerical calculations.

nonprint An impulse that inhibits line printing under machine control.

nonreflective ink Any color of ink that is recognizable to an optical character reader.

nonsequential computer A computer that must be directed to the location of each instruction.

nonswitched line A communications link that is permanently installed between two points.

nonvolatile storage A storage media that retains its data in the absence of power.

no-op An abbreviation of the term "no-operation," as in *no-operation instruction*.

no-operation instruction A computer instruction whose only effect is to advance the instruction counter. It accomplishes nothing more than to move beyond itself to the next instruction in normal sequence.

NOP (No OPeration) See *no-operation instruction*.

NOR The *Boolean operator* that gives a *truth table* value of true only when both of the variables connected by the *logical operator* are false.

normalize To adjust the exponent and fraction of a floating point quantity so that the fraction is within a prescribed range. Loosely, to *scale*.

Notebook computer. Courtesy Radio Shack, a division of Tandy Corp.

NOT A logic operator having the property that, if P is a statement, then the NOT of P is true if P is false and false if P is true.

notation See *positional notation.*

notebook computer A briefcase-size computer that uses a flat pannel liquid crystal display. It is larger than a hand-held computer but smaller than a desk-size computer.

NOT-gate A circuit equivalent to the logical operation of negation.

NOVA A designation for computers manufactured by the Data General Corporation.

NRZ (NonReturn to Zero) One of several methods for coding digital information on magnetic tape.

NS An abbreviation for nanosecond, one billionth of a second.

NTSC (National Television System Committee) A color television standard.

nucleus That portion of the control program that must always be present in internal storage.

null Pertaining to a negligible value or a lack of information, as contrasted with a zero or a blank that conveys information, such as numerals and spaces between words.

null cycle The time required to cycle through the entire program without introducing new data.

null string String with no characters. See *empty string*.

number (1) A symbol or symbols representing a value in a specific numeral system. (2) Loosely, a *numeral*.

number base See *radix*.

number crunching A term applied to a program or computer that is designed to perform large amounts of computation and other numerical manipulations of data.

number representation The representation of numbers by agreed sets of symbols according to agreed rules.

number system An agreed set of symbols and rules for number representation. Loosely, a *numeral system*.

numeral A conventional symbol representing a number; for example, six, 6, VI, and 110 are four different numerals that represent the same number.

numeralization Representation of alphabetic data through the use of digits.

numeral system A method of representing numbers. In computing, several numeral systems, in addition to the common decimal system, are of particular interest. These are the *binary, hexadecimal*, and *octal* systems. In each system, the value of a numeral is the value of the digits multiplied by the numeral system radix, raised to a power indicated by the position of the digits in the numeral. For example, the binary number 101100 may be expressed as $1 \times 2^5 + 0 \times 2^4 + 1 \times 2^3 + 1 \times 2^2 + 0 \times 2^1 + 0 \times 2^0$ or 44.

numerator In the expression a/b, a is the numerator and b is the denominator.

numeric Pertaining to numerals or to representation by means of numerals.

numerical analysis The branch of mathematics concerned with the study and development of effective procedures for computing answers to problems.

numerical control A means of controlling machine tools through servomechanisms and control circuitry so that the motions of the tools will respond to digital coded instructions on tape or to direct commands from a computer. See *APT* and *parts programmer*.

numerical indicator tube Any electron tube capable of visually displaying numerical figures.

numeric character Same as *digit*.

numeric coding Coding that uses digits only to represent data and instructions.

numeric constant Data using integer or real numbers.

numeric data Consist solely of the digits 0–9.

numeric keypad An input device that uses a set of decimal digit keys (0–9) and two special function keys. Used as a separate device or sometimes located on devices to the right of a QWERTY keyboard.

oasis A multiuser operating system used on several microcomputer systems.

obey The process whereby a computer carries out an operation as specified by one or more of the instructions forming the program that is currently being executed.

object code Output from a compiler or assembler that is itself executable machine code or is suitable for processing to produce executable machine code. Also called *object program.*

object computer A computer used for the execution of an *object program.*

object deck A set of punched cards representing the machine language equivalent of a source deck.

object language The output of a translation process. Usually, object language and machine language are the same. Contrast with *source language.* Synonymous with *target language.*

object language programming Programming in a machine language executable on a particular computer.

object program The instructions that come out of the *compiler* or *assembler*, ready to run on the computer. Also called *object code.*

OCR (Optical Character Recognition) Characters printed in a special type that can be read by both machines and people. See *optical character recognition.*

octal Pertaining to a number system with a radix of 8. Octal numbers are frequently used to represent binary numerals, with each octal digit representing a group of three binary digits (bits); for example, the binary numeral 111000010001101 can be represented as octal 70215.

octal numeral A numeral of one or more digits, representing a sum in which the quantity represented by each figure is based on a radix of eight. The digits used in octal numerals are 0, 1, 2, 3, 4, 5, 6, and 7.

OEM (Original Equipment Manufacturer) A company or organization that purchases computers and peripheral equipment for use as components in products and equipment that they subsequently sell to their customers.

office automation The application of computers and communications technology to improve the productivity of clerical and managerial office workers.

office computer A term usually applied to a microcomputer system for use in an office environment. The system is likely to include disk units, a printer, and software developed for specific office functions.

office information system A system that can include a variety of data entry terminals, word processors, graphics terminals, printers, and computer systems.

off-line A term describing equipment, devices, or persons not in direct communication with the central processing unit of a computer. Equipment that is not connected to the computer. Contrast with *on-line*.

off-line storage Storage not under control of the central processing unit.

Octal Numeral

Binary groups	Octal digit
000	0
001	1
010	2
011	3
100	4
101	5
110	6
111	7

off load To transfer jobs from one computer system to another that is more lightly loaded.

off-page connector A symbol used on a flowchart to link a symbol on one page with another symbol on a different page.

offset The difference between the value or condition desired and that actually attained.

off-the-shelf Refers to a standard, mass-produced hardware or software product that is readily available from the vendor.

OMR See *optical mark recognition*.

on-board computer A computer resident in a vehicle (e.g., in a spacecraft, an automobile, a ship, or an aircraft).

on-board regulation An arrangement in which each board in a system contains its own voltage regulator.

one-address computer A computer that employs only one address in its instruction format (e.g., ADD X, where X represents the address in the instruction).

one-address instruction An instruction consisting of an operation and exactly one address. In special cases, the instruction code of a single address computer may include both zero and multiaddress instructions. Most present-day computers are of the one-address instruction type. See *one-address computer*.

one-chip computer A complete microcomputer that is implemented on a single chip.

one-dimensional array An array consisting of a single row or column of elements.

one-for-one A phrase often associated with an assembler in which one source language statement is converted to one machine language instruction.

one-level memory Memory in which all stored items are accessed by a uniform mechanism.

one-out-of-ten code In this code, a decimal digit is represented by ten binary digits and only one of the binary digits is permitted to be a 1.

one pass compiler A language processor that passes through a source language program one time and produces an object module.

one's complement A numeral used to represent the negative of a given value. A one's complement of a binary numeral is obtained by alternating the bit configuration of each bit in the numeral. For example, 01100101 is the one's complement of the binary numeral 10011010.

1-2-3 An integrated software system whose name represents its three functions: spread sheet, data base, and graphics. It combines an electronic worksheet with data base management. To these are added the ability to produce graphics or pictures of data in the worksheet almost instantly.

on-line A term describing equipment, devices, and persons that are in direct communication with the central processing unit of a computer. Equipment that is physically connected to the computer. Contrast with *off-line*.

on-line data base A data base that can be directly accessed by a user from a terminal, usually a visual display device.

on-line problem solving A teleprocessing application in which a number of users at remote terminals can concurrently use a computing system in solving problems on-line. Often, in this type of application, a dialogue or conversation is carried on between a user at a remote terminal and a program within the central computer system.

on-line processing A system in which equipment, and people, are in direct communication with the central processing unit of a computer. Equipment that is physically connected to the computer.

on-line storage Storage under control of the central processing unit.

op A contraction for the term *operation*.

op-code See *operation code*.

open-ended Capable of accepting the addition of new programs, instructions, subroutines, modifications, terms, or classifications without disturbing the original system.

open shop A computer installation at which computer operations can be performed by a qualified person. Contrast with *closed shop*.

open subroutine A subroutine that is inserted into a routine at each place it is used. Contrast with *closed subroutine*.

operand The data unit or equipment item that is operated upon. An operand is usually identified by an address in an instruction. For example in "ADD 100 TO 400," 100 and 400 are operands. See *operation code*.

operating ratio See *availability*.

operating system (OS) A set of programs that is designed to control the input and output operations of the computer, communicate with an operator, and schedule the resources of the computer to allow for continuous operation of the computer system with minimal manual intervention. See *CP/M, MP/M,* and *UNIX*.

operation (op) A defined action. The action specified by a single computer instruction or high-level language statement.

operational management The supervisors or leaders responsible for operating details and the employees who perform them.

operation center A physical area containing the human and equipment resources needed to process data through a computer and produce desired output. Same as *data processing center*.

operation code The instruction code used to specify the operations a computer is to perform. For example, in "ADD 100 TO 400," ADD is the operation code. See *operand*.

operations analysis See *operations research*.

operations research A mathematical science devoted to carrying out complicated operations with the maximum possible efficiency. Among the common scientific techniques in operations research are the following: *linear programming, probability theory, information theory, game theory, monte carlo method*, and *queuing theory*.

operator In the description of a process, that which indicates the action to be performed on operands. See *computer operator*.

optical character A character from a special set of characters that can be read by an *optical character reader*.

optical character reader An input device that accepts a printed document as input. It identifies characters by their shape. See *OCR* and *optical character recognition*.

optical character recognition (OCR) An information processing technology that converts human readable data into another medium for computer input. Light reflected from characters is recognized by optical character recognition equipment.

optical communications The transmission of data, pictures, speech, or other information by light. An information-carrying light wave signal originates in a transmitter, passes through an optical channel, and enters a receiver, which reconstructs the original information. Optical fibers and lasers make up a technology that offers the maximum transmitting capacity using devices that occupy little physical space.

optical disk A high-density storage device that uses a laser to burn a pattern of holes into a tellurium film on a disk surface. A single optical disk can hold billions of bytes of data.

optical fiber A thread of highly transparent glass that is pulsed very rapidly to carry a stream of binary signals. As well as carrying a high volume of data, optical fibers are immune to the electrical interference that can plague conventional cables. The use of optical fibers is rapidly becoming standard in computer communications.

optical mark reader An input device that reads graphite marks on cards or pages. See *mark sensing* and *optical mark recognition*.

optical mark recognition (OMR) Refers to recognition by ma-

Optical recognition device. Courtesy Sperry Corp.

chines of written marks based on inputs from photoelectric transducers. See *optical mark reader.*

optical page reader An input device that accepts a page of printed matter.

optical printer See *electrostatic printer.*

optical reader See *optical character reader* and *optical mark reader.*

optical recognition device A device that can read symbols or marks coded on paper documents and can convert them into electrical pulses. See *optical character reader* and *optical mark reader.*

optical scanner See *optical character reader.*

optical scanning Generally defines an input method by which information is converted for machine processing by evaluating the relative *reflectance* of that information to the background on which it appears. See *optical character recognition.*

optimal merge tree A *tree* representation of the order in which strings are to be merged so that a minimum number of move operations occurs. See *string*.

optimize To write a program or design a system in such a way as to minimize or maximize the value of some parameter, especially cost, storage, and time.

optimizing compiler A compiler that attempts to correct inefficiencies in a program's logic in order to improve execution times, main storage requirements, and so forth.

optimum programming Programming in order to maximize efficiency with respect to some criterion; for example, least storage usage, least usage of peripheral equipment, or least computing time.

optimum tree search A *tree* search whose object is to find the best of many alternatives.

OR See *exclusive OR* and *inclusive OR*.

OR circuit See *OR-gate*.

organizational control The administrative procedures implemented to protect an information system from infiltration, tampering, or sabotage.

OR-gate A computer circuit containing two switches whose output is a binary one if either or both of the inputs are binary. This electrical circuit implements the *OR* operator.

origin In coding, the absolute memory address of the first location of a program or program segment.

original data Data to be processed.

original equipment manufacturer (OEM) A manufacturer who buys equipment from other suppliers and integrates it into a single system for resale.

orthoferrite A naturally occurring substance composed of alternate, snakelike regions of opposite magnetic polarity.

OS See *operating system*.

oscillating sort An external tape sort that capitalizes on a tape drive's ability to read forward and backward.

oscillography The projection of a pattern of electrical signals on the face of a cathode-ray tube.

oscilloscope An electronic instrument that produces a luminous plot on a fluorescent screen showing the relationship of two or more variables. It is used by computer maintenance technicians.

outdegree The number of directed edges leaving a *node*. See *edge*.

outdent In word processing, a line of text that extends farther to the left than other lines in the same paragraph.

out-of-line Pertaining to statements in a computer program that are not in the main line of the program; for example, closed subroutines.

output   (1) Data transferred from a computer's internal storage unit to some auxiliary storage or output device. (2) The final result of data that have been processed by the computer. Contrast with *input*.

output area   An area of storage reserved for output data. Contrast with *input area*.

output buffer   A *buffer* used to transfer data to an external device.

output channel   A channel that connects peripheral units and the central processing unit, and through which data may be transmitted for output.

output data   Data to be delivered from a device or program, usually after some processing. Synonymous with *output*. Contrast with *input data*.

output device   A unit that is used for taking out data values from a computer and presenting them in the desired form to the user. Contrast with *input device*.

output media   The physical substance upon which information is recorded; for example, paper, magnetic disk, or magnetic tape.

output stream   The sequence of data to be transmitted to an output device.

outputting   The process of producing a useful information output.

overflow   In an arithmetic operation, the generation of a quantity beyond the capacity of the register or storage location that is to receive the result.

overhead   (1) A collective term for the factors that cause the performance of a program or device to be lower than it would be in the ideal case. (2) Nonproductive effort that takes place when the operating system and programs are performing administrative tasks, but not when productive work is being done.

overlap   To do something at the same time that something else is being done; for example, to perform an input operation while instructions are being executed by the central processing unit. This approach permits the computer to work on several programs at once.

overlap processing   The simultaneous execution of input, processing, and output activities by a computer system.

overlay   To transfer segments of a program from auxiliary storage into internal storage for execution so that two or more segments occupy the same storage locations at different times. This technique is used to increase the apparent size of internal storage. This is accomplished by keeping only the programs or data that are currently being accessed within internal storage; the rest is kept on a direct storage device (magnetic disk unit) until needed.

overprint The process of printing more than once at the same position in order to emphasize or improve the type.

overpunch To add holes in a card column that already contains one or more holes.

override To force a preexisting value to change in a program by superseding it.

overrun An activity that occurs whenever I/O operations initiated by a program exceeds the capability of the I/O channel.

overscan The loss of text at the end of a line if the computer and monitor are not matched properly.

overstriking The ability of a hard-copy printer to strike a character more than once to produce a boldface effect.

overwrite To place data in a location and destroy or mutilate the data previously contained in that location.

P

PABX (Private Automated Branch eXchange) A private telephone system with automatic switching. PABX equipment provides telephone communications within an office or factory, and also links up with the public telephone system.

pack To store several short units of data into a single storage cell in such a way that the individual units can later be recovered; for example, to store two 4-bit BCD digits in one 8-bit storage location. Opposite of *unpack*.

package A program or collection of programs to be used by more than one business or organization.

packet A block of data for data transmission. Each packet contains control information, such as routing, address, error control, and so forth, as well as data.

packing The process of storing two single digit numerals in a single storage byte.

packing density The number of useful storage cells per unit of area or length; for example, the number of characters per inch.

pad The rectangular contact region around the chip where the wire is bonded.

pad character *Buffer* character used to fill a *blank*.

padding A technique used to fill out a fixed-length block of information with dummy characters, items, words, or records.

paddle A graphical input device consisting of a single potentiometer, which the user actuates with a knob.

page A segment of a program or data, usually of fixed length, that has a fixed virtual address but can in fact reside in any region of the computer's internal storage. See *virtual storage*.

page frame A location in the rear storage of the computer that can store one page (which usually consists of either 2K or 4K words) of commands or data.

page-in The process of swapping programs or data from disk storage to the computer's main storage.

page-out The process of swapping programs or data from the computer's main storage to disk storage.

page printer A printer in which an entire page of characters is composed and determined within the device prior to printing.

page reader A piece of optical scanning equipment that scans many lines of information, with the scanning pattern being determined by program control and/or control symbols intermixed with input data.

page skip A control character that causes a printer to skip the rest of the current page and move to the top of the next page.

pagination The electronic manipulation of graphics and blocks of type for the purpose of setting up an entire page. The breaking up of a printed report into units that correspond to pages.

paging A technique for moving programs back and forth from real (main) storage to virtual (auxiliary) storage.

paging rate In virtual storage systems, the average number of page-ins and page-outs per unit of time.

painting (1) Displaying the trail of movement of a graphical input device. (2) In computer graphics, filling a selected area with a solid color.

PAL (Phase Alternation Line) The color television system used in most European countries.

palette The set of available colors in a computer graphics system.

PAM (Pulse Amplitude Modulation) Modulation in which the modulation wave is caused to amplitude-modulate a pulse carrier.

panel   See *control panel* and *plugboard*.

paper feed   The method by which paper is pulled through a printer. See *tractor feed mechanism*.

paper tape   A continuous strip of paper in which holes are punched to record numerical and alphanumerical information for computer processing. For example, 8-track paper tape is 2.54 centimeters (1 inch) wide, and a character is recorded by punching a code of up to eight holes across the width of the tape.

paper tape code   The system of coding that is used to relate the patterns of holes in paper tape to the alphanumeric characters they represent.

paper tape punch   A code-sensitive output device that translates computer code into an external code on paper tape.

paper tape reader   An input device used for translating the holes in a perforated paper roll into machine-processable form.

paragraph   A set of one or more COBOL sentences making up a logical processing entity and preceded by a paragraph header or name.

parallel   The simultaneous transmission or processing of the individual parts of a whole, such as the bits of a character or the characters of a word.

parallel access   The process of obtaining information from or placing information into storage where the time required for such access is dependent on the simultaneous transfer of all elements of a word from a given storage location.

parallel adder   An *adder* that performs its operations by bringing in all digits simultaneously from each of the quantities involved.

parallel circuit   An electric circuit in which the elements, branches, or components are connected between two points with one of the two ends of each component connected to each other.

parallel computer   A computer in which the digits or data lines are processed concurrently by separate units of the computer.

parallel conversion   The process of changing to a new data processing system that involves running both the old and new systems simultaneously for a period of time.

parallel input/output   Data transmission in which each bit has its own wire. All of the bits are transmitted simultaneously, as opposed to being sent one at a time (serially). Contrast with *serial input/output*.

parallel interface   An equipment boundary where information is transferred simultaneously over a set of paths.

parallel operation   The performance of several actions, usually of a similar nature, simultaneously through the provision of individual, similar, or identical devices for each such action. Contrast with *serial operation.*

parallel printing Printing an entire line of information at one time.

parallel processing Pertaining to the concurrent or simultaneous execution of two or more processes in multiple devices, such as processing units or channels. Contrast with *serial processing.*

parallel reading Row-by-row reading of a data card.

parallel run The process of running a new system or program in parallel with the old system to ensure a smooth transition and an error-free conversion.

parallel transmission In data communications, a method of data transfer in which all bits of a character are set simultaneously. Contrast with *serial transmission.*

parameter An arbitrary constant. A variable in an algebraic expression that temporarily assumes the properties of a constant. For example, in y = mx + b, m and b are parameters if either is treated as a constant in a family of lines.

parent A file whose contents are required, and in some cases are the only sources of information available, to create new records. See *child.*

parent/child relationship The passing of information from one generation to the next. Older information (*parent*) is necessary to create new information (*child*).

parity bit An extra bit added to a byte, character, or word to ensure that there is always either an even number or an odd number of bits, according to the logic of the system. If, through a hardware failure, a bit should be lost, its loss can be detected by checking the parity. The same bit pattern remains as long as the contents of the byte, character, or word remain unchanged. See *parity checking.*

parity checking Automatic error detection by using checking bits along with the numerical bits. See *parity bit.*

parsing (1) The process of separating statements into syntactic units. (2) Analyzing a character string and breaking it down into a group of more easily processed components.

partition An area in memory assigned to a program during its execution.

partitioning Subdividing a computer storage area into smaller units that are allocated to specific jobs or tasks.

parts programmer A programmer who translates the physical explanation for machining a part into a series of mathematical steps and then codes the computer instructions for those steps. See *APT* and *numerical control.*

party-line   Used to indicate a large number of devices connected to a single line originating in the central processing unit.

Pascal   A high-level language that has gained wide acceptance as a tool for both applications programming and system development. It has been implemented for a wide range of computer systems ranging from microcomputers to large mainframe facilities. Pascal is relatively easy to use, yet it is more powerful than FORTRAN or BASIC. The language provides a flexible set of control structures and data types to permit orderly program design and development; it promotes top-down program design.

Pascal, Blaise (1623–1662)   A French mathematician who built the first desk calculator-type adding machine in 1642. See *Pascal's calculator.*

Pascal's calculator   The first adding machine, designed by Blaise Pascal in the seventeenth century. This device represented the numbers from 0 to 9 with teeth on gears and could perform addition and subtraction. See *Pascal, Blaise.*

pass   (1) A complete input, processing, and output cycle in the execution of a computer program. (2) A scanning of source code by a compiler or assembler.

passive device   A device that passes signals without altering them.

password   A special word, code, or symbol that must be presented to the computer system to gain access to its resources. It identifies the user to the system.

patch   (1) A section of coding that is inserted into a program to correct a mistake or to alter the program. (2) A temporary electrical connection.

patching   (1) A makeshift technique for modifying a program or correcting programming errors by changing the object code of the program, usually to avoid recompiling or reassembling the program. (2) Making temporary patches to hardware.

path   See *channel.*

pattern recognition   The recognition of forms, shapes, or configurations by automatic means.

PC   An acronym for Personal Computer, Pocket Computer, Portable Computer, Program Counter, Printed Circuit, Pocket Calculator, and Programmed Controlled.

PCB   (Printed Circuit Board) The plastic board into which the computer's various electronic components are soldered. These are linked by thin interconnecting wires printed on its surfaces.

P-channel MOS (PMOS)   A relatively old metallic oxide semiconductor technology for *large scale integration* (LSI) devices.

PCM   (Plug Compatible Manufacturer) A business that makes computer equipment that can be plugged into existing computer systems without requiring additional hardware or software interfaces.

P-code   A method of translating a source code to an intermediate code, called p-code, by means of a compiler, then using a special P-code interpreter on a host machine to obtain an executable object code. Several versions of Pascal use P-code. See *p-system*.

PDM   (Pulse Duration Modulation) Pulse time modulation in which the duration of a pulse is varied.

PDP   A designation for computers manufactured by Digital Equipment Corporation (e.g., PDP-8, PDP-10, PDP-11, and so forth).

PEEK   A computer language instruction that allows the programmer to look at (peek at) any location in a computer's programmable memory. See *POLK*.

peek-a-boo system   A method of checking the presence or absence of punched holes in identical locations on cards by placing one card on top of another card. See *Batten system*.

pel   Picture element. See *pixel*.

peopleware   The personnel who design, program, operate, and maintain computer equipment.

perforator   A keyboard device for punching paper tape.

perform   To execute instructions in a computer.

performance   A major factor in determining the total productivity of a system. Performance is largely determined by a combination of the following factors: availability, throughput, and response time.

performance monitor   A program that keeps track of service levels being delivered by a computer system.

perfs   Perforations in paper to facilitate removing pin-fed edges and tearing continuous paper into separate pages.

periodic report   A report that provides information to users on a regular basis.

peripheral equipment   The input/output units and auxiliary storage units of a computer system. The units are attached by cables to the central processing unit. Used to get data in and data out, and to act as a reservoir for large amounts of data that cannot be held in the central processing unit at one time. The card reader, typewriter, and disk storage unit are examples of peripherals.

peripheral equipment operator   In a busy computer room, the computer operator is assigned to the console and rarely leaves it.

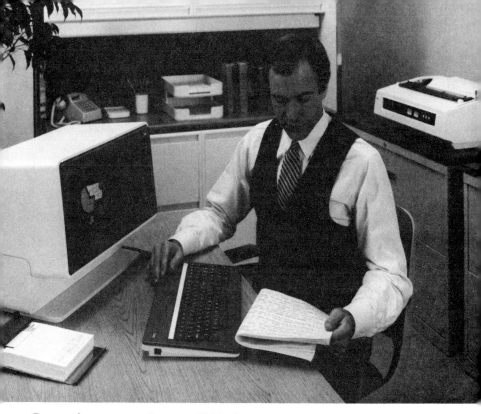

Personal computer. Courtesy NCR Corp.

Additional people assist by mounting and demounting disk packs and tapes, placing cards in the card reader, labeling outputs, and operating the various input/output devices as directed. These people are usually called peripheral equipment operators.

peripheral slots Empty slots built into the housing of some computers so that printed circuit cards can be added in order to increase capabilities without hardware modification.

permanent storage See *storage*.

personal computer A moderately priced microcomputer system that is intended for personal use rather than commercial purposes. See *microcomputer*.

personal computing The use of a personal computer (usually a microcomputer) by individuals for applications such as entertainment, home management, and education.

personal identification number (PIN) A security number that computer systems sometimes require before a user can access the system or before a point-of-sale terminal user can enter or receive information.

personalized form letter   A computer-generated form letter produced by a word processing system or a *merge-print program*.

personal microcomputer   Same as *personal computer*.

PERT   (Program Evaluation and Review Technique) A management technique for control of large-scale, long-term projects, involving analysis of the time frame required for each step in a process and the relationships of the completion of each step to activity in succeeding steps. See *critical path method*.

PET   A popular microcomputer system developed by Commodore Electronics Limited. See *microcomputer*.

petri nets   A popular and useful model for the representation of systems with concurrency or parallelism.

phased conversion   A method of system implementation in which the old information system is gradually replaced by the new one.

phonetic system   A system that uses data based on voice information (phonemes) to produce sounds that emulate speech.

phosphor   A rare earth material used to coat the inside face of cathode-ray tubes.

phosphor dots   On a cathode-ray tube display tube, the small particles of phosphor used to create an image.

photocomposition   The application of electronic processing to the preparation of print. This involves the specification and setting of type, and its production by a photographic process.

photoelectric devices   Devices that give an electrical signal in response to visible, infrared, or ultraviolet radiation.

photo-optic memory   A memory that uses an optical medium for storage. For example, a laser might be used to record on photographic film.

photoresist   The process, utilized in etching semiconductor devices, of selectively removing the oxidized surface of a silicon wafer by masking the part that is to be retained.

phototypesetter   A computer-controlled device that converts text into professional quality type. Virtually all books are typeset on a phototypesetter.

physical design   Refers to how the data is kept on storage devices and how it is accessed.

physical record   The unit of data for input or output; for example, a punched card, a tape block, or a record on a disk. One or more logical records may be contained in one physical record. Contrast with *logical record*.

pi   A number for which the symbol is π. The ratio of the circumfer-

ence to the diameter of any circle is C/D = π. An approximation
for π is 3.14159365358979932384626433 + .

pica A type size that fits ten characters into each inch of type. Also,
in phototypesetting, a sixth of an inch.

picking device An input device, such as a light pen, mouse, or
joystick, that is used to enter data on a display screen.

picosecond (*psec*) One trillionth of a second. (0.000000000001),
one thousandth of a nanosecond.

picture element See *pixel*.

picture processing See *image processing*.

picture tube A cathode-ray tube used as a television picture tube.

piezoelectric A property of some crystals that undergo mechanical
stress when subjected to voltages, or that produce a voltage when
subjected to mechanical stress.

piggyback board A small printed circuit board mounted on a
larger circuit board in order to add additional features to the larger
circuit board.

piggyback file A file capable of having records added at the end,
without having to recopy the entire file.

PILOT A textually based computer language originally designed as an
author language for *computer-assisted instruction* (CAI); however,
it is also used for teaching computer programming to beginners.
The language is composed of powerful and nearly syntax-free,
conversation-processing statements.

pilot method The act of trying a new computer system in one area
rather than on a wider range of activities. For example, the implementation of a new information system into an organization
whereby only a small part of the business uses the new system
until it has proved to be successful.

PIN See *personal identification number*.

pin compatible Chips and devices that perform identical functions
and can be substituted for one another. The devices use the same
pins for the same input/output signals.

pin feed A paper-feed system that relies on a pin-studded roller to
draw paper, punched with matching holes, into a printer.

pingpong To alternate two or more storage devices so that processing can take place on a virtually endless set of files.

pins The small metal connectors on a *DIP* that fit into sockets on a
printed circuit board.

pipeline An overlapping operating cycle function that is used to
increase the speed of computers.

pitch   The density of characters on a printed line, usually expressed in terms of characters per inch; for example, 12 pitch means twelve characters per inch.

pixel   A picture cell. The visual display screen is divided into rows and columns of tiny dots, squares, or cells. Each of these is a pixel. A pixel is the smallest unit on the display screen grid that can be stored, displayed, or addressed.

PLA   (Programmable Logic Array) An alternative to *ROM* (Read-Only Memory) that uses a standard logic network programmed to perform a specific function. PLAs are implemented in either MOS or *bipolar* circuits.

plaintext   A term used by encryption experts to denote an ordinary message in its original meaningful form.

PLANIT   (Programming LANguage for Interactive Teaching) A programming language designed for use with computer-assisted instruction (*CAI*) systems.

plasma display   A lightweight, flat, electronic display suitable for applications that demand portability and ruggedness. Dot matrix characters are produced by selectively firing cells of a neon-based gas arranged in a grid pattern. See *PLATO*.

platen   A backing, commonly cylindrical, against which printing mechanisms strike to produce an impression.

PLATO   (Programmed Logic for Automatic Teaching Operations) A computer-based instructional system that uses large computers and plasma display terminals. The system contains thousands of lessons representing sixty-five fields of study for all levels from kindergarten through graduate school. See *computer-assisted instruction* and *plasma display*.

platter   That part of a hard disk drive that actually stores the information. It is a round, flat, metallic plate covered on both surfaces with a brown magnetic substance.

PL/C   A version of the *PL/I* programming language, designed to be used in an educational environment.

PL/I   A high-level programming language designed to process both scientific and business applications. The PL/I language contains many of the best features of *FORTRAN, COBOL, ALGOL*, and other languages, as well as a number of facilities not available in previous languages.

PL/M   A programming language used to program microcomputers. The language, developed by the Intel Corporation, is a high-level language that can fully command the microcomputer to produce efficient run-time object code. PL/M was designed as a tool to help microcomputer programmers concentrate more on their problem or application and less on the actual task of programming. PL/M is derived from PL/I, a general-purpose programming language, and is usually implemented as a cross-compiler.

PL/M Plus An extended version of PL/M developed by National Semiconductor to simplify programming of their microprocessors.

plotter An output unit that graphs data by an automatically controlled pen. Data are normally plotted as a series of incremental steps. Primary types of plotters are the *drum plotter* and the *flatbed plotter*. Also called *digital plotter, incremental plotter*, and *X-Y plotter*.

plug The connector on a cable that goes to a jack on a part of the system.

plugboard A perforated board used to control the operations of unit record devices. Also called a *control panel*.

plug compatible A peripheral device that requires no interface modification in order to be linked directly to another manufacturer's computer system.

PMOS (P-channel MOS) Refers to the oldest type of MOS circuit, in which the electrical current consists of a flow of positive charges. See *NMOS*.

PN See *Polish notation*.

poaching Accessing files or program listings in search of information to which the user is not entitled.

pocket computer A portable, battery-operated, hand-held computer that can be programmed (in BASIC) to perform a wide number of applications. It is able to process small amounts of data under the control of complex stored programs. Also called a *hand-held computer*.

pointer An address or other indication of location.

point-of-sale terminal (POS) A device used in retail establishments to record sales information in a form that can be input directly into a computer. This intelligent terminal is used to capture data in retail stores (i.e., supermarkets or department stores). See *intelligent terminal* and *source data automation*.

Poisson theory A mathematical method for estimating the number of lines needed to handle a given amount of data communications traffic.

POL See *procedure-oriented language* or *problem-oriented language*.

polar A situation in which a binary 1 is represented by current flow in one direction and binary 0 by current flow in the opposite direction.

polarizing filter An accessory for terminal screens to reduce glare.

Polish notation (PN) A logical notation for a series of arithmetic operations in which no grouping symbol is used. This notation was developed by a Polish logician, Jan Lukasiewicz, in 1929. For example, the expression z = a (b + c) is represented in Polish notation as bc + a × z =, where this expression is read from left to right. Note that the operator follows the operands.

POLK A computer language instruction that is used to place a value (poke) into any location in the computer's programmable memory. See *PEEK*.

polling In data communications, scanning the networks of terminals or sensors by the computer, asking one after the other if it has any data to submit.

polyphase sort An external tape sort used for six or fewer tapes.

pooler A device for consolidating and/or converting key entry data into a form acceptable to the main computer.

pop Pulling or retrieving data from the top of a program *push down stack*. The *stack pointer* is decremented to address the last word

Pocket computer. Courtesy Radio Shack, a division of Tandy Corp.

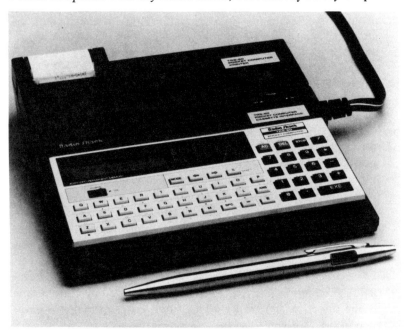

pushed on the stack. The contents of this location are moved to one of the accumulators or to another register. Also called *pull*. See *push*.

pop instruction   A computer instruction that executes the *pop* operation.

POP-2   A list processing language developed at the University of Edinburgh. See *list processing languages*.

populated board   A circuit board that contains all of its electronic components. Contrast with *unpopulated board*.

port   That portion of a computer through which a peripheral device may communicate. See *input/output channel*.

portability   Refers to the ease with which a program can be moved from one computer environment to another. Many programs written in high-level languages may be used on different machines. These programs are, therefore, portable.

portable computer   A microcomputer system that can be moved easily from one location to another. The physical size is about the same as a small typewriter. See *briefcase computer, desktop computer, microcomputer,* and *notebook computer*.

portable program   Software that can be used on different computer systems.

POS   An acronym for *point-of-sale terminal*.

positional notation   A method for expressing a quantity using two or more figures wherein the successive right-to-left figures are to be interpreted as coefficients of ascending integer powers of the radix.

positive true logic   A logic system in which a lower voltage represents a bit value of 0 and a higher voltage represents a bit value of 1.

POS systems   Department stores and supermarkets are currently using POS systems, in which the cash register is actually a special-purpose computer terminal that can monitor and record transactions directly in the store's data files for inventory control, perform checks on credit card validity, and perform other data handling functions. See *point-of-sale terminal*.

post   To enter a unit of information on a record.

post edit   To edit output data from a previous computation.

postfix notation   A notation in which operators follow the operands.

post-implementation review   Evaluation of a system after it has been in use for several months.

post mortem   Pertaining to the analysis of an operation after its completion.

post mortem dump A storage dump taken at the end of the execution of a program. See *storage dump*.

potentiometer A device used to develop electrical output signals proportional to mechanical movement.

power A symbolic representation of the number of times a number is multiplied by itself. The process is called *exponentiation*.

power amplifying circuit An electronic circuit that converts an input AC voltage into an output DC voltage.

power fail/restart A facility that enables a computer to return to normal operation after a power failure.

powerful Hardware is considered powerful if it is faster, larger, and can accomplish more work than comparable machines. Software is considered powerful if it is efficient and provides a wide range of options.

power supply Converts AC voltage to low-voltage DC. The output of a power supply is tightly regulated to keep noise pulses and voltage variations from upsetting the computer's circuits.

power surge A sudden, brief increase in the flow of current that can cause problems in the power operation of computer equipment.

pph An abbreviation for pages per hour.

PPM (Pulse Position Modulation) Pulse time modulation in which the value of each instantaneous sample of the wave modulates the position in time of a pulse.

pragmatics An investigation of the relationship between symbols and the use of those symbols.

precanned routines See *canned routines*.

precedence Rules that state which operators should be executed first in an expression. See *hierarchy*.

precision The degree of exactness with which a quantity is stated. The result of calculation may have more precision than it has accuracy; for example, the true value of π to six significant digits is 3.14159; the value of 3.14162 is precise to six digits given six digits but is accurate only to about five. See *accuracy*.

precompiler A program that checks a source program for correctness of format and sequence before the program is translated into machine language by a compiler. See *compiler*.

predefined function A standard mathematical procedure available to the user for inclusion in a program.

predefined process (1) A process that is identified only by name and that is defined elsewhere. (2) *A closed subroutine*.

predefined process symbol   A flowcharting symbol that is used to represent a subroutine.

pre-edit   See *edit.*

prefix notation   A method of forming mathematical expressions in which each operator precedes its operands; for example, in prefix notation, the expression "*x* plus *y* multiplied by *z*" would be represented by " + xy × z."

p-register   A program counter register in which the location of the current instruction is kept.

preprinted forms   Forms that can contain computer-produced output but that enter a computer system with headings and identifying information already imprinted.

preprocessor   A program that performs conversion, formatting, condensing, or other functions on input data prior to processing.

preset   To establish an initial condition, such as the control values of a loop or the initial values in index registers. See *initialize.*

pressure sensitive keyboard   A keyboard constructed of two thin plastic sheets that are coated with a circuit made of electrically conductive ink. It is an economical, flat keyboard that is used in several low-priced microcomputers.

PRESTEL   A commercial *videotex* service in Great Britain.

preventive maintenance   The process used in a computer system that attempts to keep equipment in continuous operating condition by detecting, isolating, and correcting failures before their occurrence. It involves cleaning and adjusting the equipment as well as testing the equipment under both normal and marginal conditions. Contrast with *corrective maintenance.*

primary cluster   A buildup of table entries around a single *table* location.

primary key   A unique *field* for a record. It is used to sort records for processing or to locate a particular record within a file.

primary storage   See *internal storage.*

primitive   A basic or fundamental unit, often referring to the lowest level of a machine instruction or the lowest unit of language translation.

primitive element   A graphics element, such as a line segment or point, that can be readily called up and extrapolated or combined with other primitive elements to form more complex objects or images.

print chart   A form that is used to describe the format of an output report from a printer.

Printed circuit board

print control character A control character for operations on a line printer (e.g., carriage return, page ejection, or line spacing).

print density The number of printed characters per unit of measurement (e.g., the number of characters on a page).

printed circuit (PC) An electronic circuit that is printed, vacuum deposited, or electroplated on a flat insulating sheet.

printed circuit board (PCB) A circuit board whose electrical connections are made through conductive material that is contained on the board itself, rather than with individual wires. Electrical components such as integrated circuit chips, resistors, transistors, diodes, and switches are then mounted on the board.

print element The part of a printer that actually puts the image on paper. Popular print elements are print balls, daisy wheels, and thimbles.

printer An output device that produces hard-copy output. See *electrostatic printer* and *line printer*.

printer format Printing paper divided into print zones. Only one value can be printed in each zone.

printer stand A wood or metal stand that is designed to support a printer. The stand has an opening in the top for fanfold printer paper.

Printer. Courtesy IBM Corp.

print head   The part of a printer that actually puts the image on
    paper.
print layout sheet   A chart that is used for establishing margin and
    spacing requirements for a printed report.
printout   A form of computer system output. It is printed on a page
    by a printer.
print wheel   A single element providing the character set at one
    printing position of a wheel printer.
print zone   In BASIC programming, a fixed-length area on an output
    device within which data are aligned in columns.
priority interrupt   An interrupt that is given preference over other
    interrupts within the system.
priority processing   The processing of a sequence of jobs on the
    basis of assigned priorities. See *job queue.*
private automatic branch exchange (PABX)   A private auto-
    matic telephone switching system that controls the transmission of
    calls to and from the public telephone network.
privately leased line   A communications line intended for the use
    of a single customer.
privileged instruction   A computer instruction that is not available
    for use in ordinary programs written by users; its use is restricted

to the routines of the operating system. See *storage key* and *storage protection*.

probabilistic model   A model that makes use of the mathematics of probability. It is used to analyze data whose individual values are known but whose long-range behavior can be predicted.

probability   Probability measures the odds of a given event taking place. For example, if you flip a coin, the probability is one out of two that it will show heads and one out of two that it will show tails.

probability theory   A measure of the likelihood of occurrence of a chance event. It is used to predict the behavior of a group.

problem definition   The formulation of the logic used to define a problem. A description of a task to be performed.

problem-oriented language (POL)   A programming language designed for the convenient expression of a given class of problems. Contrast with *assembly language, machine language*, and *procedure-oriented language*. See *APT, COGO, GPSS*, and *RPG*.

problem program   A program that is executed when the central processing unit is in the "problem state"; that is, any program that does not contain privileged instructions.

procedure   (1) A portion of a high-level language program that performs a specific task necessary for the program. (2) A computer program.

procedure division   One of the four main component parts of a *COBOL* program. The procedure division specifies the procedures to be performed by the *object program* by means of English-like statements.

procedure-oriented language (POL)   A high-level, machine-independent, programming language designed for the convenient expression of procedures used in the solution of a wide class of problems. Examples include *FORTRAN, COBOL*, and *PL/I*. Contrast with *assembly language, machine language,* and *problem-oriented language*. See *Ada, ALGOL, APL, BASIC, C, COBOL, FORTH, FORTRAN, JOVIAL, LOGO, NELIAC, Pascal, PILOT, PLANIT, PL/I, SIMSCRIPT, SNOBOL*, and *WATFOR*.

process   A systematic sequence of operations to produce a specified result. To transform raw data into useful information.

process bound   A situation in which the computer system is limited by the speed of the processor.

process control   The use of the computer to control industrial processes such as oil refining and steel production.

process control computer   A digital computer used in a process control system. Process control computers are generally limited in instruction capacity, word length, and accuracy. They are designed for continuous operation in nonair-conditioned facilities.

process conversion   Changing the method of running the computer system.

processing   The computer manipulation of data in solving a problem. See *data processing*.

processing symbol   A flowcharting symbol used to indicate a processing operation (e.g., a calculation). A rectangular-shaped figure is used to represent this symbol.

processor   A device or system capable of performing operations upon data; for example, *central processing unit* (hardware) or *compiler* (software). A compiler is sometimes referred to as a *language processor*.

processor bound   Refers to processes that are slowed down by the time it takes the central processing unit to perform the actual processing or computations. Contrast with *I/O bound*. Same as *compute bound*.

product   The quantity that results from multiplying two quantities.

production run   The execution of a debugged program that routinely accomplishes the purpose of the program. For example, running a payroll program to produce weekly paychecks is a production run.

productivity   A measure of the work performed by a software/hardware system. Productivity largely depends on a combination of two factors: the facility (ease of use) of the system and the performance (*throughput*, response time, and availability) of the system.

program   (1) A sequence of instructions that permits a computer to perform a particular task. (2) A plan to achieve a problem solution. (3) To design, write, and test one or more routines. (4) Loosely, a *routine*.

program card   A card that is punched with specific coding and used to control the automatic operations of keypunch and verifier machines.

program chaining   A process of linking programs or program sections together. This allows programs that are larger than *internal memory* to be executed through sequential loading and execution of successive sections or modules of that program.

program coding   The process of writing instructions in a programming lanuage.

program control   Descriptive of a system in which a computer is used to direct the operation of the system.

program correctness   See *program testing*.

program counter   A counter that indicates the location of the next program instruction to be executed by the computer. Same as *instruction counter*.

program deck   A set of punched cards containing instructions that make up a computer program.

program development cycle   The steps involved in the solution of a problem with a computer: problem analysis, algorithm development, coding, program testing, and documentation.

program flowchart   A diagram composed of symbols, directional lines, and information about how the computer will be used to solve a problem. Contrast with *system flowchart*. See *flowchart*.

program generator   See *generator*.

program graph   A graphical representation of a program.

program ID   Program identification.

program language   See *programming language*.

program library   A collection of available computer programs and routines. Same as *library*. See *disk library* and *tape library*.

program listing   See *listing*.

programmable calculator   A calculatorlike device with certain computerlike features; e.g., a calculator that can execute a program written in the BASIC programming language.

programmable communications interface   An interface board used for communications control.

programmable function key   A keyboard key whose function changes with the programs within the computer.

programmable logic array.   A device that provides the sum of a partial product with outputs for a given set of inputs.

programmable memory   A content-changeable memory, usually where most computer programs and data are stored. It is usually *RAM* or *PROM* memory. Contrast with *ROM*. See *storage*.

programmable read-only memory (PROM)   A memory that can be programmed by electrical pulses. Once programmed, it is read-only. A special machine (called a *PROM programmer*) is used to write in the new program.

program maintenance   The process of keeping programs up-to-date by correcting errors, making changes as requirements change, and altering the programs to take advantage of equipment changes.

programmed check   A check consisting of tests inserted into the programmed statement of a problem and performed by the use of computer instructions.

programmed labels   To make the identification of disk and tape files more reliable, most programs include a built-in routine that creates a label record at the beginning of the file.

programmer   A person whose job it is to design, write, and test programs and the instructions that get the computer to do a specific job. Also called *computer programmer*. See *coder* and *parts programmer*.

programmer board   A board that allows a user to program *PROM* or *EPROM* memories for use in his or her computer system. See *PROM programmer*.

programming   The process of translating a problem from its physical environment to a language that a computer can understand and obey. The process of planning the procedure for solving a problem. This may involve, among other things, the analysis of the problem, coding of the problem, establishing input/output formats, establishing testing and checkout procedures, allocation of storage, preparation of documentation, and supervision of the running of the program on a computer.

programming aids   Computer programs that aid computer users (e.g., compilers, debugging packages, linkage editors, and mathematical subroutines).

programming analyst   A person skilled in the definition development of techniques and computer programs for the solution of a problem. See *programmer* and *systems analyst*.

programming language   A language used to express computer programs. See *Ada, ALGOL, APL, APT, BASIC, C, COBOL, COGO, FORTH, FORTRAN GPSS, ICES, JOVIAL, LOGO, NELIAC, Pascal, PILOT, PLANIT, PL/C, PL/I, PL/M, problem-oriented language, procedure-oriented language, SIMSCRIPT, SNOBOL,* and *WATFOR*.

programming linguistics   Languages for communication between any two systems, be they mechanical, electrical, or human, can be described by the three interconnected concepts of *syntax, semantics*, and *pragmatics*.

programming team A group of individuals assigned to a programming project. See *chief programmer.*

program specifications A document that identifies the data requirements of a system, the files required, the input/output specifications, and the processing details.

program stack An area of computer memory set aside for temporary storage of data and instructions, particularly during an *interrupt.* See *pop, push, push down list, push down stack,* and *stack.*

program stop A stop instruction built into the program that will automatically stop the computer under certain conditions, upon reaching the end of the processing, or upon completing the solution of a problem.

program storage A portion of the internal storage reserved for the storage of programs, routines, and subroutines. In many systems, protection devices are used to prevent inadvertent alteration of the contents of the program storage.

program switch A point in a programming routine at which two courses of action are possible, the correct one being determined by a condition prevailing elsewhere in the program or by a physical disposition of the system.

program testing Executing a program with test data to ascertain that it functions as expected.

projecting Producing a two-dimensional graphics display of a three-dimensional scene.

projection An extensison of past trends into the future.

project manager A person who takes responsibility for the enforcement of a project's goals. Sometimes called a project team leader.

PROM (Programmable Read-Only Memory) A memory that can be programmed by electrical pulses. Once programmed, it is read-only. The PROM chips can be purchased blank and then programmed by using a *PROM programmer.*

PROM burner See *PROM programmer.*

PROM programmer A device used to program PROMs (Programmable Read Only Memories) and reprogram EPROMs (Erasable PROMs) by electrical pulses. Sometimes called PROM burner. See *PROM.*

prompt A character or message provided by the computer to indicate that it is ready to accept keyboard input.

proofing program Same as a *dictionary program.*

propagated error An error or mistake occurring in one operation and affecting data required for subsequent operations so that the error or mistake is spread through much of the processed data.

propagation delay   A time delay in a satellite communications system.

proportional spacing   If the horizontal space allotted to a printed character is proportional to the width of that character, the spacing is said to be proportional.

proprietary   An adjective meaning "held in private ownership" but usually applied to software to indicate that it is the property of the author and may not be occupied or resold.

protected storage   Storage locations reserved for special purposes in which data cannot be stored without undergoing a screening procedure to establish suitability for storage therein.

protocol   A set of procedures or conventions used routinely between equipment such as terminals and computers.

prototype   The first version or model of a software package or computer hardware device or system ready for preproduction testing.

proving   Testing a machine in order to demonstrate that it is free from faults, usually after corrective maintenance.

psec   An abbreviation for picosecond; one trillionth of a second.

pseudocode   An arbitrary system of symbols used to represent operators, operands, operations, index registers, and so forth.

pseudolanguage   A language, not directly understandable by a computer, that is used to write computer programs. Before a pseudoprogram can be used, it must be translated into a language that the computer understands (*machine language*). Same as *symbolic language*.

pseudo-operation   An operation that is not part of the computer's operation repertoire as realized by hardware; hence, an extension of the set of machine operations.

pseudorandom number   A number generated by a computer in a deterministic manner. These numbers have been subjected to many statistical tests of randomness and, for most practical purposes, can be used as *random numbers*.

p-system   A microcomputer operating system. One of the principal advantages of the p-system is that programs written for it will work on a wide variety of machines. It translates p-code into the machine language appropriate to a specific computer. See *p-code*.

publication language   A well-defined form of a programming language suitable for use in publications. A language such as this is necessary because some languages use special characters that are not available in common type fonts.

public domain software Software that is not protected by copyright laws and is therefore free for all to reproduce without fear of legal prosecution.

public network A communications service that is open to anyone, usually on a fee basis.

pull See *pop*.

pull instruction An instruction that pulls or retrieves data from the top of the program *push down stack*. Same as *pop instruction*.

pulse An abrupt change in voltage, either positive or negative, that conveys information to a circuit.

pulse modulation Use of a series of pulses that are modulated or characterized to convey information. Types of pulse modulation include amplitude (*PAM*), position (*PPM*), and duration (*PDM*) systems.

punched card A cardboard card, used in data processing operations, in which tiny rectangular holes at hundreds of individual locations denote numerical values and alphanumeric codes. See *Hollerith card* and *ninety-six column card*.

punched card code A code used to represent data on cards. See *Hollerith code*.

punched paper tape See *paper tape*.

punched tape code See *paper tape code*.

punching position One of the divisions of a card column into which a hole may be punched.

punching station The area on the keypunch and card punch machine where a card is aligned for the punching process.

pure procedure A procedure that never modifies any part of itself during execution.

purge To erase a file.

push Putting data into the top location of a *program stack*. The *stack pointer* is automatically incremented to point to the next location, which becomes the top of the stack. Also called *put*. See *pop*.

push down list A list written from the bottom up, with each new entry placed on the top of the list. The item to be processed first is the one on the top of the list. See *LIFO (last in-first out)*.

push down stack A set of memory locations or registers in a computer that implements a *push down list*.

push instruction A computer instruction that implements a push operation.

push-pop stack A register that receives information from the program counter and stores the address locations of instructions on a *last-in-first-out* basis. Two operations are involved in stack processing: "pushing" describes the filling of the *stack* from *registers*; "popping" involves emptying the stack for transfer to registers.

push up list A list of items in which each item is entered at the end of the list and the other items maintain their same relative position in the list.

put See *push*.

quad-density A term used to specify the data storage density of a computer disk system. Quad-density systems can store up to four items the data that can be stored on single-density disks.

quality control A technique for evaluating the quality of a product being processed by checking it against a predetermined standard and taking the proper corrective action if the quality falls below the standard.

quantify To assign numeric vlues to nonnumeric objects.

quantity A positive or negative real number.

quantum The smallest unit of measure employed in a system.

quasi language See *pseudolanguage*.

QUBE An information utility that is part of an advanced cable-TV system providing viewers everything from first-run movies to special programs for doctors and lawyers. It is an interactive *Viewdata*-type service.

query language A set of commands used to extract from a data base the data that meet specific criteria. Same as *data manipulation language*.

query response A message sent to a computer terminal in answer to a specific request from the operator.

question-answer The process of interacting with the computer. The computer asks the user a question and the user provides the answer.

queue A group of items waiting to be acted upon by the computer. The arrangement of items determines the processing priority.

queued access method Any *access method* that automatically synchronizes the transfer of data between the program using the access method and the input/output devices, thereby eliminating delays for input/output operations.

queuing A method of controlling the information processing sequence.

queuing theory A form of probability theory useful in studying delays or lineups at servicing points. A research technique concerned with the correct sequential orders of moving units. May include sequence assignments for bits of information or whole messages.

quibinary code A *binary coded decimal* code that is used to represent decimal numbers in which each *decimal digit* is represented by seven binary digits. See *binary digit* and *decimal number*.

quiescent state The time during which a circuit element is not performing its active function in the circuit.

quotient A result obtained by division.

QWERTY keyboard The name given to the normal typewriter layout for keyboards; named after the first six letters on the top row of the alpha section. This keyboard layout is found on most computer keyboards. See *Dvorak keyboard*.

R

radian A central angle subtended in a circle by an arc whose length is equal to the radius of the circle. Thus the radian measure of an angle is the ratio of the arc it subtends to the radius of the circle in which it is the central angle (a constant ratio for all such circles). A straight line (180-degree angle) has an angle of π (3.1415927 radians); a 90-degree angle is 1.5707963 radians, or $\pi/2$. Trigonometric functions in many high-level programming languages work on radians rather than degrees.

Radio Shack A manufacturer and distributor of electronic equipment, including microcomputer systems. A division of the *Tandy Corporation*.

radix The base number in a number system (e.g., the radix in the decimal system is 10). Synonymous with *base*.

radix complement See *complement*.

radix point In a number system, the character (a dot) or implied character that separates the integral part of a numeral from the fractional part; for example, *binary point, hexadecimal point*, and *octal point*.

radix sorting Same as *digital sorting*.

ragged left Refers to text printed with a straight right margin and an uneven left margin. Also called flush right.

ragged right Text printed with a straight left margin and an uneven right margin. Also called flush left.

raised flooring Elevated flooring used in computer rooms so that connecting cables can be laid directly between equipment units.

RALU (Register, Arithmetic, and Logic Unit) A major part of a microprocessor when arithmetic and logic operations are performed.

RAM (Random Access Memory) A memory into which the user can call up data (read) or enter information and instructions (write). RAM is the "working memory" of the computer into which applications programs can be loaded from outside and then executed.

RAM card A printed circuit board containing RAM chips. By plugging such a board into some computers, their internal storage can be expanded.

random access The process of obtaining data from or placing data into a storage location in which access is independent of the order of storage.

random access memory A memory whose contents can be read or written on directly without regard to any other memory location. See *RAM*.

random files Files not organized in any sequence. Data are retrieved based on the address of the record on the direct access device.

random logic design Designing a system using *discrete* logic circuits.

random number A patternless sequence of digits. An unpredictable number, produced by chance, that satisfies one or more of the tests for randomness. See *pseudorandom number*.

random number generator A computer program or hardware designed to produce a *pseudorandom number* or series of pseudorandom numbers according to specified limitations.

range check A range check is usually applied to a code in order to verify that it falls within a given set of characters or numbers.

rank (1) To arrange in an ascending or descending series according to importance. (2) A measure of the relative position in a group, series, array, or classification.

raster   A grid. A device that stores and displays data as horizontal rows of uniform grid or picture cells (*pixels*). Raster scan devices re-create or "refresh" a display screen thirty to sixty times a second in order to provide a clear image for viewing.

raw data   Data that have not been processed. Such data may or may not be on machine-readable media.

read   To get information from any input or file storage media. For example, reading punched cards by detecting the pattern of holes, or reading a magnetic disk by sensing the patterns of magnetism.

reader   Any device capable of transcribing data from an input medium.

read head   A magnetic head that is designed and used to read data from the media. Contrast with *write head*.

reading station   The part of a punched card machine where a data card is aligned for reading by a sensing mechanism.

reading wand   A device that senses marks and codes optically; for example, a device that reads price tags in a *point-of-sale terminal*.

read ink   See *nonreflective ink*.

read-only memory (ROM)   A special type of computer memory. It is permanently programmed with one group of frequently used instructions. Read-only memory does not lose its program when the computer's power is turned off, but the program cannot be changed by the user. In many microcomputers, the BASIC language interpreter and operating systems are contained in read-only memory. Several of the newer microcomputers use plug-in read-only memory modules that contain special programs (i.e., game programs, educational programs, business programs, and so on). See *EPROM, firmware, PROM, ROM*, and *solid state cartridge*.

read-only storage   See *read-only memory*.

readout   The manner in which a computer presents the processed information (e.g., *visual display, line printer, digital plotter*, and so forth).

read/write head   A small electromagnet used to read, write, or erase data on a magnetic storage device (i.e., disk, tape, drum, magnetic card). See *read head* and *write head*.

real constant   A number that contains a decimal point; that is, 26.4 or -349.0. Also called a floating-point constant.

real number   Any rational or irrational number.

real storage   The internal storage in a *virtual memory* system.

real time   Descriptive of on-line computer processing systems that receive and process data quickly enough to produce output to control, direct, or affect the outcome of an ongoing activity or process. For example, in an airline resesrvations system, a customer-booking inquiry is entered into the computer to see whether space is available. If a seat is booked, the file of available seats is updated immediately, thus giving an up-to-date record of seats reserved and seats available.

real-time clock   A piece of hardware that interrupts the processor at fixed time intervals to synchronize the operations of the computer with events occurring in the outside world, often involving human/computer interaction.

real-time image generation   Performance of the computations necessary to update an image is completed within the *refresh* rate, so the sequence appears correctly to the viewer. An example is flight simulation, in which thousands of computations must be performed to present an animated image, all within the 30–60 cycles per second rate at which the frames change.

real-time output   Output data removed from a system at a time of need by another system.

real-time systems   Computer systems in which the computer is required to perform its tasks within the time restraints of some process or simultaneously with the system it is assisting. Usually, the computer must operate faster than the system assisted in order to be ready to intervene appropriately.

reasonableness check   A technique whereby tests are made on processed data to indicate whether a gross error exists. Programming instructions would check if the data lies within present upper and lower limits and initiate some action if the data are not reasonable.

reboot   To stop and *boot* the operating system again. A reboot usually occurs by human intervention as the result of a problem. It is similar to "reset" on a home appliance.

receive only   A designation used to indicate the read-only capabilities of equipment lacking keyboards and input equipment.

recompile   To compile a program again, usually after debugging or because the program needs to be run on a different type of computer.

reconstruction   Restoring the data base system to a previous state after data have been tampered with or destroyed.

record   A collection of related items of data treated as a unit. See *item.*

record gap   See *interrecord gap.*

recording density The number of useful storage cells per unit of length or area; for example, the number of characters per inch on a magnetic tape or the number of bits per inch on a single track of a disk. Also called *packing density*. The most common magnetic tape densities are 800, 1600, and 6250 characters per inch (cpi). A recording density of 6250 cpi on tape means that there are 6250 characters per inch.

record layout The arrangement and structure of data in a record, including the size and sequence of its components.

record length A measure of the size of a record, usually specified in units such as words, bytes, or characters; for example, the number of bytes per data record in file.

recover To continue program execution after a failure.

recoverable error An error condition that can be sensed and corrected, thereby allowing continued operation of a program.

rectifier An electrical device that changes alternating current into a direct current.

recurring costs Includes personnel, supplies, equipment rental, and overhead costs associated with a computer system.

recursion A set of operations or program statements in which one of the operations or statements is specified in terms of the entire set. The continued repetition of the same operation(s).

recursive Pertaining to a process that is inherently repetitive. The result of each repetition is usually dependent upon the result of the previous repetition.

recursive procedure A procedure (*A*) that, while being executed, either calls itself or calls another procedure (*B*), which in turn calls procedure *A*.

recursive subroutine A subroutine capable of calling itself, or a subroutine that invokes another subroutine, which in turn invokes the original subroutine.

red-green-blue monitor A *high resolution* color display unit.

reduction The process of saving computer storage by eliminating empty fields or unnecessary data to reduce the size of the length of records.

redundancy The duplication of a feature in order to prevent system failure in the event of the feature's malfunction.

redundancy check A check based on the transfer of more bits or characters than the minimum number required to express the message itself, the added bits or characters having been inserted systematically for checking purposes. See *parity bit* and *parity checking*.

redundant code   A *binary coded decimal* value with an added check bit.

redundant information   A message expressed in such a way that the essence of the information occurs in several ways.

reel   A mounting for a roll of tape.

reentrant   Pertaining to a routine that can be used by two or more independent programs at the same time.

reentrant code   Assembly-generated *machine language* programs that may be shared simultaneously by any number of users.

reentrant subroutine   In a multiprogramming system, a subroutine of which only one copy resides in internal storage. This copy is shared by several programs.

reference manual   A manual designed to describe how a piece of equipment or a program works.

reflectance   In *optical scanning*, a relative value assigned to a character or color of ink when compared with the background.

reflectance ink   In *optical scanning*, ink that has a reflectance level that very nearly approximtes the acceptable paper reflectance level for a particular *optical character reader*.

reflected code   Same as *gray code*.

reformat   To change the representation of data from one format to another.

refresh   (1) A signal sent to *dynamic RAM* every few milliseconds to help it remember data. (2) To rerecord an image on cathode-ray tube screen when it begins to fade. Typically, the image must be regenerated at a rate of 30 to 60 hertz (cycles per second) to avoid flicker.

regenerate   The process of renewing some quantity. Used in storage devices to write back information that has been read in a destructive manner.

register   A high-speed device used in a central processing unit for temporary storage of small amounts of data or intermittent results during processing.

registration   The accurate positioning relative to a reference.

regression analysis   A technique in model-building that is used to define a dependent variable in terms of a set of independent variables.

regression testing   Tests performed on a previously verified program whenever it is extended or corrected.

relation   The equality, inequality, or any property that can be said to hold (or not hold) for two objects in a specified order.

relational data base   A data base organizational method that organizes data into arrays of rows (records) and columns (fields). One of the major features of a relational data base is the ability to generate a new file with data from two relational files.

relational expression An expression that contains one or more relational operators. See *relational operator.*

relational model A data base model in which items are functionally related.

relational operator A symbol used to compare two values; the operator specifies a condition that may be either true or false, such as = (equal to), < (less than), > (greater than), and so on.

relative address An address to which a *base address* must be added in order to form the *absolute address* of a particular storage location.

relative coding Coding that uses machine instructions with relative addresses. See *relative address.*

relay A magnetically operated switch used in preelectronic computers.

release version The version of a program that is currently available for purchase.

reliability A measure of the ability of a system or individual hardware device to function without failure.

relocatable addresses The addresses used in a program that can be positioned at almost anyplace in internal storage.

relocatable program A program existing in a form that permits it to be loaded and executed in any available region of a computer's internal storage.

relocate A program coded so that it may be executed anywhere in computer storage.

remainder The dividend minus the product of the quotient and divisor.

remark Verbal messages inserted into a source language program that do not cause any computer processing steps but are helpful notes for future users who may later attempt to understand or alter the program.

remote access Communication with a computer facility by a station (or stations) that is distant from the computer.

remote batch processing The processing of data in batches at a remote location by using a small computer system. See *batch processing.*

remote computing services Services offered to customers by computer service centers. Examples are batch processing, interactive problem solving, consulting, and so on.

remote job entry (RJE)   Refers to the computer programs used to submit processing jobs from remote terminals.

remote processing   The processing of computer programs through an input/output device that is remotely connected to a computer system. See *remote batch processing*.

remote station   See *remote terminal*.

remote terminal   A device for communicating with computers from sites that are physically separated from the computer, often distant enough so that communications facilities such as telephone lines are used rather than direct cables. See *terminal*.

repeat counter   A program counter that records the number of times an event takes place in a program for later comparison.

repeating decimal number   A nonterminating decimal number, such as .3333333 . . . or .31282828. . . .

repeat key   A keyboard key that can be held down so that it repeatedly makes contact without need for additional pressing.

reperforator   A paper tape punch.

repertoire   A complete set of instructions that belongs to a specific computer or family of computers.

repetition instruction   An instruction that causes one or more instructions to be executed an indicated number of times.

replacement theory   The mathematics of deterioration and failure, used to estimate replacement costs and determine optimum replacement policies.

report   Usually associated with output data; involves the grouping of related facts so as to be easily understood by the reader. A common means of presenting information to users.

report file   A file generated during data processing, usually used to print out or display desired output.

report generator   A program that converts machine-readable data into a printed report organized for a specific purpose. See *RPG*.

report program generator   See *RPG*.

reproduce   To copy information on a similar medium; for example, to obtain a duplicate disk pack from a specific disk pack.

reproducer   See *reproducing punch*.

reproducing punch   A device for duplicating decks of cards. The reproducing punch is capable of giving an exact copy of a master deck, or a copy of the deck may be punched in a different format.

reprogramming   Changing a program written for one computer so that it will run on another.

reprographics   A technique of producing output by which the computer is connected to a phototypesetting machine and the output is produced on photographic "repro" paper.

request for proposal (RFP)   A document sent to hardware/software vendors requesting them to propose equipment and software to meet system specifications.

request for quotation (RFQ)   A document sent to hardware/software vendors requesting them to quote prices for equipment and/of software that meets system requirements.

rerun   To repeat all or part of a program on a computer, usually because of a correction, a false start, or an interrupt.

reserve accumulator   An auxiliary storage register allied to the main accumulator in a central processing unit. See *accumulator*.

reserved words   Certain words that, because they are reserved by operating systems, language translators, and so on for their own use, cannot be used in an applications program.

reset   (1) To return computer components to a specified static state. (2) To place a binary cell into the zero state.

reset key   A key on a keyboard that normally is used to *reset* the parts of a computer.

resident program   A program that occupies a dedicated area of internal storage.

residual value   The value of a piece of equipment at the end of a lease term.

resilient   A system capable of continuing execution despite failure.

resistor   A component of an electric circuit that produces heat while offering opposition, or resistance, to the flow of electric current.

resolution   The density and overall quality of a video display. The number of pixels on the picture screen. A high-resolution picture looks smooth and realistic. It is produced by a large number of pixels. A low-resolution picture is blocky and jagged. It is produced by a small number of pixels. See *pixel*.

resource   Any component of a computer configuration. Memory, printers, visual displays, disk storage units, software, and operating personnel are all considered resources.

resource allocation   The sharing of computer resources among competing tasks.

resource sharing   The sharing of one central processor by several users as well as several peripheral devices.

response position   In *optical scanning*, the area designated for marking information on an OMR form.

response time   The time it takes the computer system to react to a given input. It is the interval between an event and the system's response to the event.

restart To resume the execution of a program.

retrieval The extraction of data from a data base or files.

retrieving The process of making stored information available when needed.

retrofit To update or add to an existing system in order to improve it.

return A set of instructions at the end of a subroutine that permits control to return to the proper point in the main program.

return key A key on a computer keyboard that is used to make the display cursor or a printer carriage move to the beginning of the next line.

reusable The attribute of a *routine* that permits the same copy of the routine to be used by two or more tasks.

reverse Polish notation See *Polish notation*.

reverse video A term used to indicate, in some video terminals, the ability to display black characters on a white (or green) background.

rewind To return a magnetic tape to its starting position.

rewrite To erase and reset.

RF (Radio Frequency) The general term for a broad spectrum of electromagnetic radiation ranging in frequency from 10,000 to 40 billion cycles per second. RF radiation has been used primarily for the purpose of communication.

RF modulator A device that modulates a data communication channel with an information signal.

RGB A form of color video signal (red, green, blue), distinctly different from the composite color video used in standard television sets. RGB can be displayed only on a color monitor that has a separate electron gun for each of these primary colors. Ordinary color television sets use only one gun. RGB displays are noted for their crisp, bright colors and high *resolution*.

ribbon cartridge A plastic holder that contains a printer ribbon.

right justify See *justify*.

rigid disk Same as *hard disk*.

ring A cyclic arrangement of data elements. See *circular list*.

ring network A computer network in which each computer is connected to adjacent computers.

ripple sort See *bubble sort*.

RI/SME (Robotics International of the Society of Manufacturing Engineers) This professional organization directs itself toward engineers interested in the design and use of robots.

RJE   (Remote Job Entry) Refers to the programs used to submit processing jobs from terminals.

RO   (Receive Only) A designation used to indicate the read-only capabilities of teletypewriters and other equipment lacking keyboards and of paper tape input equipment.

robot   A computer-controlled device equipped with sensing instruments for detecting input, signals, or environmental conditions, with a calculating mechanism for making decisions, and with a guidance mechanism for providing control. See *ML, ROBOTLAN,* and *VAL.*

robot control languages   Languages for programs that are designed to control robots. *VAL, AL, ML,* and *ROBOTLAN* are examples of these languages.

robotics   An area of artificial intelligence related to robots. The science of robot design and use.

ROBOTLAN   A programming language used to control robots.

rod memory   A computer storage consisting of wires coated with a nickel-iron alloy and cut in such a way as to form stacks of rods. See *thin film.*

rollback   A system that will restart the running program after a system failure. Snapshots of data and programs are stored at periodic intervals, and the system rolls back to restart at the last recorded snapshot.

roll out   To record the contents of internal storage in auxiliary storage.

rollover   A property of some keyboards. It is a feature that prevents keys from getting stuck when two or more keys are depressed.

roll paper   Printer paper in continuous form on a spool.

ROM   (Read-Only Memory) Generally, a solid state storage chip that is programmed at the time of its manufacture and cannot be reprogrammed by the computer user. Also called firmware, since this implies software that is permanent or firmly in place on a chip.

ROM cartridge   A read-only memory module that contains a preprogrammed function (i.e., a game, an educational program, a business system, and so on). The module is plugged into the computer. See *firmware* and *read-only memory.*

ROM simulator   A general-purpose device that is used to replace ROMs or PROMs in a system during program checkout. Because it offers real-time in-circuit simulation, it can be used in the engineering prototype or reproduction model to find and correct program errors or in the production model to add new features. See *PROM* and *ROM*.

rotation   In computer graphics, the turning of a computer-modeled object relative to an origin point on a coordinate system.

rotational delay   The time it takes for a record contained on one of the sectors of a disk to rotate under the read/write head.

RO terminal   A data communications machine capable only of receiving and not of transmitting.

round   See *round off*.

round off   To truncate the rightmost digit of a number, and to increase by 1 the now remaining rightmost digit if the truncated digit is greater than or equal to half of the number base. For example, the base 10 number 463.1076 would be rounded to 463.108, and the number 23.602 would be rounded to 23.60.

round-off error   The error resulting from rounding off a quantity by deleting the less significant digits and applying the same rule of correction to the part retained; for example, 0.2751 can be rounded to 0.275 with a round-off error of .0001. Contrast with *truncation error*.

round robin   A scheduling method that engages each device and process at its turn in a fixed cycle.

routine   A set of machine instructions for carrying out a specific processing operation. Sometimes used as a synonym for *program*.

routing   The assignment of a path for the delivery of a message.

row   (1) The horizontal members of one line of an array. (2) One of the horizontal lines of punching positions on a punched card. Contrast with *column*.

RPG   (Report Program Generator) A popular business-oriented programming language. The language will allow a user to program many business operations as well as to generate reports. A fairly simple RPG program can perform a rather sophisticated business task. The language is relatively easy to learn.

RPROM   An acronym for reprogrammable PROM. See *EPROM*.

RS-232   A data communicatioins industry standard for the *serial transmission* of data to a peripheral device, such as a printer, a video monitor, a plotter, and so forth. Most microcomputers provide for an RS-232 interface.

rubberbanding   A computer graphics technique that is used to construct lines and contours.

ruggedized computer   A computer designed to be used in special environments; for example, aboard a space vehicle, on a ship, in a missile, in a submarine, in a tank, in farm equipment, and so on.

run The single and continuous execution of a program by a computer on a given set of data.

run manual A manual or book documenting the processing system, program logic, controls, programs changes, and operating instructions associated with a computer run.

run time The time during which the data are fetched by the control unit and the actual processing is performed in the *arithmetic-logic unit*. Also called *execution time*. Contrast with *compilation time*.

S

sales representative A person who sells computers and related equipment and software. Most representatives work for computer manufacturers, service organizations, or computer stores.

SAM (Sequential Access Method) A method for storing and retrieving data on a disk file.

sample data A set of hypothetical data used to see if a flowchart is logical and if a program works. See *test data*.

sampling Obtaining a value of a variable at regular or intermittent intervals.

sampling rate The frequency at which *sampling* occurs.

sapphire A material used as a substrate for some types of integrated circuit chips.

satellite An earth-orbiting device that is capable of relaying communications signals over long distances.

satellite communications The use of orbiting transponders or microwave relays to transmit information around the world.

satellite computer (1) An additional computer, usually smaller, that supports a larger computer system. An economy of processing can be effected if the satellite computer handles lower-level functions such as remote terminal coordination, data validity checking, code conversion, and input/output functions. (2) An off-line auxiliary computer.

save To store a program somewhere other than in the computer's internal memory; for example, on a cassette tape or diskette.

SBC (1) An acronym for Small Business Computer, a small-sized computer capable of performing a variety of basic business applications. (2) An acronym for Single Board Computer, a board with *CPU, ROM, RAM,* and peripheral interfaces.

scalar value An integer declared as such in a programming language and possessing a value within a fixed range.

scale To adjust the magnitude of a quantity so as to fit it in the available storage location.

scale factor One or more factors used to multiply or divide quantities occurring in a problem and to convert them into a desired range, such as the range from +1 to −1.

scaling The process of changing the size of an image. For example, scaling by a factor of four multiples all dimensions of an image by 4.

scan (1) To examine point by point in logical sequence. (2) An algorithmic procedure for visiting or listing each node of a data structure. (3) The operation required to produce an image on a television screen.

scan area That area of a form or document that contains information to be scanned by an *optical character reader.*

scan line A horizontal line on a raster display screen.

scanner Any optical device that can recognize a specific set of visual symbols.

scanner channel A device that polls individual channels to see if they have data ready to be transmitted.

scanning The rapid examination of every item in a computer's list of data to see whether a specific condition is met.

scan path In *optical scanning,* a predetermined area within the clear area where data to be read must be located. The position of the scan path and the amount of data that can be read will generally depend upon the machine involved.

scatter plot Shows a two-variable frequency distribution by plotting a dot or symbol at each data point. Sometimes a line or curve is added to show the correlation (if there is one) between the variables represented on the two axes. Also called scatter diagram.

scatter read-gather write Scatter read refers to placing information from an input record into nonadjacent storage areas. Gather write refers to placing information from nonadjacent storage areas into single physical record.

SCDP (Society of Certified Data Processors) An organization formed to represent exclusively the interests and wishes of the holder of the Certificate in Data Processing (*CDP*).

scheduled report A report produced at a regular interval to provide routine information to users.

schedule maintenance Maintenance of a computer system at fixed intervals in order to increase its reliability.

scheduler A program that schedules jobs for processing.

scheduling The task of determining what the succession of programs should be in a multiprogramming computer center.

SCHEMA A high-level computer language used by the data base administrator to define the structure of the data base.

schematic A diagram of an electronic circuit showing connections and identification of compoments.

schematic symbols Symbols used in schematic diagrams:

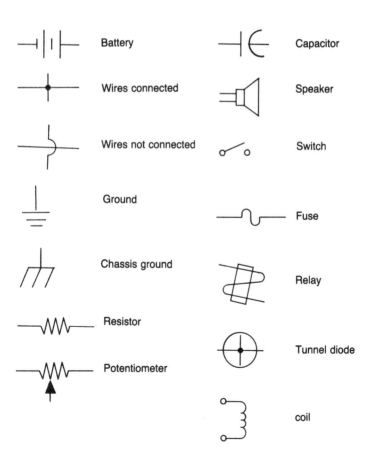

Battery	Capacitor
Wires connected	Speaker
Wires not connected	Switch
Ground	Fuse
Chassis ground	Relay
Resistor	Tunnel diode
Potentiometer	coil

scientific applications   Tasks that are traditionally numerically oriented and often require advanced engineering, mathematical, or scientific capabilities.

scientific notation   A notation in which numbers are written as a "significant digits" part times an appropriate power of 10; for example, 0.32619×10^7, or $0.32619E + 07$, to mean 3,261,900.

SCM   (Society for Computer Medicine) This organization brings together physicians and computer scientists. It emphasizes the use of automation for medical applications.

scope   See *oscilloscope*.

SCR   (Silicon Controlled Rectifier) A semiconductor device useful in controlling large amounts of DC current or voltage. Basically, it is a diode turned on or off by a signal voltage applied to a control electrode called the *gate*. Its characteristics are similar to the old vacuum tube *thyratron*, which is why it is sometimes called a *thyristor*.

scratch file   During the processing of substantial files of data, it often becomes necesary to create temporary files for later use by copying all or part of a data set to an auxiliary storage device.

scratchpad   A small, fast storage that is used in some computers in place of registers. See *cache memory*.

screen   A surface on which information is displayed, such as a video display screen. See *cathode-ray tube, display*, and *video terminal*.

screen dump   The process of transferring the information currently appearing on a display screen to a printer or other hard-copy device.

screen size   The physical dimension of a display screen, usually a diagonal measure in inches.

screen update   Changing the screen contents to reflect new information.

Scripsit   A software package used for word processing.

scrolling   The movement of data on a video display. This movement of text is repeated until the desired spot in the text has been reached. If the scroll is upward, a new line must appear at the bottom of the screen as an old one disappears at the top. See *horizontal scrolling* and *vertical scrolling*.

SCS   (Society for Computer Simulation) A professional computer science organization that is devoted primarily to the advancement of simulation and allied technology.

search   To examine a set of items for those that have a desired property.

search key   Data to be compared to specified parts of each item for the purpose of conducting a search.

search memory   See *associative storage*.

second   Base unit of time in the SI metric system; also used in the customary English system.

secondary key   A *field* that is used to gain access to records in a file; it is not required to be unique.

secondary storage   See *auxiliary storage*.

second generation computer   A computer belonging to the second era of technological development of computers, when the transistor replaced the vacuum tube. These wre prominent from 1959 to 1964, when they were displaced by computers using integrated circuitry.

sector   One of the peripheral elements into which each track of a disk surface is divided.

secure kernel   A protected segment of a systems program.

security controls   Methods to ensure that only authorized users have access to a computer system and its resources.

security program   A program that controls access to data in files and permits only authorized use of terminals and other equipment.

seed   A constant used to initiate a *pseudorandom number* generator. The seed is used to generate the first number, and all subsequent numbers are based on previous results.

seek   To position the access mechanism of a direct access device at a specified location.

seek time   The time required to position the access mechanism of a direct access storage device at a specified position. See *access time* and *transfer rate*.

segment   (1) To divide a program into parts such that some segments may reside in *internal storage* and other segments may reside in *auxiliary storage*. Each segment will contain the necessary instructions to jump to another segment or to call another segment into internal storage. (2) The smallest functional unit that can be loaded as one logical entity during execution of an *overlay* program. (3) As applied to the field of telecommunications, a portion of a message that can be contained in a *buffer* of specified size.

selecting   Extracting certain cards from a deck for a specific purpose without disturbing the sequence in which the cards were originally filed.

selection sort   A *sort* that selects the extreme value (smallest or largest) in a list, exchanges it with the last value in the list, and repeats with a shorter list.

selection structure   One of the three primary structures of a structured flowchart. It provides a choice between two alternative paths, based upon a certain condition.

selector channel   A term used in certain computer systems for an *input/output channel* that can transfer data to or from only one peripheral device at a time. Contrast with *multiplexer channel*.

self-adapting   The ability of a system to change its performance characteristics in response to its environment.

self-checking code   See *error-detection code*.

self-compiling compiler   A *compiler* that is written in its own *source language* and is capable of compiling itself.

self-complementing code   A code that has the following property: the binary one's *complement* of the weighted binary number is also the numbers nine's complement in decimal notation. For example, a decimal 843 equals a self-complementing code 111001000011.

self-correcting code   A numerical coding system in which transmission errors are automatically detected and corrected. Same as *error-correcting code*.

self-validating code   A code that makes an explicit attempt to determine its own correctness and proceed accordingly.

semantics   The study of the science of meaning in language forms. Pertains to the relationships between symbols and what they represent.

semaphores   Synchronization primitives used to coordinate the activities of two or more programs or processes that are running at the same time and sharing information. See *primitive*.

semiconductor   A solid material, usually germanium or silicon, with an electrical conductivity that lies between the high conductivity of metals and the low conductivity of insulators. Depending on the temperature and pressure, a semiconductor can control a flow of electricity. It is the material from which integrated circuits are made. See *integrated circuit*.

semiconductor device   An electronic element fabricated from crystalline materials such as silicon or germanium that, in the pure state, are neither good conductors nor good insulators and are unusable for electronic purposes. When certain impure atoms such as phosphorus or arsenic are diffused into the crystal structure of the pure metal, the electrical neutrality is upset, introducing positive or negative charge carriers. Diodes and transistors can then be implemented. See *diode* and *transistor*.

semiconductor storage   A memory device whose storage elements are formed as *solid state* electronic components on an *integrated circuit* chip.

semirandom access The method of locating data in storage that combines in the search for the desired item some form of *direct access*, usually followed by a limited sequential search.

sense (1) To examine, particularly relative to a criterion. (2) To determine the present arrangement of some element of hardware. (3) To read holes punched on a card or tape.

sense switch A computer console switch that may be interrogated by a program. Sense switches are very useful when debugging a large, complex program.

sensitivity The degree of response of a control unit to a change in the incoming signal.

sensors Devices to detect and measure physical phenomena such as temperature, stress, heartbeat, wind direction, and fire.

sequence check A check used to prove that a set of data is arranged in ascending or descending order.

sequence structure One of the three primary structures of a structured flowchart. In this structure, instructions are executed in order.

sequential The occurrence of events in time sequence, with little or no simultaneity or overlap of events.

sequential access A term used to describe files, such as magnetic tape, that must be searched serially from the beginning to find any desired record.

sequential computer A computer in which events occur in time sequence with little or no simultaneity or overlap of events.

sequential data set A *data set* whose records are organized on the basis of their successive physical positions, such as on magnetic tape.

sequential data structure A *data structure* in which each atom is immediately adjacent to the next atom. Also called *contiguous data structure*.

sequential device A peripheral device from which data are read or into which data are writen in order; nothing can be omitted.

sequential file organization The organization of records in a specific sequence based on a key, such as part number or employee ID. The records in sequential files must be processed one after another.

sequential list A list stored in contiguous locations. Also called dense list and linear list.

sequential logic A circuit arrangement in which the output state is determined by the previous state of the input. See *combination logic.*

sequential machine A mathematical model of a certain type of sequential *switching circuit.*

sequential storage *Auxiliary storage* where data are arranged in ascending or descending order, usually by item number.

serial (1) Pertaining to the sequential occurrence of two or more related activities in a single device. (2) The handling of data in a sequential fashion. Contrast with *parallel.*

serial access Descriptive of a storage device or medium in which there is a sequential relationship between access time and data location in storage; that is, the access time is dependent upon the location of the data. Contrast with *direct access.* See *serial processing.*

serial adder An adder that performs its operations by bringing in one digit at a time from each of the quantities involved.

serial computer A computer in which each digit or data word bit is processed serially by the computer.

serial input/output Data transmission in which the bits are sent one by one over a single wire. Contrast with *parallel input/output.*

serial interface An *interface* on which all the data move over the same wire, one bit after the other.

serializability When several users access data at the same time, the result must be equivalent to that which occurs when they access the data one at a time. This effect is called serializability.

serial operation A computer operation in which all digits of a word are handled sequentially rather than simultaneously. Contrast with *parallel operation.*

serial port An *input/output port* in a computer through which data are transmitted and received one bit at a time. In most cases, in personal computers, serial data are passed through an RS-232C serial interface port.

serial processing Reading, and/or writing, records on file, one by one, in the physical sequence in which they are stored. Contrast with *parallel processing.* See *serial access.*

serial reading Column-by-column reading of a punch card.

serial transmission A method of information transfer in which the bits composing a character are sent sequentially. Contrast with *parallel transmission.*

service bureau An organization that provides data processing services for other individuals or organizations. See *computer utility.*

service programs Programs that supplement the control programs of an operating system; for example, language translators, utility routines, and programmer aids.

servicer A service bureau that provides computer services to other organizations for a fee.

servomechanism A feedback control system.

set (1) To place a binary cell into the one state. (2) To place a storage device into a specified state, usually other than denoting zero or blank.

SETL A *high-level language* designed to facilitate the programming of algorithms involving sets and related structures.

setup An arrangement of data or devices to solve a particular problem.

setup time The time between computer runs or other machine operations that is devoted to such tasks as changing disk packs and moving cards, forms, and other supplies to and from the equipment.

shade In computer graphics, the quantity of black mixed with a pure color.

shadow printing On some printers, a bold character can be printed by backing up the print head to within $\frac{1}{120}$ inch of its previous position and restriking. The slight amount of misregistration between the initial impression and the overstrike produces a fatter, bolder character.

SHARE An organization of users of medium and large scale IBM data processing systems.

shared file A direct access device that may be used by two systems at the same time. A shared file may link two computer systems.

shared logic The concurrent use of a single computer by multiple users.

shared resource Computer resource shared by several users.

shielding Protection against electrical or magnetic noise.

shift To move the characters of a unit or information column-wise right or left. For a number, this is equivalent to multiplying or dividing by a power of the base of notation.

shift key The key on a computer keyboard that, when pressed, makes letters print as capitals instead of lowercase letters and allows some special characters to be printed.

SI Standard abbreviation of the worldwide International Metric System. (From French, Systeme International d'Unites—International System of Units.)

sift To extract certain desired items of information from a large amount of data.

sifting A method of internal sorting by which records are moved to permit the insertion of other records. Also called *insertion method*.

sign Used in the arithmetic sense to describe whether a number is positive or negative.

signal In communications theory, an intentional disturbance in a communications system. Contrast with *noise*.

signaling rate The rate at which signals are transmitted over a communications link.

signal-to-noise ratio In data communications, the ratio of the (wanted) signal to the (unwanted) noise.

sign digit The digit in the *sign position* of a word.

sign extension The duplication of the sign bit in the *higher-order* positions of a *register*. This extension is usually performed on *one's complement* or *two's complement* binary values.

sign flag A *flip-flop* that goes to position 1 if the most significant bit of the result of an operation has the value of 1.

significant digits If the digits of a number are ranked according to their ascending higher powers of the base, then the significant digits are those ranging from the highest-power digit (different from zero) and ending with the lowest-power digit.

signing-on The process of getting connected to a time-sharing computer network.

sign position The position at which the sign of a number is located.

silicon A nonmetallic chemical element used in the manufacture of transistors, integrated circuits, solar cells, and so forth. It is a chemical element (atomic number 14) widely found in sand and clay.

silicon controlled rectifier (SCR) A semiconductor device that, when in its normal state, blocks a voltage applied in either direction.

Silicon Valley An area south of San Francisco, California, noted for its large number of electronic, semiconductor, and computer manufacturing firms. Also known as Silicon Gulch.

silicon wafer A silicon slice on which integrated chips are fabricated. After fabrication, the wafer is cut into many individual chips, which are then mounted in *dual in-line packages* (DIPs). See *dual in-line package*.

simplex Pertaining to a communications link that is capable of transmitting data in only one direction. Contrast with *full duplex* and *half duplex*.

SIMSCRIPT A *high-level language* specifically designed for programming simulation applications.

simulation To represent the functioning of one system by another; that is, to represent a physical system by the execution of a computer program, or to represent a biological system by a mathematical model. See *mathematical model*.

simulator A device, computer program, or system that represents certain features of the behavior of a physical or abstract system.

simultaneous processing The performance of two or more data processing tasks at the same instant of time. Contrast with *concurrent processing*.

single address See *one-address instruction*.

single board computer A computer that contains all its circuitry on one board.

single density A format for putting information on a floppy disk.

single-sided A floppy disk system that can store data on only one side of a diskette.

single step The operation of a computer in such a manner that only one instruction is executed each time the computer is started.

sixteen-bit chip A CPU chip that processes data sixteen bits at a time.

sketching A computer graphics technique in which a trail of lines is drawn or sketched along the path of the cursor.

skew In *optical scanning*, skew refers to a condition in which a character, line, or reprinted symbol is neither parallel with nor at right angles to the leading edge.

SLA (Special Library Association) This international organization of libraries and information specialists promotes the establishment of resource centers for interest groups such as banks, museums, law firms, and other businesses.

slab A part of a *word*.

slave A device controlled by another device.

slave tube A cathode-ray tube connected to another in such a way that both tubes perform identically.

slew To move paper through a printer.

slice A special type of chip architecture that permits the cascading of devices to increase word bit size.

slot A single board position in a *backplane*.

SLSI (Super Large Scale Integration) Refers to ultra-high density chips that contain 100,000 or more transistors per chip.

SLT (Solid Logic Technique) A term coined by IBM to refer to a microelectronic packaging technique for producing a circuit module.

slug A metal casting that carries the image of a printable character. The slug prints by striking the paper.

small business computer A stand-alone data processing system built around a digital computer system that is dedicated to the processing of standard business applications such as payroll, accounts receivable and payable, order entry, inventory, and general ledger. See *stand-alone system.*

small scale integration (SSI) The class of integrated circuits that has the fewest number of functions per chip.

SMALLTALK A very advanced operating system designed to make computer use as easy as possible for the layperson. It presents possible choices of operation in the form of pictures or "icons" on the screen. The user selects one by moving a pointer with the aid of a *mouse* to the appropriate position and then presses a button on top of the mouse to inform the computer of the choice.

smart card A credit card with a built-in computer.

smart machines Machines that use microprocessors as their control elements.

smart terminal A terminal that contains some capacity to process information being transmitted or received. See *local intelligence.*

smash The destruction of an area of storage by overwriting with another program.

smooth To apply procedures that decrease or eliminate rapid fluctuations in data.

smooth scrolling The ability to *scroll* text without it jerking from one line to the next.

SNA See *systems network architecture.*

snapshot dump A *dynamic dump* of the contents of specified storage locations and/or registers that is performed at specified points or times during the running of a program.

SNOBOL (StriNg Oriented symBOLic Language) SNOBOL has significant applications in program compilation and generation of symbolic equations. It is a unique language that provides complete facilities for the manipulation of strings of characters. It is particularly applicable to programs associated with text editing, linguistics, compiling, and symbolic manipulation of algebraic expressions. It was developed by Bell Laboratories.

SO (Send Only) A designation used to indicate the send-only capabilities of equipment.

soft copy Data presented as a video image, in audio format, or in any other form that is not hard copy. See *hard copy.*

soft fails *Noise* bursts in microelectronic circuits caused by cosmic-ray particles that result in spontaneous changes in the information stored in computer memories. These changes are called soft fails. This sensitivity to cosmic rays is one of the unanticipated results of the ever-decreasing size of the components of integrated microelectronic circuits, and it presents new considerations in the development of very large scale integrated circuits.

soft sector A method of marking sectors or sections on a disk using information written on the disk. Soft sectoring is a method of determining positioning of data on the disk by software calculations rather than by physical monitoring of the disk. See *hard sector.*

software A set of programs, procedures, routines, and documents associated with the operation of a computer system. Software is the name given to the programs that cause a computer to carry out particular operations. The software for a computer system may be classified as applications programs and systems programs. Contrast with *hardware.* See *firmware.*

software broker An individual who specializes in marketing software packages.

software compatibility Refers to the ability to use programs written for one system on another system with little or no change.

software documents The written or printed material associated with computer equipment and software systems.

software encryption The encoding or decoding of computerized data using programming techniques rather than hardware devices such as scramblers.

software engineering The process of engineering software; that is, not only the programs that run on a computer but also the requirements definition, functional specification, design description, program implementation, and test methods that lead to this code.

software flexibility A property of software that enables it to change easily in response to different user and system requirements.

software house A company that offers software support services to computer users.

software license A contract signed by the purchaser of a software product in which he/she is usually made to agree not to make copies of the software for resale.

software maintenance The ongoing process of detecting and removing errors from existing programs.

software monitor A program used for performance measurement purposes.

software package A collection or set of related computer programs. A package usually includes the programs, stored on a storage media (floppy disk, cassette, and so on), and documentation or a *tutorial.*

software piracy The copying of commercial software without the permission of the originator.

software portability Refers to the ease with which a program can be moved from one computer environment to another.

software protection Resistance to unauthorized copying of software.

software publisher A business that publishes and sells software packages.

software resources The program and data resources that represent the software associated with a computing system.

software science A discipline concerned with the measurable properties of computer programs.

software system The entire set of computer programs and their documentation used in a computer system.

software transportability The ability to take a program written for one computer and run it without modification on another computer.

solar cell A semiconductor electrical *junction* device that absorbs and converts the radiant energy of sunlight directly and efficiently into electrical energy.

solicitation A request to vendors to submit bids for hardware, software, or services. See *request for proposal (RFP)* and *request for quotation (RFQ).*

solid state Descriptive of electronic components whose operation depends on the control of electric or magnetic phenomena in solids such as integrated circuits and transistors. See *integrated circuit* and *transistor.*

solid state cartridge A preprogrammed plug-in module that contains a program stored in ROM. See *firmware* and *ROM.*

solid state device A device built primarily from solid state electronic circuit elements.

S-100 bus A standard means of interconnection between a microcomputer and peripheral equipment.

son file See *father file.*

SOP An acronym for Standard Operating Procedure. The status quo.

sort (1) To arrange records according to a logical system. On a computer, most sorting is done using magnetic disks, drums, or tapes.

(2) A utility program that sorts records held on disk, drum, or tape.

sort effort   The number of steps needed to order an unordered list.

sorter   A device that arranges a set of card records in a preselected sequence.

sorting   The process of arranging data according to a logical system.

sort generator   A program that generates a sort program for production running.

sort/merge program   A generalized processing program that can be used to sort or merge records in a prescribed sequence.

SOS   (Silicon On Sapphire). The process of fabricating integrated chips on layers of silicon and sapphire.

source   One of three terminals or electrodes of a *field effect transistor* (FET). The source is the origin of the charge carriers.

Source, The   A popular commercial data base accessible to the general public. It features stock market reports, software reviews, news features, electronic mail, shopping, and so on. Personal computer users can use The Source network via a common telephone hookup. It is operated by The Source Telecomputing Corporation.

source code   *Symbolic coding* in its original form before being processed by a computer. The computer automatically translates source code into a code the computer can understand.

source/computer   A computer used to translate a *source program* into an *object program*.

source data automation   In source data automation, the data that are created while an event is taking place are entered directly into the system in a machine-processable form. See *point-of-sale terminal*.

source deck   A card deck comprising a computer program in source language.

source document   An original document from which basic data is extracted (e.g., invoice, sales slip, inventory tag).

source language   The original form in which a program is prepared prior to processing by the computer; for example, a program written in FORTRAN or assembly language. Contrast with *object language*.

source program   A computer program written in a source language such as BASIC, FORTRAN, COBOL, Pascal, or assembly language. It is converted to the machine code object program by a special processing program, such as a compiler or assembler.

source register   The *register* that contains a data word that is being transferred.

SPA (Systems and Procedures Association) A professional organization whose purpose is to promote advanced management systems and procedures through seminars, professional education, and research.

space (1) One or more blank characters. (2) The state of a communications channel corresponding to a binary zero.

spacebar At the bottom of a keyboard, the long, narrow key that generates spaces.

span The difference between the highest and lowest values in a range of values.

spanning tree A subgraph of a graph with two properties: (a) it is a *tree*; and (b) it contains all the nodes of the original graph. See *node*.

sparse array An array in which most of the entries have a value of zero.

spatial data management A technique that allows users access to information by pointing at pictures on a display screen. The pictures represent data bases, document files, or any category of information.

spec An abbreviation for specification.

special character A graphics character that is neither a letter, a digit, nor a blank; for example, plus sign, equal sign, asterisk, dollar sign, comma, period, and so on.

special interest groups Special groups within an organization that hold meetings, sponsor exhibits, and publish documents related to some special interest, topic, or subject. The Association for Computing Machinery (ACM) has more than thirty Special Interest Groups (SIGs). These groups elect their own officers, set their own dues, and are self-supporting. *See page 252.*

special-purpose computer system A computer system capable of solving only a few selected types of numerical or logical problems.

special-purpose programming language A programming language designed to handle one specific type of problem or application.

specification A detailed description of the required characteristics of a device, process, or product.

specification sheet A form used for coding *RPG* statements.

speech recognition The ability of a computer to match the pattern of signals coming into it from a "microphone" with stored "voice patterns" held in its memory and thus recognize spoken words.

speech synthesis The arranging of coded speech components into

SPECIAL INTEREST GROUPS IN THE
ASSOCIATION FOR COMPUTING MACHINERY (ACM)

SIGACT
Automata and
  Computability
  Theory

SIGAPL
APL

SIGARCH
Architecture of Computer
  Systems

SIGART
Artificial Intelligence

SIGCOMM
Data Communications

SIGCPR
Computer Personnel
  Research

SIGCSE
Computer Science
  Education

SIGCUE
Computer Uses in
  Education

SIGDA
Design Automation

SIGDOC
Systems Documentation

SIGGRAPH
Computer Graphics

SIGBDP
Business Data
  Processing

SIGBIO
Biomedical Computing

SIGCAPH
Computers and the
  Physically
  Handicapped

SIGCAS
Computers and Society

SIGCHI
Computer and Human
  Interaction

SIGOA
Office Automation

SIGOPS
Operating Systems

SIGPC
Personal Computing

SIGPLAN
Programming Languages

SIGPLAN/Ada TEC
Technical Committee on
  Ada

SIGPLAN/FORTEC
Technical Committee on
  Fortran

SPECIAL INTEREST GROUPS IN THE
ASSOCIATION FOR COMPUTING MACHINERY (ACM)

SIGIR Information Retrieval	SIGSAC Security, Audit, and Control
SIGMAP Mathematical Programming	SIGSAM Symbolic and Algebraic Manipulation
SIGMETRICS Measurement and Evaluation	SIGSIM Simulation
	SIGSMALL Small Computing Systems and Applications
SIGMICRO Microprogramming	
SIGMOD Management of Data	SIGSOFT Software Engineering
	SIGUCCS University and College
SIGNUM Numerical Mathematics	Computing Services

---

real words and sentences. Speech synthesis constructs words for phonemes.

speech synthesizer   A device that converts numerical code into recognizable speech, which is played over a loudspeaker. In other words, a peripheral that converts output signals into an artificial human voice that "speaks."

spelling checker   A computer program, usually associated with word processing, that compares typed words against a word list and informs the user of possible spelling mistakes.

spike   A sharp-peaked, short-duration voltage *transient*. A brief sudden surge of electricity.

spinwriter   A particular type of high-quality computer printer.

split screen   A display screen that can be partitioned into two or more areas (called windows) so that different screen formats can be shown on the screen at the same time.

spool   (1) A reel of magnetic tape. (2) To wind a magnetic tape.

Speech synthesizer. Courtesy Radio Shack, a division of Tandy Corp.

spooler A program or peripheral device that allows a computer to produce hard copy on a printer while doing something else.

spooling (1) The process by which various input/output devices appear to be operating simultaneously, when actually the system is inputting or outputting data via buffers. (2) Temporarily storing data on disk or tape files until another part of the system is ready to process it. See *buffer.*

spreadsheet An applications program that allows financial forecasting and similar applications to be performed by using a large electronic grid of numbers and formulas. It is a simulation modeling tool most useful to business management but applicable to any numeric manipulations of rows and columns of numbers.

squeezer The person who lays out LSI and VSLI circuits in their original "large" form.

SSI See *small scale integration.*

stack A sequential data list stored in internal storage. Rather than addressing the stack elements by their memory locations, the computer retrieves information from the stack by "popping" elements from the top (LIFO) or from the bottom (FIFO). See *program stack* and *stack pointer.*

stacked job processing A technique that permits multiple jobs to be stacked for presentation to the system and automatically processes the jobs, one after the other. A series of jobs to be executed is placed in a card reader. The computer system executes the jobs automatically in accordance with the job control cards for each job.

stacker   See *card stacker*.

stack pointer   A register that is used to point to locations in the stack. A stack pointer is incremented by one before each new data item is "pulled" or "popped" from the stack, and decremented by one after a word is "pushed" onto the stack. See *stack*.

stair stepping   A technique used on *raster* displays to represent a line drawn at any angle other than 45 degrees, horizontal or vertical.

stand-alone graphics system   A graphics system that includes a microcomputer or minicomputer, storage, terminal, and other input/output devices.

stand-alone system   A self-contained computer system that can work independently. It is not connected to or under the control of another computer system.

standard   A yardstick used to measure performance of the computer system function. See *ANSI*.

standard interface   A standard physical means by which all peripheral devices are connected to the central processing unit (e.g., a standard form of plug and socket).

standby equipment   A duplicate set of equipment to be used if the primary unit becomes unusable because of malfunction.

standby time   (1) The period between placing an inquiry into the equipment and the availability of the reply. (2) The period between the setup of the equipment for use and its actual use. (3) The period during which the equipment is available for use.

star bit   A bit used in *asynchronous transmission* to precede the first bit of a character transmitted serially, signaling the start of the character.

star network   A network configuration consisting of a central host computer and satellite terminals, which connect to the computer to form a star pattern.

stat   An abbreviation for statistical.

state   Used most often to refer to the condition of bistable devices, which are used to represent binary digits. By definition, such devices can have only two states; the state of a switch describes whether it is on or off. See *bistable device*.

statement   An expression of instruction in a computer language.

statement label   A line number of the symbolic name of a statement in a *source language* program.

state-of-the-art   A phrase that implies being up-to-date in technology.

static analysis   Analysis of a program that is performed without executing the program.

static dump   A storage dump that is performed at a particular point in time with respect to a machine run, often at the termination of a run.

static memory   A memory that retains its programmed state as long as power is applied.

static RAM   A memory that doesn't need to be refreshed many times a second, as is required with dynamic RAM. It does not lose its contents as long as power to the computer is on. Once the computer puts a value into a static memory location, it remains there. Contrast with *dynamic RAM*.

static storage   A specific type of semiconductor memory that does not require periodic refresh cycles. Data is held by changing the position of an electronic "switch," a transistor *flip-flop*, contained in integrated circuits.

station   One of the input or output points on a data communications system. See *terminal*.

statistics   The branch of mathematics that collects information and tabulates and analyzes it.

statizing   The process of transferring an instruction from computer storage to the instruction registers and holding it there, ready to be executed.

status   The present condition of a system component.

step   (1) To cause a computer to execute one instruction. (2) One instruction in a computer routine.

stochastic procedures   Trial and error, as opposed to algorithmic procedures.

stochastic process   Dealing with events that develop in time or space and that cannot be described precisely, except in terms of *probability theory*.

stop bit   A bit used in *asynchronous transmission* to signal the end of a character transmitted serially and representing the quiescent state in which the line will remain until the next character begins.

storage   Descriptive of a device or medium that can accept data, hold them, and deliver them on demand at a later time. The term is preferred over memory. Synonymous with *memory*. See *auxiliary storage, internal storage, PROM, protected storage, RAM*, and *ROM*.

storage allocation   The assignment of specific programs, program segments, and/or blocks of data to specific portions of a computer's storage. Sometimes called *memory allocation*. See *program storage*.

storage block   A contiguous area of *internal storage*.

storage capacity   The number of items of data that a storage device is capable of containing. Frequently defined in terms of computer words, bytes, or characters.

storage circuit   Refers to a circuit that can be switched into either of two stable states, 0 or 1.

storage device   A device used for storing data within a computer system (e.g., integrated circuit storage, magnetic disk unit, magnetic tape unit, magnetic drum unit, floppy disk, tape cassette, and so on).

storage dump   A printout of all or part of the contents of the internal storage of a computer. The printout is often used to diagnose errors. Also called *memory dump*. See *post mortem dump* and *snapshot dump*.

storage key   An indicator associated with a storage block or blocks; it requires that tasks have a matching protection key to use the blocks. See *privileged instruction* and *storage protection*.

storage location   A position in storage where a character, byte, or word may be stored. Same as *cell*.

storage map   A diagram that shows where programs and data are stored in the storage units of the computer system.

storage pool   A group of similar storage devices; the disk drives in a computer installation are collectively referred to as the disk pool.

storage protection   Protection against unauthorized writing in and/or reading from all or part of a storage device. Storage protection is usually implemented automatically by hardware facilities, usually in connection with an operating system. Sometimes called *memory protection*. See *storage key*.

storage tube   An electron tube, used in older computers, into which information can be introduced and then extracted at a later time.

storage unit   See *storage device*.

store   (1) The British term for storage. (2) To place in storage.

store-and-forward   In data communications, the process of handling messages used in a message-switching system.

stored program computer   A computer capable of performing sequences of internally stored instructions and usually capable of modifying those instructions as directed by the instructions. Same as *digital computer*.

stored program concept   Instructions to a computer as well as data values are stored within the internal storage of a computer. The instructions can thus be accessed more quickly and may be more easily modified. This concept was introduced by John von Neumann in 1945. It is the most important characteristic of the digital computer.

straight line code The repetition of a sequence of instructions by explicitly writing the instructions for each repetition. Generally, straight line coding will require less execution time and more space than equivalent loop coding. The feasibility of straight line coding is limited by the space required as well as by the difficulty of coding a variable number of repetitions. Contrast with *loop code.*

streamer A tape deck that operates at a continuous high speed rather than starting and stopping between separate blocks of data.

STRESS (STRuctural Engineering System Solver) A problem-oriented language used for solving structural engineering problems.

string A connected sequence of characters or bits that is treated as a single data item.

string length The number of characters in a string.

string manipulation A technique for manipulating strings of characters.

string processing languages Programming languages designed to facilitate the processing of strings of characters. *COMIT* and *SNO-BOL* are examples of string processing languages.

string variable A string of alphanumeric string.

stringy floppy A small cartridge containing a continuous tape loop that provides the computer with a random access capability similar to, but still slower than, a floppy disk. The price of a stringy floppy is comparable to that of a cassette.

stroke writer A *vector* graphics terminal that represents objects on a screen by a series of lines (vectors).

structural design The overall organization and control logic of processing.

structure chart A design tool for documenting the organization of program modules and the *control logic* that relates them to one another. A graphic representation of *top-down programming.* See *module.*

structured coding A method of writing programs with a high degree of structure.

structured design The methodology for designing programs and systems through *top-down,* hierarchical partitioning and logical control structures.

structured English An approach to languages that is based on replacing symbols with recognizable English words.

structured flowchart A method of representing problem solutions in terms of three flowcharting structures: the sequence structure, the decision structure, and the loop structure.

Example of a Structured Flowchart

Open Files	
Set EOF-FLAG to Zero	
Read Record; if None, Set EOF-FLAG to 1	
While EOF-FLAG = 0	
	Process Record
	Read Record; if None Left, Set EOF-FLAG to 1
Close Files	
Stop	

structured programming A programming technique used in the design and coding of computer programs. The approach assumes the disciplined use of a few basic coding structures and the use of *top-down* concepts to decompose main functions into lower-level components for modular coding purposes. The technique is concerned with improving the programming process through better organization and programs, and with better programming notation to facilitate correct and clear descriptions of data and control structures.

structured walkthrough A formal review process in which the programmer explains the design and/or logic that he or she used in the preparation of the program.

STRUDL (STRUctural Design Language) A programming language used for the design and analysis of structures.

stylus A pen-shaped instrument used in input devices; for example, a penlight device used with a graphics tablet.

subprogram A segment of a program that can perform a specific function. Subprograms can reduce programming time when a specific function is required at more than one point in a program. If the required function is handled as a subprogram, the statements for that function can be coded once and executed at the various points in the program. Subroutines and functions may be used to provide subprograms. See *function* and *subroutine*.

subroutine   A subsidiary routine within which initial execution never starts. It is executed when called by some other program, usually the main program. Also called *subprogram*. See *closed subroutine* and *open subroutine*.

subroutine reentry   Initiation of a subroutine by one program before it has finished its response to another program that called for it. This is what may happen when a *control program* is subjected to a *priority interrupt*.

subschema   The logical organization of data required for a particular program. Contrast with *schema*.

subscript   The *integer* value, appended to a variable name, that defines the storage elements composing an *array*.

subscripted variable   A symbol whose numeric value can change. It is denoted by an *array* name followed by a subscript; for example, CHESS (2,4) or A(7). See *subscript* and *variable*.

subset   A set contained within a set.

substrate   In *microelectronics*, the physical material on which a circuit is fabricated.

substring   A portion of a character string.

subsystem   A system subordinate to the main system.

subtrahend   The quantity that is subtracted from another quantity. In the subtraction $a - b$, b is the subtrahend and a is the minuend.

suite   A set of programs that are closely related.

sum   The quantity that results from adding two quantities.

supercomputer   The largest, fastest, and most expensive computer available. Used by businesses and organizations that require extraordinary amounts of computing power. Sometimes called "number crunchers" because they perform hundreds of millions of operations per second.

superconductor   An ultra-fast electronic circuit.

superconducting computers   High-performance computers whose circuits employ superconductivity and the Josephson effect to reduce cycle time. See *Josephson junction*.

super-minicomputer   A minicomputer that uses 32-bit words. The longer word length leads to increased *throughput*, more precise computations, and easier program development. The processing power of a super-minicomputer approaches that of a large scale *mainframe* computer.

superscript A letter or digit written above a symbol to denote a power or to identify a particular element of a set (e.g., x^3)

supervisory system See *operating system.*

supply company A company that offers a number of supplies that may not be produced and distributed by computer manufacturers; for example, printer paper or printer ribbons.

suppress To eliminate zeros or other insignificant characters from a computer printout.

suppression The elimination of some undesired components of a signal.

surge A sudden sharp increase in voltage.

surging A sudden and momentary change of voltage or current in a circuit.

surge protector A device that protects electrical equipment from being damaged by short surges of high voltage. A computer or other device is plugged into the surge protector, which itself is plugged into a standard 110-volt electrical outlet. See *line surge.*

swapping (1) In virtual storage, swapping occurs when a new page is brought into internal storage from auxiliary storage and swapped for an existing page. (2) In a time-sharing system, bringing the program into internal storage or storing it on a storage device. (3) Transferring out a copy of what is in internal memory to auxiliary storage while simultaneously transferring in what is in auxiliary storage to internal memory.

swarm Several program bugs.

switch See *program switch.*

switched line Typically a telephone line that is connected to the switched telephone network.

switching algebra The name given to *Boolean algebra* when it is applied to switching theory.

switching circuit A constituent electric circuit of switching or digital systems. Well-known examples of such systems are digital computers, dial telephone systems, and automatic inventory systems.

switching theory The theory applied to circuits that have two or more discrete states.

symbol (1) A letter, numeral, or mark that represents a numeral, operation, or relation. (2) An element of the computer's character set.

symbolic address An *address*, expressed in symbols convenient to the program writer, that must be translated into an *absolute address* (usually by an *assembler*) before it can be interpreted by a computer.

symbolic coding Coding in which the instructions are written in nonmachine language; that is, coding using symbolic notation for operation codes and operands.

symbolic device A name used to indicate an input/output file; for example, SYSDSK, used to specify the magnetic disk unit.

symbolic editor A system program that helps computer users in the preparation and modification of source language programs by adding, changing, or deleting lines of text.

symbolic I/O assignment A name used to indicate an input/output unit; for example, RDR used to specify the card reader.

symbolic language A *pseudolanguage* made up of letters, characters, and numbers that are not the internal language of the computer system. See *assembly language, fabricated language*, and *high-level language*.

symbolic logic The discipline that treats *formal logic* by means of a formalized *artificial language* whose purpose is to avoid the ambiguities and logical inadequacies of natural language.

symbolic name See *name*.

symbolic programming Using a *symbolic language* to prepare computer programs.

symbolic table A *mapping* for a set of symbols to another set of symbols or numbers; for example, in an *assembler*, the symbol table contains the symbolic label address of an assembled *object program*.

symbol string A string consisting solely of symbols.

symbol table A list of names used in a program with brief descriptions and storage addresses.

sync character A character transmitted to establish character *synchronization* in *synchronous communications*.

synchronization Adjustment of the chronological relationships between events either to cause them to coincide or to maintain a fixed time difference between them.

synchronization check A check that determines whether a particular event or condition occurs at the proper moment.

synchronous communications A method of exchanging data at very high speeds between computers. It involves careful timing and special control codes.

synchronous computer A computer in which each operation starts as a result of a signal generated by a clock. Contrast with *asynchronous computer*.

synchronous network   A computer network in which all the communications channels are synchronized to a common clock.

synchronous operation   The operation of a system under the control of clocked pulses.

synchronous transmission   Data transmission in which the bits are transmitted at a fixed rate. The transmitter and receiver both use the same clock signals for synchronization.

synonym   Two or more keys that produce the same table address when hashed.

syntax   The grammatical and structural rules of a language. All assembly and high-level programming languages possess a formal syntax.

syntax error   The breaking of a rule governing the structure of the programming language being used. For example, typing RIAD A instead of READ A results in the computer failing to understand what is meant. Usually, the computer will respond to such an instruction by displaying an error message; for example, "syntax error at line 110."

synthesizer   A machine that generates and processes sound automatically. Some synthesizers include microprocessors, which are used as controlling devices. A voice synthesizer produces sounds that closely resemble a person speaking.

SYSGEN   (SYStems GENeration) The process of modifying the generalized operating system received from the vendor into a tailored system meeting the unique needs of the individual user.

system   A composite of equipment, skills, techniques, and information capable of performing and/or supporting an operational role in attaining specified management objectives. A complete system includes related facilities, equipment, material, services, personnel, and information required for its operation to the degree that it can be considered a self-sufficient unit in its intended operational and/or support environment.

system analyzer   A portable device that can be used as a troubleshooting unit for field service of complex equipment and systems.

system chart   A type of flowchart. See *system flowchart.*

system commands   Special instructions given to the computer when one operates in the conversational time-sharing mode. System commands direct the computer to execute (RUN) programs, list them (LIST), save them (SAVE), and to do other operations of a similar nature.

system diagnostics   A program used to detect overall system malfunctions.

system disk   A disk that contains the operating system.

system flowchart   A graphic representation of an entire system or portion of a system consisting of one or more computer operations. It is composed of interconnected flowcharting symbols arranged in the precise sequence that the various system operations are performed. The system flowchart is essentially an overall planning, control, and operational description of a specific application. Contrast with *program flowchart*. See *flowchart*.

system follow-up   The continuing evaluation and review of the newly installed system to see that it is performing according to plan.

system generation (SYSGEN)   The process of initiating a basic system at a specific installation.

system implementation   The final phase in the creation of a new system. It is during this phase that a system is completely debugged and it is determined whether it is operational and accepted by the users.

system interrupt   A break in the normal execution of a program or routine that is accomplished in such a way that the usual sequence can later on be resumed from that point.

system loader   A supervisory program used to locate programs in the system library and load them into the internal storage of the computer.

system maintenance   The activity associated with keeping a computer system constantly in tune with the changing demands placed upon it.

system priorities   The priorities established to determine the order in which information system projects will be undertaken.

systems programmer   (1) A programmer who plans, generates, maintains, and controls the use of an operating system with the aim of improving the overall productivity of an installation. (2) A programmer who designs programming systems.

systems analysis   The examination of an activity, procedure, method, technique, or business to determine what must be accomplished and how the necessary operations may best be accomplished by using data processing equipment.

systems analyst   One who studies the activities, methods, procedures, and techniques of organizational systems in order to determine what actions need to be taken and how these actions can best be accomplished.

systems design   The specification of the working relationships between all the parts of a system in terms of their characteristic actions.

system security   The technical innovations and managerial procedures applied to the hardware and software (programs and data) in order to protect the privacy of the records of the organization and its customers.

systems engineer   One who performs systems analysis, programming, and/or systems programming functions.

systems house   A company that develops hardware and/or software systems to meet user requirements.

systems manual   A document containing information on the operation of a system. Sufficient detail is provided so that management can determine the data flow, forms used, reports generated, and controls exercised. Job descriptions are generally provided.

systems network architecture (SNA)   The design of the network of computers and peripheral devices.

systems programmer   One who understands the interaction between the application software and the systems software on a specific computer system.

systems programming   The development of programs that form operating systems for computers. Such programs include assemblers, compilers, control programs, input/output handlers, and so forth.

systems programs   Programs that control the internal operations of the computer system. Included would be operating systems, compilers, interpreters, assemblers, graphics support programs, and mathematical routines. Contrast with *applications programs*.

systems resource   Any resource of a computer system that is under the control of the operating system.

systems software   Computer programs that provide a particular service to the user; for example, compilers, assemblers, operating systems, sort/merge programs, emulators, linkage editor programs, graphics support programs, and mathematical programs.

systems synthesis   The planning of the procedures for solving a problem.

systems testing   The testing of a series of programs in succession to make sure that all of the programs, including input and output, are related in the way the systems analyst intended.

T

tab A carriage control that specifies output columns.

table A collection of data in a form suitable for ready reference. The data are frequently stored in consecutive storage locations or written in the form of an array of rows and columns for easy entry. An intersection of labeled rows and columns serves to locate a specific piece of information.

table look-up A procedure for using a known value to locate an unknown value in a table.

tablet In computer graphics, an input device that converts graphics and pictorial data into binary inputs for use in a computer.

tabulate (1) To print totals. (2) To form data into a table.

tag A portion of an instruction. The tag carries the number of the *index register* that affects the address in the instruction.

tail A special data item that locates the end of a list.

talking computer A computer system that uses a speech synthesizer to produce speech.

tandem computers Two computers connected together and working on the same problem at the same time.

Tandy Corporation Parent company of *Radio Shack*, a manufacturer of microcomputer systems.

tape A strip of material that may be punched or coated with a magnetically sensitive substance and used for data input, storage, or output. The data are usually stored serially in several channels across the tape, transversely to the reading or writing motion.

tape cartridge See *magnetic tape cartridge*.

tape cassette A *sequential access* storage medium used in microcomputer systems for digital recording.

tape code See *magnetic tape code* and *paper tape code*.

tape deck See *magnetic tape unit*.

tape drive See *magnetic tape drive*.

tape handler See *magnetic tape unit*.

tape label Usually the first record on a magnetic tape reel, containing such information as the date the tape was written, identification name or number, and the number of records on the tape.

tape librarian A person who has responsibility for the safekeeping of all computer files; for example, programs and data files on magnetic tapes, disk packs, microfilm, diskettes, punched cards, and so on.

tape library A special room that houses a file of magnetic tape under secure, environmentally controlled conditions.

tape mark A special code used to indicate the end of a tape file.

Tape Operating System (TOS) An operating system in which the operating system programs are stored on magnetic tape.

tape-to-card converter A device that converts information directly from magnetic tape to punch cards, usually *off-line*.

tape unit See *magnetic tape unit, paper tape punch*, and *paper tape reader*.

target language The language into which some other language is to be properly translated. Usually has the same meaning as *object language*.

target program Same as *object program*.

tariff In data communications, the published rate for a specific unit of equipment, facility, or type of service provided by a communications common carrier.

tb (*terabyte*) One trillion bytes, 1000 gb.

technical writer A person who prepares proposals, training manuals, reference manuals, programming manuals, books, and reports that are associated with computer equipment and software.

telecommunications The transfer of data from one place to another over communications lines. See *data communications* and *teleprocessing*.

telecommunications specialist A person responsible for the design of data communications networks.

telecommuting Working at home with telecommunications between the office and the home.

teleconference An "electronic meeting" conducted among people at distant locations through the use of telecommunications. Considered an alternative to travel and face-to-face meetings, a teleconference is conducted with two-way video, audio, and, as required, data and facsimile transmission.

telecopying Long-distance copying. Same as *facsimile*.

Telematics The convergence of telecommunications and automatic information processing.

telemedicine The use of telecommunications, particularly television, for transmitting medical data, such as X rays or live images of a patient, to a distantly located specialist for consultation.

telemetry Transmission of data from remote measuring instruments by electrical or radio means; for example, data can be telemetered from a spacecraft circling the moon and recorded at a ground station located on Earth.

Telenet   A communications network that enables many varieties of user terminals and computers to exchange information.

telephotography   The transmission of photographs over electrical communications channels. The channels are generally those provided by common carrier communications companies.

teleprinter   An automatic printing device.

teleprocessing   The use of telephone lines to transmit data and commands between remote locations and a data processing center or between two computer systems. The combined use of data communications and data processing equipment. See *data communications* and *telecommunications*.

telesoftware   Computer programs sent by telephone line or television as part of the teletext signal.

teletext   A one-way communications medium. Images, each constituting a single frame of TV data in a special, compressed format, are transmitted in a continuous sequence. Users indicate which frame they would like to see by interaction with the decoding unit in their local TV set. See *Viewdata*.

teletypewriter (TTY)   A teletype unit. A generic term referring to teleprinter equipment and to the basic equipment made by the Teletype Corporation. A device used widely as an input/output unit in older computer systems.

telex   A telegraph service provided by Western Union.

telpak   A service offered by communications common carriers for the leasing of wide band channels between two or more points.

template   A plastic guide used in drawing flowcharting symbols.

temporary storage   In programming, storage locations reserved for intermediate results. Synonymous with *working storage*.

ten's complement   A number used to represent the negative of a given value. A ten's complement number is obtained by subtracting each digit from a number containing all 9s and adding 1; for example, 654 is the ten's complement of 346 and is obtained by performing the computation $999 - 346 + 1$.

terabit storage   A general term applied to storage devices whose capacity is of the order of 10^{12} bits.

terabyte   One trillion bytes. More accurately, 1 009 511 627 776, or 2^{40}.

terminal   A keyboard/display or keyboard/printer device used to input programs and data to the computer and to receive outputs from the computer.

terminal emulation   A situation in which special software makes a computer behave as though it were a terminal connected to another computer.

terminal symbol A flowcharting symbol used to indicate the starting point and termination point or points in a procedure. An oval-shaped figure is used to represent this symbol:

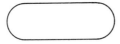

ternary (1) Pertaining to a characteristic or property involving a selection, choice, or condition in which there are three possibilities. (2) Pertaining to the numeration system with a *radix* of 3.

test data Data especially created to test the operation of a given program. Usually, one or more hand-calculated results, or otherwise known results, will be associated with test data so that the program under test may be validated.

test driver A program that directs the execution of another program against a collection of test data sets.

testing Examination of a program's behavior by executing the program on sample data sets. See *debug* and *systems testing*.

test run A run carried out to check that a program is operating correctly. During the run, test data generate results for comparison with previously prepared results.

text That part of the message that contains the information to be conveyed.

text editor A program that facilitates changes to computer-stored information and assists in the preparation of text.

text editing The general term that covers any additions, changes, or deletions made to electronically stored material.

text processing The manipulation of alphabetic data under program control.

theorem proving Two approaches to automated theorem proving are proof-finding and consequence-finding. A proof-finding program attempts to find a proof for a certain given theorem. A consequence-finding program is given specific axioms for which to deduce consequences. Then, "interesting" consequences are selected.

theory of numbers A branch of mathematics concerned generally with the properties and relationships of integers.

thermal printer A hard-copy device that produces output on heat-sensitive paper. Thermal printers have slow speeds, mediocre quality reproduction, and use an expensive paper. The device itself, however, is relatively inexpensive.

thimble A printing element (in the form of a thimble) used for letter-quality printing. Character slugs are arranged around the perimeter of the thimble. As the slug for the character to be printed spins into the correct position, a hammer drives it forward to print the impression on paper.

thimble printer Similar in function to a daisy wheel printer, the thimble printer uses type wheels in the shape of a thimble instead of a daisy. The thimble rotates, positioning the spokes so that the striking device can hit the spoke tip against the ribbon, thus printing the character on paper.

thin film A computer storage made by placing thin spots of magnetic materials on an insulated base (usually a flat plate or wire); electric current in wires attached to the base is used to magnetize the spot. See *rod memory*.

thin window display A one-line display that is used on keyboards, pocket computers, and so on.

third generation Computers that use integrated circuitry and miniaturization of components to replace transistors, reduce costs, work faster, and increase reliability. The third generation of computers began in 1964.

third party lease An agreement by which an independent firm buys equipment from the manufacturer and in turn leases it to the end user.

thirty-two-bit chip A CPU chip that processes data thirty-two bits at a time.

thrashing *Overhead* associated with memory *swapping* in a *virtual memory* system. Also called *churning*.

threaded A program consisting of calls to several separate subprograms.

threaded tree A *tree* containing additional pointers to assist in the scan of the tree.

three-address computer A computer that employs three addresses in its instruction format. For example, in the instruction "ADD A B C," the values represented by *A* and *B* are added, and the result is assigned to *C*.

three-dimensional array An array that provides a threefold classification: row, column, and layer.

throughput The total amount of useful processing carried out by a computer system in a given time period.

thumb wheel Dials that provide input into a computer system.

thyratron See *SCR.*

thyristor A *bistable device* comprising three or more junctions. See *SCR.*

TICCIT (Time-shared, Interactive, Computer-Controlled, Instructional Television) A computer-aided instruction system that uses minicomputers and modified color television sets as terminals to provide individual instruction to many students simultaneously. See *computer-assisted instruction* and *PLATO.*

tie-breaker Refers to circuitry that resolves the conflict that occurs when two central processing units try to use a peripheral device at the same time.

tie line A leased communications channel.

tightly coupled Computers that are dependent upon one another.

time division multiplexing (TDM) The merging of several bit streams of lower bit rates into a composite signal for transmission over a communications channel of higher bit-rate capacity. See *bit rate* and *bit stream.*

time quantum In a time-sharing system, a unit of time allotted to each user.

timer The computer's internal clock.

time-sharing A method of operation in which a computer facility is shared by several users for different purposes at (apparently) the same time. Although the computer actually services each user in sequence, the high speed of the computer makes it appear as though the users are all handled simultaneously.

time-slicing The allotment of a portion of processing time to each program in a multiprogramming system to prevent the monopolization of the central processing unit by any one program.

T²L See *TTL.*

toggle Pertaining to any device having two stable states. Synonymous with *flip-flop.*

token A symbol representing a name or entity in a programming language.

tone In computer graphics, the degree of tint and shade in color.

top-down program design A technique for designing a program or system according to its major functions and breaking these down into even smaller subfunctions. See *modular programming* and *structured programming.*

topology The physical layout of a computer network.

touch-sensitive panel A finger-operated device that is used to input data to a computer.

touch-sensitive screen   A display device that allows a user to communicate with a computer simply by touching characters that appear on the display screen.

touch-tone   A service mark of the AT&T Company that identifies its push-button dialing service.

touch-tone telephone   A push-button telephone used in teleprocessing systems.

TPI   (Tracks Per Inch) A measure of storage density in magnetic disks.

trace   (1) The scanning path of the beam in a *raster* display. (2) An electrical pathway on circuit boards that connects electronic components.

tracing routine   A routine that provides a time history of the contents of the computer operational registers during the execution of the program. A complete tracing routine would reveal the status of all registers and locations affected by each instruction each time the instruction is executed.

track   A path along which data are recorded on a continuous or rotational medium, such as magnetic tape, or magnetic disk or drum.

track ball   A track ball is similar to a joystick, but it uses a ball moved by the palm of the hand instead of a lever held by the fingers. As the ball is moved, the display cursor moves at the speed of and in the direction of the ball's motion.

tractor feed mechanism   A pair of pin-studded belts that rotate in unison and pull paper, punched with holes, into a printer.

traffic intensity   The ratio of the insertion rate to the deletion rate of a queue.

tradeoff   The balancing of factors in a computer system.

trailer record   A record that follows a group of records and contains pertinent data related to the group.

trailing edge   The edge of a punched card that is opposite the leading edge relative to the direction of motion of the card as it passes along the card track preceding, during, or after reading or punching. Contrast with *leading edge*.

transaction code   One or more characters that form part of a record and signify the type of transaction represented by the record.

transaction file   A collection of records containing data pertaining to current business activities. Synonymous with *detail file*.

transaction-oriented processing   Activities related to the processing of transactions as they occur.

transborder   Data communications between computer systems located across national borders.

transcribe   To copy from one external storage medium to another. The process may involve *translation*.

transducer   Any device or element that converts an input signal into an output signal of a different form.

transfer   (1) To copy or read, transmit, and store an item or block of information. (2) To change control. See *branch, conditional transfer, jump*, and *unconditional transfer*.

transfer address   See *entry point*.

transfer rate   The speed at which accessed data can be moved from one device to another. See *access time* and *seek time*.

transformation   In computer graphics, one of the modifications that can be made to the placement or size of an on-screen image. The three basic transformations are *translation, scaling*, and *rotation*.

transformer   An alternating current device used in computer power supplies to reduce 115 volts 60 Hertz to a lower, more suitable voltage usable by computer equipment.

transient   (1) A phenomenon caused in a system by a sudden change in conditions and that persists for a relatively short time after the change. (2) A momentary surge on a signal or power line. It may produce false signals and cause component failures.

transistor   A semiconductor device for controlling the flow of current between two terminals, the emitter and the collector, by means of variations in the current flow between a third terminal, the base, and one of the other two. It was developed at Bell Laboratories by William Shockley, Walter Brattain, and John Bardeen.

transistor-transistor logic (TTL)   A family of integrated circuits characterized by relatively high speed and low power consumption.

transit error   A type of error that occurs only once and cannot be made to repeat itself.

translate   To change data from one form of representation to another without significantly affecting the meaning. See *language translation*.

translation   In computer graphics, the movement of an image to a new position on the screen. Under translation, every point in the image moves in the same direction with the same speed at any given instant.

translator   A computer program that performs translations from one language or code to another; for example, a compiler. See *assembler, compiler, interpreter*, and *translation*.

transmission   The sending of data from one location and the receiving of data in another location, usually leaving the source data unchanged. See *data transmission*.

transmission facility The communications link between remote terminals and computers. Examples are communications lines, telephone lines, private lines, microwave transmission, communications satellites, lasers, waveguides, and fiber optics.

transmit To send data from one location and to receive the data at another location.

transparent A process that is not visible to the user or to other devices. Transparent memory refresh is an example.

transponder An amplifier located on a satellite that receives signals from an earth station and reflects them to a receiving station.

transpose To interchange two items of data.

trap A programmed conditional jump to a known location that is automatically executed when program execution reaches the location where the trap is set. See *interrupt*.

trapping A hardware provision for interrupting the normal flow of control of a program while transfer to a known location is made. See *interrupt*.

traversal The execution of each statement of a program for debugging purposes.

tree A connected graph with no cycles.

tree sort A sort that exchanges items treated as nodes of a tree. When an item reaches the root *node*, it is exchanged with the lowest *leaf* node. Also called *heap sort*.

tree structure A hierarchical structure with many branches.

triad A group of three bits, bytes, or characters.

trichromatic Three-colored. In computer graphics, trichromatic generally refers to the three primary colors (red, green, and blue) combined to create all others.

trigonometry The branch of mathematics that deals with the sides and angles of triangles and their measurements and relationships.

triple precision The retention of three times as many digits of a quantity as the computer normally uses.

tristimulus values Relative amounts of three primary colors that are combined to create other colors.

tron A popular high-tech suffix; for example, dayatron and cyclotron.

troubleshoot A term applied to the task of finding a malfunction in a hardware unit or a mistake in a computer program. Synonymous with debug. See *bug, debugging aids*, and *test data*.

TRSDOS An acronym for Tandy-Radio Shack Disk Operating System, the operating system for Radio Shack TRS-80 microcomputers.

TRS-80 microcomputer The trade name of several microcomputer systems manufactured by Radio Shack, a division of the Tandy Corporation. See *home computer, microcomputer,* and *personal computer.*

True BASIC   A structured version of the BASIC programming language.

true complement   Synonymous with *ten's complement* and *two's complement.*

truncate   To drop digits of a number or terms of a series, thus lessening precision; for example, 3.14159 truncates the series for π, which could conceivably be extended indefinitely.

trunk   The direct line between two telephone switching centers.

truth table   A systematic tabulation of all the possible input/output combinations produced by a binary circuit.

TTL   An acronym for *transistor-transistor logic.*

TTY   An abbreviation for *teletypewriter.*

tunnel diode   An electronic device with switching speeds of fractional billionths of seconds. Used in high-speed computer circuitry and memories.

TRS-80 microcomputer. Courtesy Radio Shack, a division of Tandy Corp.

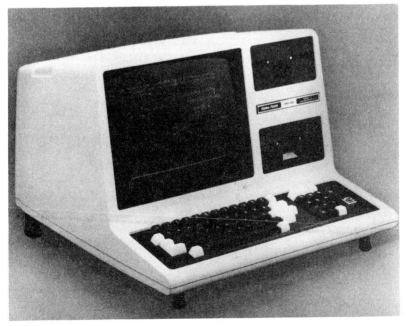

turnaround To reverse some process.

turnaround form An output document that serves as an input medium during a subsequent phase of processing.

turnaround time The time it takes for a job to travel from the user to the computing center, to be run on the computer, and for the program results to be returned to the user.

turnkey system A computer system containing all the hardware and software needed to perform a given application.

turtle graphics Graphics accomplished by a simulated robot that have been incorporated into *LOGO* and other computer languages. Turtle graphics is used to teach geometry and computer graphics concepts to children.

tutorial A training manual.

TVT (TeleVision Typewriter) A keyboard and electronics specially designed to convert a television into a computer terminal. A video terminal.

TV terminal A common television set used as a computer output device. See *video terminal.*

tweak To fine tune or adjust a piece of equipment.

twelve-punch A punch in the top row of a Hollerith punched card. Synonymous with *Y-punch.*

twinkle box An input device consistsing of optical sensors, lenses, and a rotating disk, and capable of determining the three-dimensional position of a light-emitting object by angular light sensing.

two-address computer A computer that employs two addresses in its instruction format. For example, in the instruction "ADD A B," the values represented by *A* and *B* are added, and the result replaces the old value of *B*.

two-dimensional array An arrangement consisting of rows and columns. See *matrix.*

two's complement A method of representing negative numbers. A positive or negative number is changed to the opposite sign by changing all 1s to 0s and all 0s to 1s, then binarily adding 1. Synonymous with *true complement.*

TWX (TeletypeWriter EXchange Service) An American Telephone and Telegraph Service that connects user's teleprinter equipment with the common telephone network.

typeball A typewriter striking element that contains all the usable characers. It looks like a golf ball with raised characters set around the surface. It is mounted on a moveable axis and acts as a hammer, striking the ribbon against the paper to produce the character image.

typeface See *type font.*

type font A type of face of a given size. See *font.*

typewriter An input/output device that is capable of being connected to a computer and used for communications purposes.

U

μ A common abbreviation for micro. Greek letter for mu.

UART (Universal Asynchronous Receiver/Transmitter) A device that converts parallel data into serial form for transmission along a serial interface, and vice versa.

μC An abbreviation for microcomputer (μ is the Greek letter for mu).

UCSD (University of California at San Diego) The developer of p-code and the p-system for making software portable. See *p-code* and *p-system.*

UCSD Pascal A popular version of the *Pascal* programming language. It was developed at the University of California at San Diego.

ULSI (Ultra Large Scale Integration) Refers to silicon chips containing the equivalent of 100,000 or more components on one chip.

ultrafiche Microfiche holding images reduced a hundredfold or more.

ultrasonic Above the human audio range; that is, above 20 kilohertz.

ultraviolet light Used to erase data or instructions stored in an erasable PROM (EPROM). Once the EPROM has been "erased," it can be reprogrammed by using PROM programmer. See *EPROM* and *PROM programmer.*

unary See *monadic.*

unattended operation Data transmission and/or reception without an operator.

unbundled The services, programs training, and so on sold independently of the computer hardware by the computer hardware manufacturer. Contrast with *bundled.*

unconditional transfer In program control, an instruction that always causes a branch away from the normal sequence of executing instructions. Contrast with *conditional transfer*.

uncontrolled loop   A program loop that does not reach a logical end.

underflow   (1) The condition that arises when a computer computation yields a result that is smaller than the smallest possible quantity the computer is capable of storing. (2) A condition in which the exponent plus the excess become negative in a floating point arithmetic operation.

underpunch   In a punched card column, a second hole that is immediately under the original standard code hole punched in the column.

undo   A word processing command that undoes the effect of previous commands and puts the text back the way it was.

unibus   A high-speed data communications bus structure shared by the CPU, internal memory, and peripherals.

unipolar   Refers to having one pole. See *bipolar*.

unit   A device having a special function (e.g., arithmetic unit, central processing unit, or magnetic tape unit).

unit position   The extreme right position of a *field*.

unit record system   A data processing system that uses electromechanical processing machines (sorters, collators, and so on) operated by technicians, as contrasted with a more automated computerized system. Most unit record installations have been replaced with modern computer equipment.

UNIVAC I   The first commercial electronic digital computer. It was used by the Census Bureau for processing some of the data from the 1950 census. Forty-eight of these computers were built.

universal asynchronous receiver/transmitter   An integrated circuit that converts serial data into parallel form and parallel data into serial form.

universal identifier   A standard multidigit number assigned to an individual to be used in verifying her or his identity.

universal language   A programming language that is available on many computers, such as *FORTRAN, COBOL*, and *BASIC*. Same as *common language*.

universal product code   An 11-digit computer readable code that is used in labeling retail products. The code includes a 5-digit manufacturer identification number and a 5-digit product code number.

UNIX   A minicomputer operating system that is now available for some microcomputers. It provides many advanced features, including the *C* programming language. UNIX was developed by Bell Laboratories.

unpack   To separate short units of data that have previously been packed. Opposite of *pack*.

unpopulated board   A circuit board whose components must be supplied by the purchaser. Contrast with *populated board*.

unset   To change the value of a bit (or a group of bits) to binary zero.

μP   An abbreviation for microprocessor (μ is the Greek letter mu).

up-and-running   Used to indicate that a computer system or a peripheral device has just been put into operation and that it is working properly.

UPC   (Universal Product Code) Developed by the supermarket industry for identifying products and manufacturers on product tags. A variety of manufacturers produce printers to print the 10-digit bar symbols and optical scanning devices to read the codes during supermarket checkout.

upgrade   To reconfigure a computer system in order to increase its computing power.

upload   To transfer information from a user's system to a remote computer system. Opposite of *download*.

uptime   The period of time that equipment is working without failure.

upward compatible   A term used to indicate that a computer system or peripheral device can do everything that the previous model could do, plus some additional functions. See *compatibility*.

μs   An abbreviation for microsecond; one millionth of a second (μ is the Greek letter mu). Same as μsec.

user   (1) Anyone who utilizes a computer for problem solving or data manipulation. (2) Anyone who requires the services of a computer system.

user-defined function   A function that has been defined by the user.

user-defined key   A computer keyboard key that either has a predefined function or whose function can be changed by a program. The function is performed by the computer whenever the key is depressed.

user-friendly   The term applied to software and/or hardware that has been designed to be easily used, without the user having to remember complex procedures. User-friendly software is very easy for the inexperienced person to use.

user-oriented language   See *problem-oriented language* and *procedure-oriented language.*

users group   A group of computer users who share the knowledge they have gained and the programs they have developed on a computer or class of computers of a specific manufacturer. They usually meet to exchange information, share programs, and trade equipment.

user's manual   A document describing a hardware device, a software product, or a system.

user terminal   See *terminal.*

utility   See *computer utility.*

utility routines   Software used to perform some frequently required process in the operation of a computer system (e.g., sorting, trigonometric functions, and so on). See *systems programs.*

V

VAB   (Voice Answer Back) An audio response device that can link a computer system to a telephone network, thus providing voice response to inquiries made from telephone-tape terminals.

vacuum tube   The dominant electronic element found in computers prior to the advent of the transistor. Those computers using vacuum tubes are referred to as *first generation computers.*

VAL   (Vicarm Arm Language) A computer language for controlling robots.

validation   The examination of data for correctness against certain criteria such as format (patterns of numbers, spaces, and letters), ranges (upper and lower value limits), check digits, equivalent entries on a master file, and so on.

value   A constant or quantity that is stored in a computer's memory.

variable   A quantity that can assume any of a given set of values. See *subscripted variable.*

variable-length record   Pertaining to a file in which the records are not uniform in length. Contrast with *fixed-length record.*

variable name   An alphanumeric term that identifies a data value in a program. The term can assume one of a set of values.

variable word length Pertaining to a machine word or operand that may consist of a variable number of bits, bytes, or characters. Contrast with *fixed word length*.

VAX A designation for large minicomputer systems manufactured by the Digital Equipment Corporation.

VDL (Vienna Definition Language) A language for defining the syntax and semantics of programming languages.

VDT (Video Display Terminal) A device that provides a visual representation of information.

VDU (Visual Display Unit) A peripheral device on which data are displayed on some type of screen.

vector (1) A list or table of numbers, all of which are expressed on the same line. (2) A quantity having magnitude and direction. (3) In computer science, a data structure that permits the location of any item by the use of a single index or subscript. Contrast with a *table, two-dimensional array*, or *matrix*, which require two subscripts to uniquely locate an item.

vendee A person or business that purchases a hardware or software system.

vendor A company that sells computers, peripheral devices, time-sharing service, or computer services.

Venn diagram A diagram to picture sets and the relationships between sets.

verifier machine A device used to detect keypunching mistakes by rekeying.

verify (1) To determine whether a data processing operation has been accomplished accurately; for example, to check the results of keypunching. (2) To check data validity.

version A specific release of a software product of a specific hardware model. Usually numbered in ascending order. For example, DOS 3.3 is a later version of a disk operating system than is DOS 3.1 or DOS 1.0.

vertex A point.

vertical scrolling The ability of a system to move up and down through a page or more of data that is displayed on the video screen.

very large scale integration (VLSI) The process of placing a large number (usually between 10,000 and 100,000) of components on one chip.

vetting The process of making a background investigation to reduce security risks.

VHSIC program (Very High Speed Integrated Circuit program) A joint government-private industry effort, the purpose of which is to provide the Department of Defense with advanced integrated circuits for use in future weapons and armaments.

video   A visual display.

video digitizer   An input device that converts the signal from a video camera into digital form and stores it in computer storage, where it can be analyzed or modified by the computer.

videodisk   A plastic platter resembling a phonograph record that uses low-intensity laser beams to store visual materials that will appear on a display screen.

video game   An interactive game of skill and strategy in which the player operates a picking device (joystick, paddle, and so on) while observing the graphics of the action on the display screen. A popular activity on personal computers.

video game machine   A microprocessor-controlled machine designed principally for running commercially produced cartridges that contain games and educational programs.

video generator   A device that generates the signals that control a television display.

video monitor   A device that is functionally identical to a television set, except that it has no channel selector. It receives its picture signal from an external source, such as a video terminal board.

video terminal   A device for entering information into a computer system and displaying it on a screen. A typewriterlike keyboard is used to enter information. See *cathode-ray tube, display*, and *screen*.

videotex   The generic term for electronic home information delivery systems. Within this broad term, there are two specific approaches, called Viewdata and teletext. See *teletext* and *Viewdata*.

videotext   Same as *Viewdata*.

vidicon   The tube inside a TV camera that converts the image of a scene into an electrical signal.

Viewdata   A home information delivery system through which users can access a central data base interactively from their local TV. Users may request specific frames of information. More importantly, they can directly access what they want, meaning quicker response time and a more structured usage of the medium. Users can communicate with other users via the system (electronic mail). They can also utilize transactional services, including shopping or banking based on information provided by the system. Also called *videotext*. See *teletext*.

virtual address   In virtual storage systems, an address that refers to *virtual storage* and must, therefore, be translated into a *real storage* address when it is used.

virtual memory   See *virtual storage*.

virtual storage   A technique for managing a limited amount of internal storage and a (generally) much larger amount of lower-speed storage in such a way that the distinction is largely transparent to a computer user. The technique entails some means of *swapping* segments of the program and data from the lower-speed storage (which would commonly be a drum or a disk) into the internal storage, where it would be interpreted as instructions or operated upon as data. The unit of program or data swapped back and forth is called a *page*. The high-speed storage from which instructions are executed is called *real storage*; the lower-speed storage (drums or disks) is called *virtual storage*.

Virtual Storage Operating System (VS)   An operating system that uses a computer system's virtual storage capability.

VisiCalc   A popular elecronic spreadsheet program. It stands for visible calculation. VisiCalc displays information on a display as an electronic sheet or grid. Locations within the grid are treated

Video terminal. Courtesy NCR Corp.

as variables. To manipulate a variable, the user applies an operation to the variable's location in the grid.

visual display A visual representation of data; that is, a picture or diagram drawn on a display screen, a diagram produced by a plotter, or a printed report.

visual scanner See *optical character reader*.

VLDB (Very Large Data Base) A data base that is distributed among multiple computers with different data base management systems.

VLSI (Very Large Scale Integration) Usually means chips that contain between 10,000 and 100,000 components.

vocabulary Codes or instructions that can be used to write a program for a particular computer.

voder A speech synthesizer.

voice communciations The transmission of sound in the human hearing range. Voice or audio sound can be transmitted either as *analog* or *digital* signals.

voice grade channel Telephone grade communications channels that provide for medium-speed transmission of data.

voice input An input device that permits a human voice to be used as input to a computer.

voice output An audio response output device that permits the computer to deliver answers by the spoken word.

voice recognition system A system that is designed to recognize and understand the voice and vocabulary of the user.

voice response Computer output in spoken form.

voice synthesis The ability of the computer to use stored patterns of sounds within its memory in order to assemble words that can be played through a loudspeaker.

volatile storage A storge medium whose contents are lost if power is removed from the system.

voltage Electrical pressure. High voltage in a computer circuit is represented by "1"; low (or zero) voltage is represented by "0."

voltage regulator A circuit that holds an output voltage at a predetermined value or causes it to vary according to a predetermined plan, regardless of normal input-voltage change or changes in the load *impedance*.

voltage surge protector A device that protects electrical equipment from being damaged by short surges of high voltage. A computer or other device is plugged into the surge protector, which itself is plugged into a standard 110-volt electrical outlet. See *line surge*.

volume A physical unit of a storage medium (disk pack, diskette,

Wafer

tape reel, and so on) capable of having data recorded on it and subsequently read.

VS   An acronym for *virtual storage*.

vulnerability   Weaknesses in a computer system that pose security hazards.

W

wafer   The thin, round piece of silicon from which integrated circuits are made. After the circuitry has been applied on the wafer, the wafer is sawed into pieces to make individual chips.

wait state   A condition in which the central processing unit is idle, not executing instructions.

wait time   The time during which a program or a computer waits for the completion of other activities.

walkthrough   A peer review session in which a phase of system or program development is reviewed to identify errors.

WAMI   An acronym for World Association for Medical Informatics.

wand   A penlike device able to read optically coded labels.

warm-up time   The interval between the energizing of a device and the beginning of the application of its output characteristics.

WATFIV   See *WATFOR*.

WATFOR   A version of *FORTRAN* developed at the University of Waterloo in Ontario, Canada. WATFIV is a revision of WAT-FOR.

WATS   (Wide Area Telephone Service) A service that permits an unlimited number of calls from one point to any location in a large area. The United States is divided into six WATS zones.

weed   To discard currently undesirable or needless items from a file.

weighted code   A code in which each bit position of the code has a weighted value. In the 8-4-2-1 weighted code system, the decimal numeral 529 = 0101 0010 1001.

West Coast Computer Faire   A major microcomputer trade show held annually in San Francisco.

What if?   The premise on which most electronic spreadsheet programs operate. New values may be substituted to determine the resultant effect on the other values.

wheel printer   A printer with a printing mechanism that contains the printing characters on metal wheels. A type of *line printer*.

whole number   A number without a fractional part (e.g., 63, -47, 88.0).

Wide Area Telephone Service (WATS)   A service provided by telephone companies that permits a customer, by use of an access line called a WATS line, to make data communications in a specific zone on a dial basis for a flat monthly charge.

wideband   In data communications, a channel wider in bandwidth than a *voice grade channel*.

widow   The last line of a paragraph setting alone at the top of a page of text.

wildcard   A method of file-naming conventions that permits an operating system to perform utility functions on multiple files with related names, without the programmer or user having to specify each file by its full, unique name. For example, if a word processor is directed to search for "Don," it might locate "Donald" as well as "Donna" if both were present in the file.

Winchester disk   A fast, auxiliary storage device. Consists of a rigid magnetic disk in a sealed container.

window   A portion of the video display area that is dedicated to some specific purpose.

wire board   See *control panel.*

wired program computer   A computer in which the instructions that specify the operations to be performed are specified by the placement and interconnection of wires. The wires are usually held by a removable control panel, allowing limited flexibility of operation. The term is also applied to permanently wired machines that are then called *fixed program computers.*

wire wrap   A type of circuit board construction. Electrical connections are made through wires connected to the posts that correspond to the proper component lead.

Wirth, Nicklaus   Developed the computer language Pascal, a popular high-level language that facilitates the use of structured programming techniques.

wizard   An experienced hacker.

word   A group of bits, characters, or bytes considered as an entity and capable of being stored in one storage location. See *keyboard.*

word length   The number of bits, characters, or bytes in a word.

word processing   A technique for electronically storing, editing, and manipulating text using an electronic keyboard, computer, and printer. The text is recorded on a magnetic medium, usually floppy disks. The final output is on paper.

word processing center   A central facility that contains the word processing equipment and personnel that prepare written communications for an organization.

word processing operator   An individual who operates word processing equipment.

word processing program   Software that guides the computer system in writing, editing, and formatting text.

word processing supervisor   The person who oversees the work performed in a word processing center.

word processing system   An information processing system that relies on automated and computerized typing, copying, filing, dictation, and document retrieval that are used in modern offices.

Wordstar   A popular word processing system that is available on most microcomputer systems.

word wrap   A feature that automatically moves a word to the beginning of the next line if it will not fit at the end of the original line.

workbench A programming environment in which hardware and software items are shared by several users.

working storage Same as *temporary storage.*

workspace A loosely defined term that usually refers to the amount of internal storage available for programs and data.

work station A configuration of computer equipment designed for use by one person at a time. This may have a terminal connected to a computer, or it may be a stand-alone system with local processing capability.

WP (Word Processing) Involves the use of computerized equipment and systems to facilitate the handling of words and text.

WPM (Words Per Minute) A measure of data transmission speed.

WPS (Word Processing Society) This organization encourages word processing educational programs in schools to promote word processing as a profession.

wraparound The continuation of an operation, such as a change in the storage location from the largest addressable location to the first addressable location; or a visual display cursor movement from the last character position to the first position.

write (1) The process of transferring information from the computer to an output medium. (2) To copy data, usually from *internal storage* to *auxiliary storage* devices.

write head A magnetic head that is designed and used to write data onto the media. Contrast with *read head.*

write-inhibit ring Used to prevent data from being written over on magnetic tapes.

write protect notch Floppy disks (diskettes) may be protected from the possibility of undesired recording of data by application of a gummed tab over the "write protect notch." An uncovered write protect notch will allow writing onto the diskette. See *file protection.*

X

xerographic printer A device for printing an optical image on paper in which light and dark areas are represented by electrostatically charged areas on the paper. A powdered ink dusted on the paper adheres to the charged areas and is melted into the paper by heat.

XOR An acronym for *Exclusive OR.*

X-punch A punch in the eleventh punching position (row 11) of a Hollerith punched card. Synonymous with *eleven-punch.*

X-Y plotter See *plotter.*

Y

yoke The part of the electron beam deflection system used for addressing a video display.

Y-punch A punch in the twelfth position (row 12) of a Hollerith card. Also called a high-punch. Synonymous with *twelve-punch.*

Z

Z80 The name of a popular 8-bit microprocessor chip used as a base for microcomputers. It forms the heart of most of today's CP/M-80 machines.

zero A numeral normally denoting lack of magnitude. In many computers, there are distinct representations for plus and minus zero.

zero flag A *flip-flop* that goes to logic 1 if the result of an instruction has the value of zero.

zeroize To initialize a program with zeros.

zero suppression The suppression (e.g., elimination) of nonsignificant zeros in a numeral, usually before or during a printing operation. For example, the numeral 00004763, with zero suppression, would be printed as 4763.

zone bits Special bits used along with numeric bits to represent alphanumeric characters in *ASCII* and *EBCDIC* codes.

zone punch A punch in the *O,X,* or *Y* row on a Hollerith card.

zooming The changing of a view on a graphics display by either moving in on successively smaller portions of the currently visible picture or moving out until the window encloses the entire scene.

Zulu time The international point of reference for the time of day— Greenwich Meridian Time.